D1726914

Christopher Kopper and Stephanie Tilly

150 Years of BRENNTAG

Christopher Kopper and Stephanie Tilly

150 Years of BRENNTAG
From Berlin out into the World

Siedler

In cooperation with the Gesellschaft für Unternehmensgeschichte
www.unternehmensgeschichte.de

Penguin Random House Verlagsgruppe FSC® N001967

First published in 2024
Copyright © 2024 by Siedler Verlag, Munich
a member of Penguin Random House Verlagsgruppe GmbH,
Neumarkter Strasse 28, 81673 Munich
All rights reserved
Translation: Richard Pettit; Preface: Brenntag Global Communications
Editing: Dr. Claudia Rapp, Berlin
Design Cover: Büro Jorge Schmidt, Munich
Cover Images: front © Mayk Azzato; back: see Picture Credits on p. 246, Figure 18
Typesetting: Markus Miller, Munich
Printing and binding: Alföldi Nyomda Zrt., Debrecen
Printed in Hungary
ISBN 978-3-8275-0194-3
www.siedler-verlag.de

Contents

Preface

A company – our company – is 150 years old. How can this be achieved?

Planning? Hardly. Luck? Yes, that too. Performance? Sure.

"From an egg wholesaler to the world market leader in chemical distribution" – this description has often been used in the past to describe the development of our company. But how did Brenntag really go down this path?

It was a matter close to my heart to have the development of Brenntag historically reviewed and illuminated – unfiltered, i.e., also and especially where dark shadows weigh on our history.

The process was challenging. We only had access to a few existing documents. Christopher Kopper and Stephanie Tilly spent over two years researching and consulting numerous archives in order to reconstruct our company's history as completely as possible. Nevertheless, some topics and conclusions had to remain open.

150 years of Brenntag – a cause for joy and pride? Of course.

Brenntag's history is not linear; it is characterized by decisive events, often very courageous decisions, but also by forced steps. The historical events in Germany have had a profound impact on our company – both positive and negative.

This is precisely why it is so important to be aware of our company's history, to look at it again from today's perspective, and to categorize it.

The people – our employees – were and are the driving force, the never-ending engine of our company. In its long history, Brenntag has acquired countless companies and has grown through and with these acquisitions. Coming from different countries, regions, and cultures, the people behind these companies have brought their own cultural values and experiences with them, thus helping to shape our Brenntag culture.

New colleagues, our customers, and suppliers confirm time and again the special warmth, openness, and partnership with which we treat them at Brenntag.

This is our DNA, the result of a great melting pot of cultures, experiences, and knowledge that we can be proud of. And it is a wonderful counterpoint to what was once supposed to be in the darkest of times.

The willingness to break new ground and try out new business models led to great successes but also to failure time and again. However, giving up was never the answer but rather rethinking and reinventing. And despite all the change, there was our will to always focus and refocus on our strengths. This is what "Focus in change," the motto of our anniversary year, stands for.

I see it as our task to take the lessons and experiences of the last 150 years seriously. We want to preserve them, including by setting up a comprehensive company archive and further historical research. But above all, we see them as the basis for our orientation toward the future. Many of the key questions – what were the success factors, what were the criteria for important decisions, how were risks and opportunities weighed? – are questions we will be asking ourselves time and again.

Openness, consistency, expansion, and focus – for me, these complementary values represent the experience and characteristics that have made Brenntag successful for over 150 years.

These are also the values that I personally and as CEO, together with my team at Brenntag, want to carry forward into the future.

Christian Kohlpaintner
Chairman of the Board of Brenntag SE

1.

Introduction

"From an egg wholesaler to the world market leader in chemical distribution" – behind this catchy, one-line summation of *Brenntag's* history, there is a striking and eventful development process. Over time, a family-run trading company with a local sales market grew into the global corporation *Brenntag*. This contrast between its current global status and its beginnings in the local egg trade seems quite remarkable. How did *Brenntag* become what it is today? The ability to change is a fundamental and indispensable prerequisite for the continued existence of a company. "Success in Change" (Erfolg im Wandel) – the company itself conceived this motto on the occasion of a previous anniversary.

If you look at *Brenntag's* ownership structures, stability and transformation stand side by side: In *Brenntag's* history, there was an era of almost 60 years as a family-run company with largely constant ownership structures, but also phases in which the owners changed in rapid succession. In addition, *Brenntag* was part of the corporate conglomerate of the Stinnes family of entrepreneurs for several decades and is closely linked to both the history of *Hugo Stinnes OHG* and the history of *Stinnes AG*.

What were the most important stages and turning points in the company's history? These will be outlined below. The book breaks new ground in various respects. While there is extensive historical research on the German chemical industry, the history of chemical distribution has so far remained unexplored.

For nonspecialists outside the industry, the way chemical products are distributed on the market is a barely visible process. This is also reflected in the *Brenntag* history. The expansion and global presence of the company do not necessarily correspond to a high level of awareness of the company among the general public. To this day, *Brenntag* still appears to be a hidden champion despite its placement in the DAX stock index and its position as the world market leader in chemical distribution. This may have something to do with the fact that chemical distribution is a B2B business and is, therefore, much less in the public eye than the production of chemicals. Nevertheless, it represents an essential link between producing chemicals and large parts of the industry as a whole. The division of tasks within the chemical industry has also been characterized by upheavals over time, which are reflected in *Brenntag's* history.

The growth of chemical markets and the differentiation of product diversity in the chemical industry also strengthened the role of chemical distributors within the industry. What was *Brenntag's* specific path? There is much to suggest that *Brenntag* underwent a fundamental transformation process several times in order to adapt to changing conditions. In doing so, they were able to use historically developed resources, but at the same time, they also burned bridges with the past and broke new ground.

A quick run through *Brenntag's* 150-year history shows that it reflects various dimensions of economic change. Before the start of the First World War, *Brenntag's* business manifested the beginning of the chemicalization of the world. In the 1920s and 1930s, the beginning of motorization was reflected in investments and sales, before the policies of the National Socialist regime forced the Jewish owners to sell. After the Second World War, the boom of the 1950s and 1960s, known as the "economic miracle," was reflected in the strong growth of the chemical trade and the mineral oil business. *Brenntag* gradually changed its product portfolio and gained a foothold in new markets. In addition, its development over six decades was closely linked to the name Stinnes. In some parts of *Brenntag's* history, aspects of the eventful history of various companies in the Stinnes family of entrepreneurs become apparent, since *Hugo Stinnes OHG* and *Hugo Stinnes AG* (later *Stinnes AG*) had a decisive influence on *Brenntag's* business in some phases. However, in the economic history research literature, there is surprisingly little information about the development of the Stinnes companies in the second half of the 20th century, so this context is also included in some chapters – where the sources are available.

The history of *Brenntag* is also a history of globalization. It shows how a distribution and logistics company operating initially locally, then regionally, then throughout Germany, opened up more and more new markets by modernizing means of conveyance and transport and expanded its market from Germany across Europe to the United States by founding foreign subsidiaries and making numerous company acquisitions across the whole world. A family-run, medium-sized company with simple and direct decision-making processes developed into a corporation with a complex organizational structure and international management. Decision-making processes were increasingly based on business management, technical, and scientific knowledge and less and less on experience-based knowledge.

Brenntag's story also has a political dimension. During the division of Germany, as a leading chemical trading company, it was predestined to play a prominent role in business transactions between the Federal Republic and the German Democratic Republic (GDR). Since the 1960s, it had also been involved in other strictly confidential transactions between the federal and GDR governments that served a humanitarian purpose: the release of political prisoners from GDR prisons. To this end, networks and procedures were used that had already been established in church-initiated goods transfers. As early as the 1950s, *Brenntag* was one of a few trusted companies that commissioned the Diakonisches Werk of the Protestant Church to deliver goods, the equivalent value of which went to the Protestant regional churches in the GDR.

This book, consequently, addresses a number of pertinent questions, but at the same time, it will not be able to provide all the answers. For the period up to 1945, there is a dearth of surviving documents. While the annual financial statements are available without a gap, important questions about strategic decisions, operational business policy, and sales organization can only be answered rudimentarily and, in some cases, only hypothetically. This also applies largely to the period after 1945, as documents relating to *Brenntag's* business operations are, for the most part, missing, and those of the parent company cease to exist at the end of the 1950s. There are only cursory references to questions that concern the firm's internal perspective over time – for example, the role of human resources in a growing company.

Since only a few files have survived from *Brenntag* itself, its history was reconstructed using a document puzzle from files in public archives. The holdings of the Stinnes companies in the Archive for Christian Democratic Politics, which offer comprehensive insights into the period from 1937 to the end of the 1950s, proved to be particularly helpful. The Federal Archives, the Diakonie Archives, and the Stasi Records Archive contain important files on specific aspects of *Brenntag's* business. Essential information on business development was collected from various files in numerous other archives and through research in the contemporary press. Examples include the North Rhine-Westphalia State Archives, the Berlin State Archives, the *Commerzbank AG* Archives, the *Deutsche Bahn AG* Archives, the Brandenburg State Main Archives, the Hamburg State Archives, the Rhenish-Westphalian Economic

Archives, and the archives of various companies. In addition, the written record was supplemented by interviews with some contemporary witnesses.[*]

How has the company overcome the various challenges in its 150 years of existence? In twelve chapters, this book takes a look at the central phases of the company's historical development and traces how *Brenntag* shaped its business model and built an increasingly global network.

Over time, the name of the company changed repeatedly. At times, *Brenntag AG* and *Brenntag GmbH* existed side by side. *Brenntag* later constituted a division within *Stinnes AG*, which in turn included various *Brenntag* sub-companies. The contemporaneous names are used in the book if a clear attribution is possible. Nevertheless, as is the case on these pages and in the following, the term "Brenntag" will often be used in short, provided that the company's business with its various roots or sectors is meant as a whole. This is particularly true for the decades after 1965, as the few sources here – for example, the supervisory board minutes – often do not differentiate between individual companies.

[*] We would like to express our considerable thanks to those who have helped us in our research! Without their extensive support in the archives and other research institutions, the interviews with witnesses of certain time periods at Brenntag, and the savvy preliminary studies by the staff at the Gesellschaft für Unternehmensgeschichte, it would not have been possible to present the book in this form. In particular, we would like to thank Fabian Engel, Michael Bermejo-Wenzel, Dennis Blum, Dirk Ullmann, Michael Hansmann, Peter Craemer, Ulrich Soénius, Dietmar Bleidick, Josephin Hensel, Susanne Kill, Paul Hahn, Rotraut Neumann, Gabriele Roolfs-Broihan, Rainer Herrmann, Gabriele Rausch, Ulrike Schöppner, Carola Schmitt-Köpke, Robert Moser, and Marco Fernschild.

2.

From Trading in Agricultural Products to Chemicals and Mineral Oil Trading: Philipp Mühsam oHG in Berlin as a Pioneering Company

The Origins of the Mühsam Family

The history of *Brenntag* begins in a small town in Upper Silesia. In the year of the German Revolution of 1848, its future founder Philipp Mühsam was born on November 14 in the small town of Pitschen (Byczyna) into a large Jewish merchant family.[1] His father Abraham Adolph Mühsam (November 21, 1816 – November 30, 1875) earned his money trading grain and other agricultural products, which he bought in the rural area surrounding Pitschen. Philipp's mother was Henriette Mühsam, née Neumann (September 22, 1823 – April 18, 1896).

Of course, the infant and toddler failed to notice that the revolutionary attempt to establish a parliamentary monarchy in 1848/49 had failed and that the Prussian king had dashed the bourgeoisie's hopes for a liberal and parliamentary kingdom and a German national state. However, the emancipation, that is to say the liberation of the Jewish citizens in Prussia through the gradual lifting of discriminatory legal restrictions, was not stopped by this political setback. Philipp Mühsam's generation was the first in the family to receive the same rights as Christians and to grow up with this new social status.

Abraham Adolph Mühsam was one of the respected residents of Pitschen. After the end of monarchical absolutism, when the first Prussian constitution of 1850 made Jews formally equal citizens, he was given the position of an honorary member of the magistrate.[2] In 1856 he moved with his family from Pitschen and relocated to Berlin. Since very little documentary evidence about the Mühsams has survived from this time, one can only develop factually based hypotheses about the motive for the move. While the population of Pitschen stagnated and economic development showed little momentum, the rapidly growing Prussian metropolis promised merchants from the province a steadily growing sales

---

1   Unless otherwise stated, the genealogical information about the Mühsam family is based on the genealogical database www.geni.com and the Mühsam family chronicle in the archives of the Leo Baeck Institute, archives.cjh.org/repositories/5/archival_objects/811130 [last accessed September 5, 2023].

2   Christoph Hamann, *Die Mühsams. Geschichte einer Familie*, Berlin 2005, 43 f. (= Jüdische Memorien, Vol. 11).

Figure 1: The company founder, Philipp Mühsam (1848–1914).

market. The no less rapidly developing railway network also connected Berlin with all parts of Prussia and the German Customs Union, the free trade area that included almost all states of what would, from 1871, be the German Empire.

The Mühsam family moved to what used to be called the Spandauer Vorstadt, a relatively central Berlin neighborhood between Oranienburger and Rosenthaler Strasse, where many Jewish families lived and numerous Jewish institutions such as synagogues and schools were located. Philipp Mühsam and his six siblings grew up in a house at Linienstrasse 112. But his father's business developed so well that the family was able to buy a two-story house at Oranienburger Strasse 73 in 1863.[3] The sale price of 67,500 marks indicates two factors. On the one hand, real estate prices in Berlin were higher than in all other cities of the future German Empire. On the other hand, one needed a higher net income and a high credit rating with the banks if one wanted to buy a house at that price.

Unfortunately, no documents have survived about Philipp's schooling and professional training, but there is much to suggest that his father was able to provide him with post-secondary education. At least one of his brothers, Benno, born in 1855, graduated from high school, studied law, and graduated with the prestigious doctorate. The Mühsam family was quite typical in this respect. Jewish Germans, right down to the middle and lower bourgeoisie, were extremely education-oriented and were significantly overrepresented in institutions of higher education. While they comprised only one percent of the entire population, the Jewish proportion of the total number of university students was over 5 percent.[4]

---

3   Ibid., 50, footnote 64; Allgemeiner Wohnungs-Anzeiger nebst Adreß- und Geschäftshandbuch für Berlin, dessen Umgebungen und Charlottenburg 1863, Berlin 1863 (online digital.zlb.de).

4   Simone Lässig, *Jüdische Wege ins Bürgentum. Kulturelles Kapital und sozialer Aufstieg im 19. Jahrhundert*, Göttingen 2004.

The Jewish Germans were among the winners of the social modernization process in the second half of the 19th century. In the Jewish bourgeoisie, entrepreneurial skills, higher education, and academic studies were seen as a means of social advancement in a society in which the importance of traditional class barriers was diminishing. Striving for education and entrepreneurial ability promoted recognition by the non-Jewish environment and the acquisition of civic respectability. The Mühsam family became part of the educated and economic middle class, the bearers of economic, cultural, and political progress in this era.

The Mühsams were not religious. When the extended family from all parts of the empire met in November 1911 for a family gathering in a good Berlin restaurant, dishes such as turtle soup and poached trout with butter sauce were on the table, which were clearly not kosher.[5] The dignified ambience showed that the Mühsams had made their way into upper middle-class circles as entrepreneurs, lawyers, and pharmacists. In order to prevent arguments, the organizers of the family day decided not to discuss religious or political issues. There were reasons for this, as political views differed widely within the extended family. While Philipp Mühsam was probably close to the National Liberals, his distant Munich relative Erich Mühsam (1878–1934) was politically far to the left and was a well-known anarchist writer.[6]

The Founding of the Philipp Mühsam Company

There is much to suggest that Philipp Mühsam worked initially in his father's business and learned the grain and agricultural products trade from scratch. When he was not quite 26 years old, he started his own business with a wholesale firm for agricultural products, "Commissions business for local produce" (Commissons-Geschäft für Landes-Producte). On October 9, 1874, the company *Philipp Mühsam* was entered in the company register of the Royal City Court of Berlin under number 8335.[7]

The company was founded during a turbulent economic phase. In 1873, the speculative boom of the founding years ended with the bursting of a temporary bubble and a drastic fall in the completely inflated price level for shares. The real economy was not spared, as prices for real estate and industrially

5   Menu sequence at the Mühsam family gathering on November 12, 1911, in: Der erste Mühsam'sche Familientag am 12. November 1911 (printed), archive.org/details/siegfriedseligmannf015/page/n26/mode/1up?view=theater [last accessed September 5, 2023].

6   Erich Mühsam was imprisoned in the Oranienburg concentration camp in 1933 and murdered by the SS on July 10, 1934.

7   *Berliner Börsen-Zeitung*, October 10, 1874.

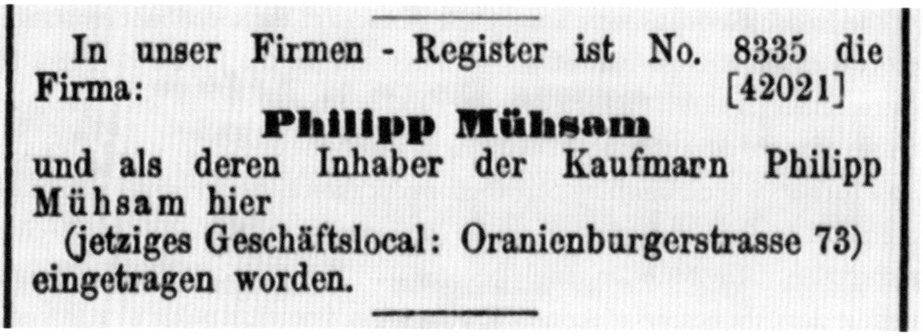
In unser Firmen - Register ist No. 8335 die Firma: [42021]

Philipp Mühsam

und als deren Inhaber der Kaufmarn Philipp Mühsam hier

(jetziges Geschäftslocal: Oranienburgerstrasse 73) eingetragen worden.

Figure 2: Official notification of the founding of the Philipp Mühsam company on October 9, 1874.

produced goods also fell. However, the bursting of the bubble did not lead to an economic recession, and the starting conditions for company founders had not worsened compared to previous years. Even for newly founded companies, the opportunities for growth were still not bad. Mühsam was thus able to succeed with his fledgling company.

The quite significant starting capital of 21,000 marks did not come from Philipp Mühsam alone. It was typical of a family business that his younger brother Carl (1849–1892) and his mother Henriette (1823–1896) participated as silent partners with contributions of 7,000 marks each.[8] And when his older brother Ismar (1847–1911) joined the company as a partner in 1880, it was transformed into *Philipp Mühsam oHG,* a general partnership.[9]

One piece of evidence suggests that Mühsam's business was getting off to a good start. According to the balance sheet that has been preserved, in 1875, in his first business year, he achieved a gross income of 56,000 marks.[10] Although his small company initially operated as a "grain and commission business"[11] according to the Berlin address book, it made most of its sales in the wholesale trade of eggs. The "Eggs Account" in the balance sheet shows a profit of 49,896.83 marks in 1875. This sum suggests a high sales volume, as an egg cost around five pfennigs in retail at the time.[12] In its second year of business, Mühsam sold a considerable number of eggs in Berlin.

8 Balance sheet book of Philipp Mühsam AG 1875–1934, Brenntag SE Essen.

9 *Berliner Börsen-Zeitung*, June 3, 1880.

10 Balance sheet of Philipp Mühsam AG; Hamann, *The Mühsams*, 56.

11 Allgemeiner Wohnungs-Anzeiger für Berlin 1876, Berlin 1876.

12 Thomas Rahlf (ed.), *Deutschland in Zahlen. Zeitreihen zur historischen Statistik*, Bonn 2023, 210.

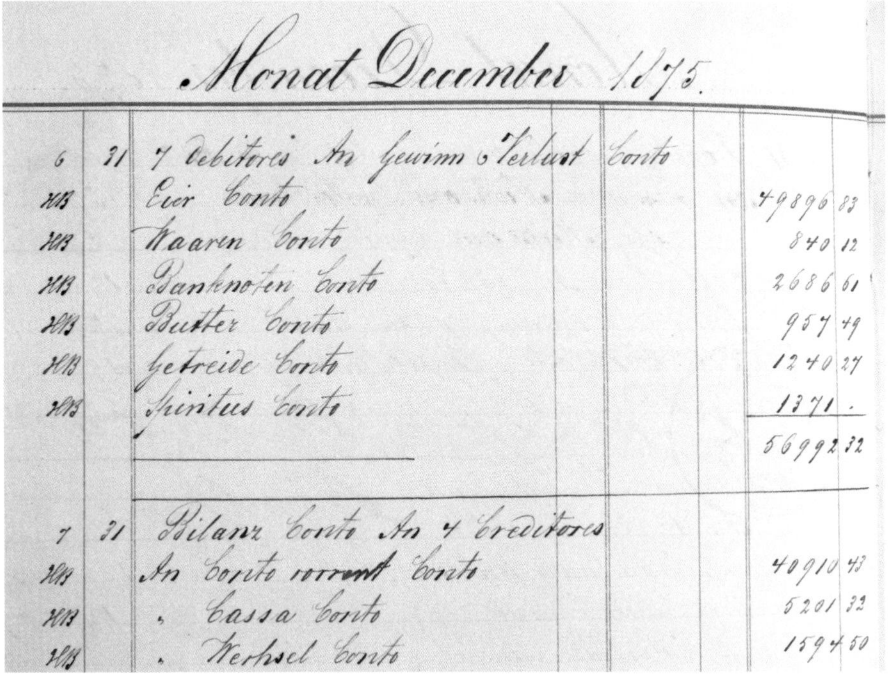

Monat December 1875.

6	31	7 Debitores An Gewinn & Verlust Conto	
HB		Eier Conto	49896 83
HB		Waaren Conto	840 12
HB		Banknoten Conto	2686 61
HB		Butter Conto	957 49
HB		Getreide Conto	1240 27
HB		Spiritus Conto	1371 .
			56992 32
7	31	Bilanz Conto An 4 Creditores	
HB		An Conto corrent Conto	40910 43
HB		" Cassa Conto	5201 32
HB		" Wechsel Conto	1594 50

Figure 3: The egg account from 1875.

The success was due to the fact that his potential local clientele continued to grow. While grain sales increasingly shifted to larger mills with steam-powered machines that purchased grain from large grain dealers, Mühsam's customers were small retailers. The rapid increase in population in Berlin caused the sales market for eggs and other agricultural products to grow steadily. In just 24 years, from 1871 to 1895, the population doubled from 826,000 to 1,677,000 people. Never before and never since did a major city in Germany grow as quickly as Berlin did before the turn of the century. In just a few decades, the then still independent municipalities of Charlottenburg, Wilmersdorf, Schöneberg, and Rixdorf (now Neukölln) developed into larger cities that coalesced with the core city.

Growth and a New Business Model: The Drug and Chemicals Trade

In 1879, Mühsam took into account his new successfull business area of egg trading and renamed the company the "Grain, Agricultural Products, Eggs, and Butter Commission Business."[13] The business premises were at Oranienburger Strasse 73,

13 "Getreide-, Product-, Eier- und Butter-Kommissionsgeschäft," in: Allgemeiner Wohnungs-Anzeiger für Berlin 1879, Berlin 1879.

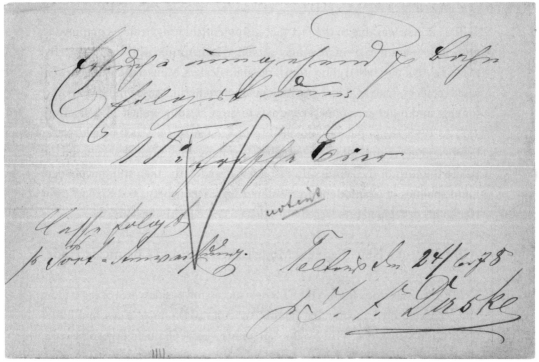

Figure 4: An order for fresh eggs dated June 24, 1878.

very close to his apartment at number 60 on the same street. Surprisingly, there was even a branch in London for eleven years starting in 1877, but unfortunately, no documents about its operations have survived.[14] It was founded in 1877 with a considerable capital expenditure of 122,400 marks, but in the following eleven years, it only generated a total profit of 114,200 marks, of which, according to the balance sheet for 1888, it did not distribute anything to the owners. It was closed in 1888 because of its low income and excessive capital commitment.[15]

Increasing sales and the capital investment from his brother Ismar enabled Mühsam's company to move to Friedrichstrasse 105a in 1881, a more central and prestigious address than Oranienburger Strasse in the Spandauer Vorstadt.[16] Mühsam also moved his apartment to the sought-after Schiffbauerdamm on the Spree River, directly opposite the newly built Friedrichstrasse train station. Since the Philipp Mühsam family's estate apparently does not exist, or at least cannot be found, his private life can only be reconstructed in rough outlines. It is very likely that he married his wife Berta,[17] née Samson (1857–1939) in 1881. Their daughter Eva was born on December 16, 1881, and their son Kurt on December 31, 1887.

The Berlin address book reveals a decision Mühsam made in 1881 that would prove important for the entire future of his company. Only two years after the last name change, *Philipp Mühsam oHG* traded as a "drugs, paints, chemicals, eggs, and produce store," a sign that it had started trading in chemicals and pharmaceutical raw materials. The increasingly precise natural science of chemistry had only developed since the end of the 18th century, producing applicable results in the technical sector, in agriculture, and in medicine. Since the second half of the 19th century, chemicals had been produced industrially and in larger quantities, making them an important part of economic life.

In the absence of any relevant documentation, it can be assumed that Mühsam realized how relatively easy he could expand his flourishing business model as a link between wholesalers and retailers of agricultural products to the trade in chemicals. The fact that sales in this area grew significantly faster thanks to economic and technical progress certainly played to his hand. Here he could expect significantly higher returns than in the more heavily populated and economically less dynamic agricultural produce trade.

---

14   Balance sheet book of Philipp Mühsam AG, annual financial statements for 1879.

15   Balance sheet book of Philipp Mühsam AG 1888.

16   Allgemeiner Wohnungs-Anzeiger für die Stadt Berlin 1881, Berlin 1881.

17   The sources are not consistent regarding the spelling of Berta/Bertha Mühsam's first name. This seems to be due to the orthography reform around 1900. The authors follow the spelling on her gravestone inscription, cf. Fig 16.

Mühsam initially focused on the textile industry. The manufacturers of textiles needed products to bleach the fabrics before dyeing them. By the end of the 19th century, synthetically produced dyes from the manufacturers *BASF, Bayer,* and *Hoechst* replaced natural plant dyes. The chemical raw materials required for this, such as soda, hydrochloric, sulfuric, and nitric acid, were supplied to wholesalers by the chemical industry. Mühsam bought the products in appropriate batch sizes in order to sell them to the medium-sized textile companies. In addition to chemical products for the textile industry, from 1881, he also traded in paints, purchasing industrially produced interior and textile paints from manufacturers, which he sold to painting and smaller textile companies.

In addition to the chemical trade, the term "Droguen" (i.e., drugs) appeared in the commercial address book for the first time in 1881. This contemporary term meant pharmaceutical raw materials that Mühsam now purchased from the chemical industry and sellers of herbal remedies and delivered to small entrepreneurs such as Berlin pharmacists and druggists. Another important group of substances was industrially produced alcohols and carbolic acid, which were used to produce solvents and disinfectants.

Even though Mühsam essentially retained his business model, the switch from trading in agricultural products to trading in chemicals was certainly a considerable change. Despite the significant increase in operating expenses, the shift proved to be a success.[18] In the strict sense of the word, Mühsam was not a pioneer entrepreneur, as there were already numerous competitors in this industry. However, although the Berlin commercial address book of 1880 listed 140 chemical manufacturers and dealers, Mühsam was able to hold his own in the crowded field of trade rivals.[19] From 1891, the company was called "Philipp Mühsam Drug, Paint and Chemical Wholesaler", a definitive indication that it had completely given up trading in agricultural products around 17 years after it was founded.[20]

From 1883 onward, *Philipp Mühsam oHG* resided again in the Spandauer Vorstadt, on the ground floor of the house at Linienstrasse 132.[21] Mühsam was tech-savvy and used the possibilities of modern communication technology early on. *Philipp Mühsam oHG* had a telephone as early as 1882, when there

---

18 Balance sheet book of Philipp Mühsam AG, annual financial statements for 1882.

19 Allgemeiner Wohnungs-Anzeiger für die Stadt Berlin 1880, Berlin 1880. The Berlin address book from 1891 lists 100 chemical stores.

20 Allgemeiner Wohnungs-Anzeiger für die Stadt Berlin 1891, Berlin 1891. As early as 1888, the egg sales account in the Mühsam company's balance sheet recorded only very low income.

21 Allgemeiner Wohnungs-Anzeiger für die Stadt Berlin 1883, Berlin 1883.

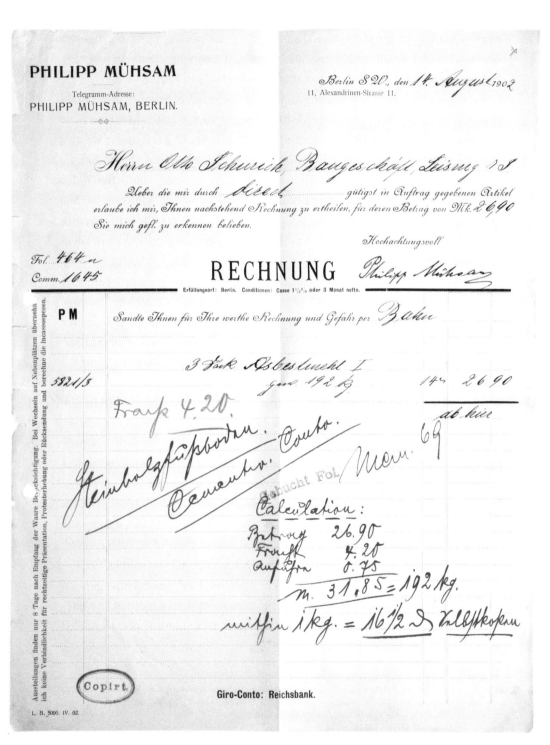

Figure 5: An invoice from 1902 for asbestos powder, to be used as a binder and pigment in xylolite floors.

were only a few hundred connections in Berlin.[22] Telephones were an expensive commodity that usually only larger and successful companies could buy or rent. Just four years later, there were over 4,000 connections in Berlin.

Even after the switch to trading in chemicals, hired coachmen and horse-drawn carts were initially responsible for transporting the goods to the end-use customers. In the first two decades of the 20th century, cars were rare and expensive luxury goods, purchased either for the leisure of the economic elite or as an investment in the future of mobility. It wasn't until the 1920s that cars would become widespread on the streets of Berlin. Mühsam, on the other hand, purchased the company's first car in 1910 for the stiff price of 17,000 marks, which corresponded to the annual income of a district president (Regierungspräsident).[23]

Thanks to the growth of his company, Mühsam was able to buy a new commercial building at Alexandrinenstrasse 11 in the Kreuzberg district in 1886. The large four-story building with a balance sheet value of 201,000 marks and a floor area of 2,150 square meters was by far the company's most valuable capital investment. Thanks to his reputation with the banks, Mühsam was able to finance almost the entire purchase price with a mortgage loan.[24] The building was not in a residential and business district and was a little further away from the center of old Berlin, but it had significantly greater expansion potential than the previous quarters. While the Mühsams occupied the rooms on the ground floor for their business, the apartments on the three upper floors were rented out.[25] The regulations for the storage of flammable and corrosive dangerous goods, which were still very loose at the time, did not rule out combined residential and commercial use. As his company continued to expand, Mühsam had the house, built in 1883, enlarged in 1901 with two side wings, amounting to a balance sheet value of 293,000 marks.[26] It remained their place of business until *Philipp Mühsam AG* was sold in 1937.

On April 1, 1888, Mühsam's younger brother Carl joined the general partnership as a partner.[27] In 1898, the balance sheet total exceeded the one-million mark for the first time.[28] The increasing business success enabled

---

22 Berlin Telephone Book, May 1882, www.geschichte-telefonbuecher.de/ [last accessed September 5, 2023].

23 Balance sheet book of Philipp Mühsam AG, annual financial statements for 1910; Rainer Fattmann, *Bildungsbürger in der Defensive. Die akademische Beamtenschaft und der "Reichsbund der höheren Beamten" in der Weimarer Republik*, Göttingen 2001.

24 Balance sheet book of Philipp Mühsam AG, annual financial statements for 1886.

25 Allgemeiner Wohnungs-Anzeiger für die Stadt Berlin 1888, Berlin 1888.

26 Balance sheet book of Philipp Mühsam AG, annual financial statements for 1901.

27 *Berliner Börsen-Zeitung*, April 7, 1888.

28 Balance sheet book of Philipp Mühsam AG, annual financial statements for 1898.

Mühsam to rise into the Berlin upper middle class. When, at the suggestion of the Berlin Chamber of Commerce, he was appointed honorary commercial judge at the Berlin I Regional Court by the Prussian Ministry of Justice in 1901, it was a sign of the civic respectability he had acquired.[29] In 1903, the Chamber of Commerce elected him for the first time to the Chemicals, Drugs, Paints, and Varnishes Committee, which can be seen as an indication that he had also found access to the circle of large chemical and paint dealers.[30]

Mühsam used the increasing net income of his company to diversify his business area, and in December 1904, he founded *Heymann & Schmidt Luxuspapierfabrik AG* in Berlin with four partners. The new firm was based at Schönhauser Allee 164, was specialized in the production of calendars, postcards, and greeting cards, as well as advertising articles and posters, and had a fairly high nominal capital of 1.5 million marks. Since Mühsam was elected as one of the three members of the supervisory board, his share of the capital in the paper factory and his reputation in business circles were probably significant.[31]

It was not the first company that Mühsam helped found. In 1895, he and four other entrepreneurs founded the "stock corporation for chemical products" (Aktiengesellschaft für Chemische Produkte) which, in addition to traditional chemical products made from natural substances (glue, fats, soaps, and horn meal) as well as chemical raw materials such as glycerin, hydrochloric acid, sulfuric acid, and superphosphate, also produced end products such as pharmaceutical preparations, soaps, and stearin.[32] Mühsam was a member of the supervisory board until his death and was followed on the board by his son Dr. Kurt Mühsam.[33] With the other companies, Mühsam had become not only a seller but also a producing entrepreneur, although the business area of *Philipp Mühsam oHG* was still limited to trading.

---

29   *Berliner Börsen-Zeitung*, May 26, 1901.

30   *Berliner Börsen-Zeitung*, January 13, 1903.

31   *Berliner Börsen-Zeitung*, January 6, 1905. Heymann & Schmidt ceased operations as a printing company.

32   *Berliner Börsen-Zeitung*, August 12, 1922.

33   This emerges from various reports in the *Berliner Börsen-Zeitung*.

The Move to Britz and into the Mineral Oil Business

In 1906, Mühsam made a decision that would keep his company on a long-term growth path. In the then independent community of Britz, now part of the Neukölln district, he acquired a large piece of land near Tempelhofer Weg, which bordered on the Teltow Canal. With foresight, Mühsam bought it at the right time: The canal was still under construction and was scheduled to open in early 1907. *Philipp Mühsam oHG* had a large four-story warehouse building with two staircases and nine window axes built, which was designed to accommodate the growing business volume.

Although it was a purely functional building, he had the gables of the stairwells and upper wall ends decorated with historical decorative elements such as the dentil cut. The warehouse and a tank depot, which were completed by 1908, offered optimal conditions for the storage of hazardous substances.[34] At that time, Britz was still on the outskirts of Berlin and had fewer than 10,000 residents. A distance of several hundred meters to the nearest residential buildings offered sufficient safety in the event of fire and explosions. The building survived the bombing raids during the Second World War, has remained the property of the company to this day, and is still in use.

In addition to a railway siding, the property on the Teltow Canal also had a jetty that connected the company to the Havel river, the Elbe-Havel Canal, the Elbe River, and the Hamburg seaport, and thus to the international oil market. The jetty helped

---

34 Balance sheet book of Philipp Mühsam AG, annual financial statements for 1906, 1907, and 1908. The copies of the sectional drawing and the frontal view of the building at the time of construction acceptance (May 28, 1907) are kept at the Brenntag site in Berlin-Britz.

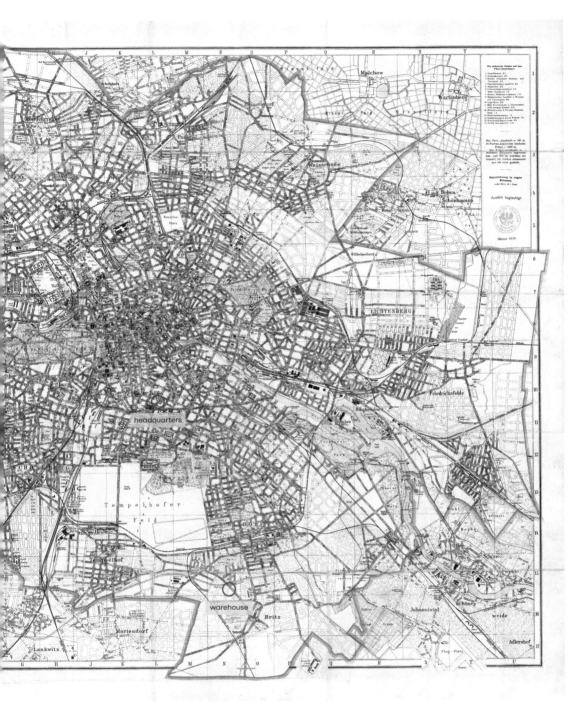

Figure 6: 1910 map of Berlin, with the headquarters at Alexandrinen-Strasse 11 and the warehouse by the Teltow canal in Britz clearly marked.

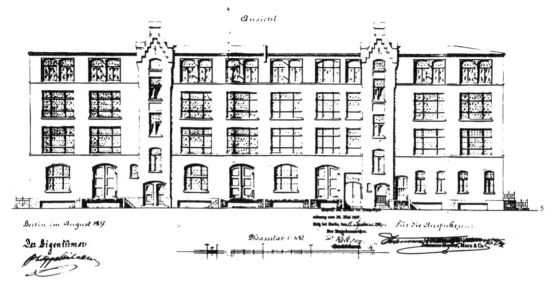

Figure 7: The generously dimensioned warehouse in Britz after its completion (1908).

Philipp Mühsam oHG to reduce the transport costs for purchasing mineral oils. A large part of the lamp petroleum and gasoline used in Germany at that time was imported from the USA and transshipped through the port of Hamburg. Inland waterway vessels transported the petroleum products to Britz via the Elbe, the Havel, and the Teltow Canal. *Philipp Mühsam oHG* also entered into further processing in the mineral oil trade by refining oil itself: In 1913, the firm was able to become partially independent of the price policy of the oil processors by building a small refinery on the Britz site.[35]

In addition to trading in paints, chemicals, and raw materials for medicines, *Philipp Mühsam oHG* developed mineral oil trading as a new business area. There were several reasons for this. Firstly, electric light was still not very common in private homes after the turn of the century. While commercial buildings were already somewhat more commonly equipped with electric lighting, living spaces were illuminated either with gaslight or by burning petroleum in lamps. On the other hand, it can be assumed that when Mühsam built the tank depot, he was thinking less about the gradually shrinking market for lamp petroleum than about the rapidly growing demand for gasoline for stationary combustion engines and motorized vehicles, the use of which was gradually spreading in the imperial capital. But while cars, as already mentioned, were only affordable for

35   Balance sheet book of Philipp Mühsam AG, annual financial statements for 1913.

a few rich vehicle owners, motor-driven buses and delivery vans were already rolling through Berlin. Gasoline also played an increasingly important role as a cleaning agent for commercial businesses.[36] By entering the mineral oil trade, Mühsam made a decision that would shape the company's profile for over 80 years until the 1980s.

Philipp Mühsam oHG's sales grew steadily. In 1906, shortly before the completion of the warehouse and tank depot in Britz, it had already achieved sales of 1.6 million marks. There is a good deal of evidence to suggest that Mühsam financed the buildings predominantly from retained profits and only to a lesser extent with outside capital, i.e., bank loans. The "Yearbook of Millionaires in the Province of Brandenburg," published in 1913, generously estimated his net worth at two to three million and his annual income at 150,000 marks, which, based on its purchasing power in 2022, would have corresponded to an income

Figure 8: Even warehouse buildings were not without decorative façade, as this picture from 2023 shows. The warehouse is still in use.

36   Rainer Karlsch/Raymond G. Stokes, *Faktor Öl. Die Mineralölwirtschaft in Deutschland 1859–1974*, Munich 2003, 49–92.

of 885,000 euros.[37] At this point, Mühsam was once again the sole owner of the company, as his brothers Carl and Ismar had died prematurely. After Ismar's death in 1911, he continued to run the previously open trading company as a sole proprietor without partners.[38]

In December 1912, the Philipp Mühsam company was rocked by a series of thefts. On January 5, 1913, readers of the *Berliner Börsen-Zeitung* learned that "valuable paints, lacquers, and varnishes" had been stolen from the commercial building on Alexandrinenstrasse and sold to paint dealers and painters.[39] The article left it unclear whether the theft was discovered when the delivery notes were checked, when goods were shipped, or during an inventory. Since the public prosecutor's office had already brought charges against the resellers and the end buyers of the stolen goods, the investigations by the criminal police and the public prosecutor's office were already advanced at this point. Two weeks later, the defendants appeared before the 4th criminal chamber of the Berlin I Regional Court. After a trial lasting several days, the judges sentenced seven men to prison sentences of up to two and a half years:[40] Two workers and two coachmen from the company were found guilty of theft; two innkeepers who were also convicted had bought varnishes and paints worth 40,000 marks from the thieves and sold them to a paint dealer who was also convicted as a buyer of the stolen goods. On the other hand, several painters who were co-accused went unpunished because the court could not prove that they had not purchased the paints in good faith.

On June 30, 1914, the Philipp Mühsam company was hit by a much larger accident. A fire broke out in their tank depot in Britz, cause undetermined, and threatened to spread to the rest of the company premises. The Tempelhof and Britz fire departments already had two motorized fire engines, but the horse-drawn carriages with the firefighting pumps took a long time to arrive at the scene of the fire. On the southern edge of the site, a storage room in which ether, acids, and gasoline were stored caught fire. The *Berliner Börsen-Zeitung* reported that the Mühsams, their workers, and the residents were lucky in the misfortune and were saved from worse harm. The westerly wind prevented it from spreading to the main building, which was north of the storage room. The report concluded with the words: "Nobody was reported to have been injured."[41]

---

37 Hamann, *Die Mühsams*, 58; Deutsche Bundesbank, *Kaufkraftäquivalente historischer Beträge in deutschen Währungen*, Frankfurt a. M. 2022.

38 Familienchronik der Familie Mühsam, *Berliner Börsen-Zeitung*, June 26, 1911.

39 *Berliner Börsen-Zeitung*, January 5, 1913.

40 *Berliner Börsen-Zeitung*, January 19, 1913.

41 *Berliner Börsen-Zeitung*, July 1, 1914.

The Second Generation in the Family Business

The family had already had to part with the company's founder a month earlier. Philipp Mühsam died on May 17, 1914, at the age of 65 under circumstances that cannot be further determined.[42] The reputable liberal daily newspaper *Vossische Zeitung* published an obituary for the family, a funeral notice for the authorized representatives and employees, and a notice for the coachmen and workers. The class society of the German Empire with its strict "collar line" between workers and employees was thus also manifested in the mourning for the deceased head of the company. At the same time, the number of obituaries indicates the high status that Mühsam must have had as the founder and owner of the company. This is not surprising when you look back at its history. Mühsam was a successful entrepreneur who managed to rise into Berlin's economic elite by developing a small trading company for agricultural products into a successful chemicals dealership with its own refinery.

Mühsam was mourned by his widow Berta who survived her husband by 24 years; his daughter Eva Kantorowicz (1881–1971); his son-in-law, the liqueur manufacturer Dr. Franz Kantorowicz (1872–1954), cousin of the historian Ernst Kantorowicz; and his son Dr. Kurt Mühsam (1887–1928).

For his higher education, Kurt Mühsam initially attended the *Königliches Wilhelms-Gymnasium* in Berlin, which, over the course of its long history, produced numerous prominent personalities such as the chemist Franz Oppenheim, the industrialist Walther Rathenau, the journalist Theodor Wolff, and the writer Kurt Tucholsky.[43] For unknown reasons, Kurt Mühsam moved to the similarly named *Königliches Gymnasium* in Wetzlar, Hesse, and passed his Abitur there in February 1906. Like almost all high school graduates from upper middle-class circles, he completed his compulsory military service in the form of a one-year voluntary service in the cavalry, during which his father had to pay for living expenses and equipment. He was not granted the otherwise usual appointment of lieutenant in the reserve in this elitist and arrogant unit. Although Jews had equal rights under the law, they were still subject to some social discrimination. In all German states except Bavaria, Jews were denied the prestigious position of reserve officer.[44]

---

42 *Vossische Zeitung*, May 19, 1914.

43 Kathrin Chod et al., König-Wilhelm-Gymnasium, in: Hans-Jürgen Mende/Kurt Wernicke (eds.), *Berliner Bezirkslexikon*, Mitte, Berlin 2003.

44 Curriculum vitae of Kurt Mühsam in his dissertation: "*Der gewerbliche Lohnkampf im heutigen Strafrecht*," Diss. Heidelberg 1910.

Figure 9: Obituary for Philipp Mühsam in the *Vossische Zeitung* of May 19, 1914.

From 1907 to 1910, Kurt Mühsam studied law in Berlin and Heidelberg, where he received his doctorate on the subject of "Commercial wage struggle in today's criminal law, taking into account the preliminary draft of a German penal code" under Professor Karl von Lilienthal. It was a treatise typical of the time, in that the sons of entrepreneurs liked to address legal remedies involving employees. Since his doctoral supervisor was one of the leading German criminal lawyers, and the topic of his dissertation touched on a very current and relevant problem, he might have imagined a career in law. After completing his doctorate, however, he forewent the bar exam, and thus further training to become a fully qualified lawyer, and joined his father's company, where he initially received a modest salary of only 800 marks per year. One can assume that his father wanted to make him his successor after the death of his brothers, to ensure family succession and consistency for the company. After the death of his uncle Ismar, his father granted Kurt Muhsam power of attorney in June 1911 and involved him in the distribution of profits from 1912 onward.[45] In January 1913, at the age of 25, he became a personally liable partner, thus his father's business partner, and received a third of the distributed profits.[46] Until then, his had been the typical career path of an entrepreneur's son – but he now had to accept his father's inheritance perhaps earlier than expected.

---

45   Balance sheet book of Philipp Mühsam AG, annual financial statements for 1910, 1911, and 1912; *Berliner Börsen-Zeitung,* June 26, 1911.

46   Balance sheet book of Philipp Mühsam AG, annual financial statements for 1913; *Berliner Börsen-Zeitung,* January 18, 1913.

3.

War and Hyperinflation:
On the Path to Philipp Mühsam AG

The Challenge of the First World War

Kurt Mühsam's entry into the company ensured the continuation of the firm after Philipp Mühsam's death. Immediately after the start of the war in August 1914, he gave his senior employee Julius Herz general power of attorney, the power of representation in all business matters.[47] In this way, Mühsam took precautions in the event that he had to go to war and delegate decision-making authority to his employees.

As was usual with many medium-sized and large companies, *Philipp Mühsam oHG* founded a welfare fund for its workers and employees in 1915, which was endowed with a capital of 30,000 marks. The surviving documents contain no information about the occasion, but it is quite possible that its founding was based on Philipp Mühsam's last will. The fund was, in any case, certainly set up to support the families of its employees who were called up for military service.[48] At the time of its founding, initial hopes for a quick German victory in the war on the Western Front against France and Great Britain had generally weakened. It can be assumed that Kurt Mühsam wanted to provide for the future of his staff and wanted them to indirectly share in part of his rapidly increasing profits.

A year after his father's death and his taking over the company, Kurt Mühsam was actually called up for military service. Unfortunately, the few surviving documents do not provide any information about how long the "serving" reservist Mühsam had to serve in the army during the First World War. When he added Julius Herz to the circle of partners in November 1915 with a capital share of 25 percent in the general partnership and made him a personally liable partner, his call-up was apparently imminent.[49] His decision showed that he trusted Herz and wanted to permanently bind him to the company through an equity investment. Contrary to widespread anti-Semitic accusations, Mühsam fought at the front like many other Jewish Germans and did not serve in the

---

47 *Berliner Börsen-Zeitung*, August 5, 1914.

48 Balance sheet book of Philipp Mühsam AG 1915.

49 Balance sheet book of Philipp Mühsam AG, annual financial statements for 1915; *Berliner Börsen-Zeitung*, November 10, 1915.

safer, non-combat zones. For his service at the front, he was promoted to lieutenant, an honor that his regiment's anti-Semitic officer corps had previously denied him.[50]

The First World War initially brought the company strong growth in sales and profits. The increasing need for transport behind the front caused the demand for fuels and lubricants to grow steadily. Since the German Reich was cut off from important supplies of raw materials from overseas due to the British naval blockade, natural materials had to be replaced as much as possible by chemically produced synthetic materials. Income from the sale of chemicals and fuel rose from 451,000 marks in 1913 to 533,000 marks in the first year of the war in 1914 and almost reached the one-million mark in 1915 with 947,000 marks, which was then significantly exceeded in 1916 with 1,532,000 marks. The strong demand and the lack of effective government price controls allowed companies to achieve excessive profit margins, from which *Philipp Mühsam oHG* also benefited. Since the low prewar income tax rates were not increased significantly during the war, revenues grew appreciably. Because of the producers' increasing supply bottlenecks under the conditions of the war economy, earnings fell to 1,051,000 marks in 1917 and fell further to 839,000 marks in the last year of the war, 1918.[51]

These figures show that until 1917, the company clearly benefited from the sharp increase in demand for fuel and chemicals caused by the war. From 1915 to 1917, Mühsam and his partners subscribed to war bonds worth 450,000 marks, an indication of the company's good earnings and high liquidity, for which he was looking for investment opportunities.[52] Mühsam not only wanted to benefit from the good interest on the war bonds but also demonstrated his patriotic spirit and his hope for a military victory for the Reich. The war bonds did not have a fixed repayment date but rather were supposed to be repaid only after the end of the war.

50 "Von Mühsams Nachfahren," in: *Der Schild. Zeitung des Reichsbundes jüdischer Frontsoldaten*, July 24, 1935.

51 Balance sheet book of Philipp Mühsam AG, annual financial statements for 1913 to 1918.

52 *Berliner Börsen-Zeitung*, September 10, 1915; March 20, 1916; April 8, 1917; and October 15, 1917.

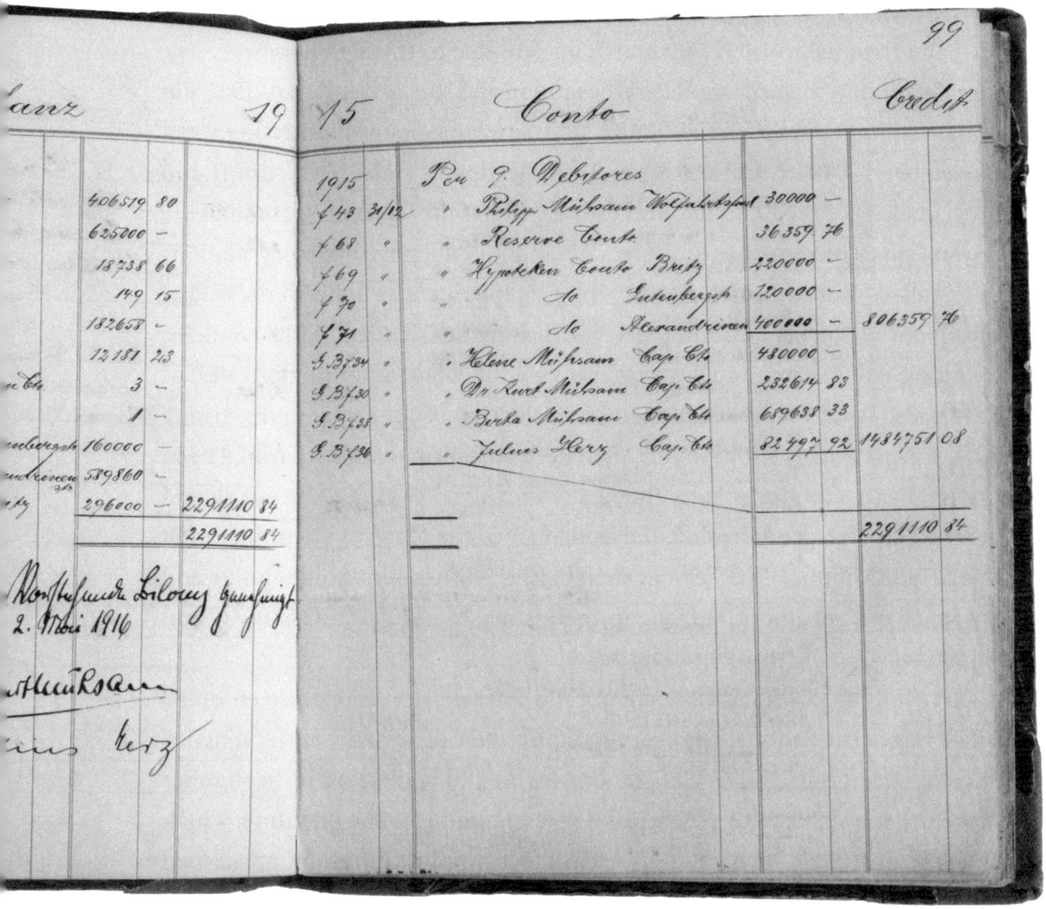

Figure 10: The welfare fund in the balance sheet of Philipp Mühsam oHG.

However, in 1918, soaring inflation and shortages of goods caused profits to shrink sharply. The rationing of chemical products, which had been introduced in 1915, was purely a regulation to combat shortages in the last year of the war. Because of the ammunition manufacturers' great need for nitrogen, sulfur, and chlorine, fewer and fewer chemicals were left for the needs of the civilian economy. The war economy was running out of resources.[53] While the owners of *Philipp Mühsam oHG* had distributed a profit of 421,000 marks in 1917, the corresponding amount fell to 10,700 marks in 1918.[54] And even this small profit distribution had to be paid for from capital reserves. From 1912 to 1917, the

53 Marcel Boldorf, *Ordnungspolitik und kriegswirtschaftliche Lenkung*; Werner Plumpe, "Chemische Industrie," in: Marcel Boldorf (ed.), *Deutsche Wirtschaft im Ersten Weltkrieg*, Berlin 2020, 23–66 and 193–226.

54 Balance sheet book of Philipp Mühsam AG, annual financial statements for 1918.

balance sheet value of capital contributions rose from 1,297,000 to 1,849,000 marks – and then fell to 1,092,000 marks in 1918 due to the high losses.

After the military defeat, the end of the empire and the Revolution of 1918 did not remain without impact on the relationship between employers and employees. On November 15, 1918, six days after the abdication of Kaiser Wilhelm II and the proclamation of the Republic, and four days after the German surrender, the employers had to recognize the unions' demand for collective wage negotiations in the so-called Stinnes-Legien Agreement. Employers could no longer resist the establishment of workers' committees, which were later called works councils. The working day became much more humane for workers and employees, as employers also had to accept the general introduction of the eight-hour working day, whereas previously a nine-hour, often even ten-hour, working day had been common. On the employer side, the heavy industrialist Hugo Stinnes signed the agreement; on the union side, the chairman of the General Commission of German Trade Unions, Carl Legien, signed. The Stinnes sons Hugo junior and Otto were to play an important role in the history of *Philipp Mühsam AG* and later *Brenntag*.

In Kurt Mühsam's own industry, chemical wholesale, the unions also enforced collective wage negotiations. They successfully argued against the entrepreneurs' claim to be able to set wages as they saw fit. At the beginning of September 1919, there was a strike in the chemical wholesale trade for the first time, which the Reich Ministry of Labor had to settle according to the legally prescribed procedure. The *Berliner Börsen-Zeitung* reported that Mühsam was one of the negotiators on the employer side.[55] One can make reasonable assumptions as to why the employers entrusted the chemical wholesaler with this task: As a lawyer with specialist knowledge of labor law, he was particularly suitable for the position of negotiator. The wage dispute of 1919 showed that authoritarian paternalism in the world of work had weakened, and the relationship between employers and employees was undergoing increasing legal regulation.

The Consequences of the First World War

In August 1919, the Reich government signed the Versailles Peace Treaty, which was dictated to it by the victorious powers. The greatest long-term burden on Germany were the Allies' high demands for financial reparations, which drove

---

55   *Berliner Börsen-Zeitung*, September 5, 1919.

up its national debt and added to inflation. Only after the treaty came into force did the British Navy lift the naval blockade against the Reich that had existed since the beginning of the war, after which imports of crude oil and petroleum products from the USA returned to normal. Income from sales at *Philipp Mühsam AG* rose from 839,000 to 1,090,000 marks in this first year of peace but in real terms remained behind the previous year due to inflation. The profits distributed were far below the exorbitant values of the first three years of the war, but at 114,000 marks, they reached a somewhat normal level again.[56] In 1920, Mühsam dissolved the welfare fund set up during the First World War, which in 1919 comprised 40,000 marks. It can be assumed that this decision was not only made because of the end of the war but was also due to the company's deteriorated equity ratio. For the years 1920 to 1923, the annual financial statements are only of limited informative value due to increasing inflation. Since the owners did not adjust the book value of the properties to the price increases, the balance sheets showed an equity ratio that was too low.[57] Only the regularly adjusted balance sheet values of mobile assets (machinery, tank wagons, and trucks) and current assets in the form of inventories approximated the increase in value on paper in increasingly worthless market amounts.

Inflation, which accelerated into hyperinflation in 1922, had drastic consequences for everyday business life.[58] The increasing devaluation of money and rising purchasing prices forced the company to increase its sales prices ever faster. Money lost its function as a store of value; cash, money in checking and savings accounts, and fixed-interest securities were completely devalued. To avoid inflation-related losses, the company was forced to shorten its customers' payment terms and collect outstanding debts more quickly. From the spring of 1923, as was common practice, prices at *Philipp Mühsam oHG* were calculated in the no longer existing gold mark or in dollars and converted into the devalued mark according to the daily exchange rate.

In a trading company, the consequences of inflation were easier to bear than in goods-producing companies, where months passed between order receipt, completion, and invoicing. *Philipp Mühsam oHG* issued its invoices for mineral oil products and chemicals immediately after delivery, insisted on immediate payment, and did everything to minimize the consequences of currency devaluation through rapid goods turnover. Because of the high

---

56 Balance sheet book of Philipp Mühsam AG, annual financial statements for 1919.

57 Balance sheet book of Philipp Mühsam AG, annual financial statements for 1920.

58 Sebastian Teupe, *Zeit des Geldes. Die deutsche Inflation zwischen 1914 und 1923*, Frankfurt a. M. 2022.

proportion of tangible assets in the company's total assets, their asset losses due to hyperinflation were limited. *Philipp Mühsam oHG* was, therefore, not among the big losers from the effects of inflation. While on the one hand, it lost all of its cash reserves, on the other hand, it benefited from the complete cancellation of its mortgage debt.

4.

Philipp Mühsam AG in the Volatile Economic Development of the Weimar Republic

At the beginning of November 1923, shortly before the absolute peak of hyperinflation, Mühsam and his partner Herz made an important decision about the future legal form of the company. They had gathered from the press reporting on inflation and the unsuccessful struggle against it that the completely devalued and effectively functionless market currency (Papiermark) was about to be replaced by a currency with stable value. Because of the imponderables of the upcoming currency reform and its impact on the company's share capital, they did not wait for the Papiermark to be replaced and decided to convert the general partnership into a joint stock corporation. This step would not only reduce the liability risk of the owners but also make it easier to accept new co-owners if necessary. Mühsam and Herz hoped that this would also facilitate the company's efforts to cover its capital needs in the future.[59]

When the stock corporation was entered in the commercial register on November 10, 1923, the wholly devalued Papiermark was on its last legs. Ten days before its replacement with the stable Rentenmark (starting 1924: Reichsmark), the owners set the share capital of *Philipp Mühsam AG* at the fictitious amount of 100 million marks. However, one can see from the following comparison that this assessment had already been overtaken by inflationary developments at the time of its publication in the commercial register: When the Papiermark was replaced by the stable Rentenmark on November 20, 1923, the Germans received for the seemingly gigantic amount of one trillion Papiermark just one Rentenmark. In addition to the two board members, Mühsam and Herz, the company had a third shareholder, Berta Mühsam, who held a significant share of the capital. The two authorized representatives, the chemist Dr. Ernst Brühl and the lawyer Ernst Höhne, only received a symbolic capital investment of 20,000 marks each.

Mühsam was able to recruit Henry Nathan (1862–1932), one of the leading bankers of his time, to chair the supervisory board.[60] Born in Hamburg, he had been a board member since 1903 and from 1920 even chairman of the

---

59 *Berliner Börsen-Zeitung*, November 23, 1923.

60 For Nathan's biography, see Rolf Wiegand, "Henry Nathan," in: *Neue Deutsche Biographie* (NDB), Vol. 18 (1997), 745 f.

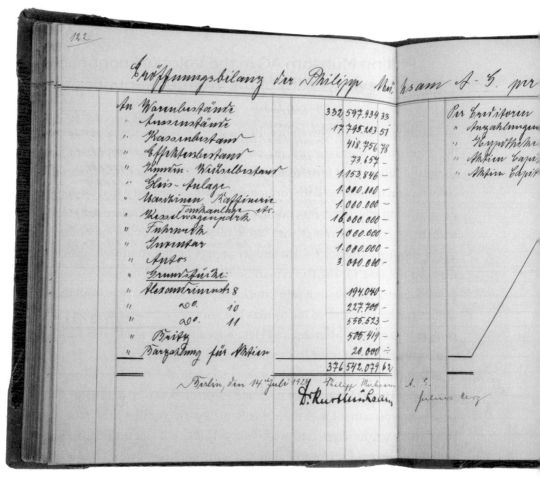

Figure 11: Inflation drove the opening balance sheet of Philipp Mühsam AG to dizzying heights.

board of *Dresdner Bank*, one of the five major banks in Germany at the time. Nathan's appointment as chairman of the supervisory board of *Philipp Mühsam AG* suggests that *Dresdner Bank* was the company's lender and chief banking connection, and that it processed a large part of its payment transactions through them. Although Nathan and other leading bankers held dozens of board seats, and their number was not yet limited by law, the appointment of a prominent banker as chairman of the board of a relatively small company was unusual. In addition, *Dresdner Bank* did not own any capital shares in *Philipp Mühsam AG* and was only at risk with relatively small loans. In other words, Nathan operated in significantly higher entrepreneurial spheres than Mühsam. Apparently, as a good credit customer and thanks to his entrepreneurial reputation, Mühsam

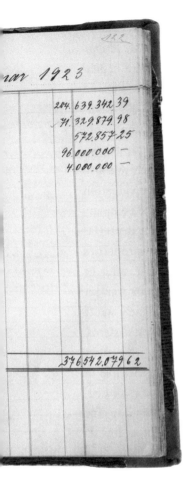

had been able to build up such a good relationship with the management of *Dresdner Bank* that they did not refuse his request to send one of their board members to his company's supervisory board. With his "enthralling personality" and his "noble character," which his business partner Herz attested to, Mühsam won over the much-courted Nathan and thus also secured his support for *Philipp Mühsam AG*.[61]

Conversely, Mühsam used his charm and networking skills to obtain supervisory board mandates in companies in the chemical industry. Although he did not own any shares, he became chairman of the supervisory board of *Gyrorector GmbH* and of *Concernos-Vertriebsgesellschaft für chemische Produkte mbH*, which competed with *Philipp Mühsam AG*. In 1927, he even took over the chairmanship of the *Aktiengesellschaft für chemische Produkte* that his father had founded.[62]

All in all, *Philipp Mühsam AG* had survived the total currency devaluation caused by hyperinflation in good shape. The majority of their assets consisted of real estate, gas stations, a small refinery, and tank cars, which were protected from inflationary devaluation and retained their intrinsic value and their earnings value. On January 1, 1924, the key date of their opening balance in the new currency, the cash balance in the account had shrunk to 11,260 Rentenmark. Only the foreign currency holdings worth 52,700 Rentenmark ensured sufficient liquidity for daily business. As an importing company, *Philipp Mühsam oHG* had regularly exchanged Papiermark for stable dollars in order to pay for its mineral oil imports, thereby saving part of its current monetary assets from inflation. While their equity interests in other companies had retained their value, the war bonds had become worthless.[63] On the other hand, *Philipp Mühsam oHG* was able to unload all mortgage debts during the inflation period and start the post-hyperinflation period debt-free.

61   These characterizations can be found in Julius Herz's obituary for Kurt Mühsam in the *Vossische Zeitung* from March 22, 1928.

62   *Berliner Börsen-Zeitung*, August 12, 1922; *Berliner Tageblatt*, August 11, 1927; *Vossische Zeitung*, March 22, 1928.

63   Rentenmark opening balance sheet of Philipp Mühsam AG as of January 1, 1924, in: Balance sheet book of Philipp Mühsam AG.

Vorstehende in das Register unter Nummer 11 Jahr

PHILIPP MÜHSAM A.-G.
BERLIN SW 68 – ALEXANDRINENSTR. 11

Geschäftsbericht für 1927

Figure 12: Balance sheet from 1927 with the Philipp Mühsam AG logo.

When it restarted its balance sheet on January 1, 1924, *Philipp Mühsam AG* had a share capital of one million Rentenmark and modest reserves of 125,000 Rentenmark. Compared to the boom years up to 1917, the capital account had shrunk, which was also due to the conservative valuation of their fixed assets. The company took significantly higher depreciation on its commercial properties on Alexandrinenstrasse and its warehouse in Britz than was required by law. It completely wrote off its refinery and tank systems, the railway tracks, and the entire fleet according to the principle of caution, which was not at all necessary under accounting law. The actual intrinsic value of its investment assets was significantly higher than the balance sheet revealed.

From 1924 to 1927, *Philipp Mühsam AG* only achieved low annual profits of 12,700 to 25,600 Reichsmark (RM), which did not allow for profit distributions. From 1925 onward, profits were squeezed by a government-imposed mortgage revaluation debt of 250,000 RM, which the company had to pay interest on and gradually repay. Like all inflation winners who were freed from their mortgage debt through hyperinflation, it had to make a financial contribution to compensate the inflation losers: The proceeds from the mortgage appreciation debt were used to compensate savers who had lost their entire savings due to inflation. The owners Mühsam and Herz therefore refrained from sharing profits and only paid themselves salaries that were significantly lower than their profit withdrawals in previous years.[64] Investments in tankers for the transport of gasoline and the accelerated repayment of the revaluation debt were given

---

64   Balance sheet book of Philipp Mühsam AG, annual financial statements for 1924 to 1927.

priority. The time of six-figure annual incomes was irretrievably over for the Mühsam family.

The balance sheet totals of 2.1 to 2.5 million RM in the years 1925 to 1931 corresponded approximately to the level from 1910 to 1913 but were lower in real terms due to the devaluation of money. Unfortunately, the surviving balance sheet does not show any sales figures. Up to and including 1933, the low annual surpluses were not sufficient to pay dividends.

As the motorization of private and commercial road transport made progress after the First World War, sales of fuels and mineral oils rose steadily in the 1920s. In 1925, the reduction in the prohibitively high car tax helped reduce the cost of owning automobiles and thereby promoted their spread among the upper middle class and among the self-employed. *Philipp Mühsam AG's* sales benefited from the acceleration of motorization through the increased demand for fuels and mineral oils, so its business outcomes improved significantly from 1928 onward. In that year the company recorded a profit of 38,500 RM, which it was able to increase to 52,300 RM in 1929 and to 58,200 RM in 1930.[65] With the exception of 1930, the good business results were not achieved by foregoing necessary depreciation. The company wrote off its mobile assets relatively quickly and used rising profits to reduce its debt to banks.

Philipp Mühsam AG sold its gasoline under the brand names Autophil and Benzophil to car repair shops, gas stations, and commercial end-users, to whom it paid a sales commission based on sales.[66] In addition to lubricating oils and greases, their other products for the growing motor vehicle market included the antifreeze Glysantin and brake fluid, both products from the *IG Farben* factory in Schkopau, the largest chemical company in

Figure 13: Giveaways were already available in the 1920s: a deck of cards with advertising for Philipp Mühsam AG and its Autophil petrol brand.

---

65   Balance sheet book of Philipp Mühsam AG, annual financial statements for 1928 to 1930
66   Letter from Philipp Mühsam AG to the freight forwarder Otto Kliems, Rathenow, July 17, 1937, in: Files from the Brenntag Berlin site.

the world. Even back then, *Philipp Mühsam AG* relied on an extensive product range.[67]

The contracts with the gas stations were designed in quite different ways. Some of the owners were only connected to the company through a supply contract. In other cases, the firm built a filling station on the property of a gas station owner at its own expense. In return, the owner had to undertake to purchase gasoline and all other operating materials such as motor oil from *Philipp Mühsam AG* for a period of four years. The filling station became the property of the gas station owner as soon as he had purchased 120,000 liters of gasoline. There were also cases in which *Philipp Mühsam AG* provided a credit guarantee for the customer in return for a longer-term delivery contract.[68]

The End of the Family Era

On March 20, 1928, the chronicle of the Philipp Mühsam family of entrepreneurs came to a tragic end. Kurt Mühsam died at the age of just 40 as a result of an operation. His wife, his business partner, his "dear friend" Julius Herz, the workers and employees, and the supervisory board members of *Philipp Mühsam AG* paid their respects to him in eight obituaries in the *Vossische Zeitung*.[69] In addition to his 29-year-old wife Ellen Mühsam, née Löwenstein, he left behind his daughters Irene (* 1920) and Andrea (* 1923).[70] Herz was the only board member left because Ellen Mühsam had no appropriate training or professional experience and did not feel capable of filling the necessary leadership role. In the patriarchal society of that time, she would hardly have been accepted as a company manager. Like her mother-in-law Berta, her role in the company was limited to a mandate on the supervisory board. In 1931, due to the poor business situation and the lack of dividends for years, she sold her majority stake, with the exception of a few shares, at the very low price of 25 percent to Herz, who thus became the company's controlling majority shareholder.[71] After selling her

---

67 Letter Brenntag AG to Walter Zimmerhöcker, Berlin-Wilmersdorf, dated 15.9.1937, in: Akten der Brenntag-Niederlassung Berlin. The original letter is no longer extant, but was reissued on 10.9.1947, following the request of the addressee. Due to the missing original, it cannot be ascertained whether the company still operated as "Philipp Mühsam AG" in 1937, or already as "Brenntag."

68 Contract between Philipp Mühsam AG and Martin Lorenz, Brandenburg/Havel, January 30, 1934; Guarantee agreement between *Philipp Mühsam AG* and the company Excursionsschifffahrt Adolf Lübeck, 1930, in: Brenntag SE, Berlin branch.

69 *Vossische Zeitung*, March 22, 1928

70 The possible death dates of his wife and children could not be reconstructed. The widow and children emigrated to Chile in 1936 (Hamann, *Die Mühsams*, 240).

71 Letter from Hugo Stinnes to the restitution office of the city of Berlin, January 16, 1950, in: *Landesarchiv Nordrhein-Westfalen*, quoted hereafter as LA NRW, Abt. Rheinland, BR 336 m No. 20799.

Telegramm-Adresse:
Philipp Mühsam, Berlin.

PHILIPP MÜHSAM

Reichsbank-Giro-Conto.

Berlin S. 14

Alexandrinen-Strasse 11

Fernsprecher: Amt IV, 2900, 2901, 2902, 2891.

„Autophil"

Unter der Bezeichnung

„Autophil"

bringe ich ein Automobilbenzin in den Handel, das sich von den bisher verwendeten Benzinsorten dadurch unterscheidet, daß es stets gleichmäßig geliefert werden kann und sich durch ein leichtes spezifisches Gewicht auszeichnet.

Der Preis für mein

„Autophil"

stellt sich bei Abschlüssen von mindestens 2000 kg.

in Eisenfässern auf M. 36.— per 100 kg.
in Kannen „ „ 38.— „ 100 „

bei geringeren Quantitäten:

in Eisenfässern Mk. 37.— per 100 kg.
in Kannen „ 39.— „ 100 „

Auch mit Offerten in billigeren Benzinsorten stehe ich gern zu Diensten und erbitte Ihre werten Anfragen.

Gleichzeitig teile ich Ihnen mit, daß ich Sie auch in **Motoröl**, dünn-, mittel- und dickflüssig, **Carbid, Putzwolle, Solarine-Putzwasser, Consistentem Fett** etc. sehr vorteilhaft bedienen kann und bitte auch bei Bedarf hierin um gefl. Berücksichtigung.

Ich erwarte gern Ihre werten Nachrichten und zeichne

Hochachtungsvoll

Philipp Mühsam.

Figure 14: Philipp Mühsam's first steps in petroleum trading under the trade name Autophil, 1906.

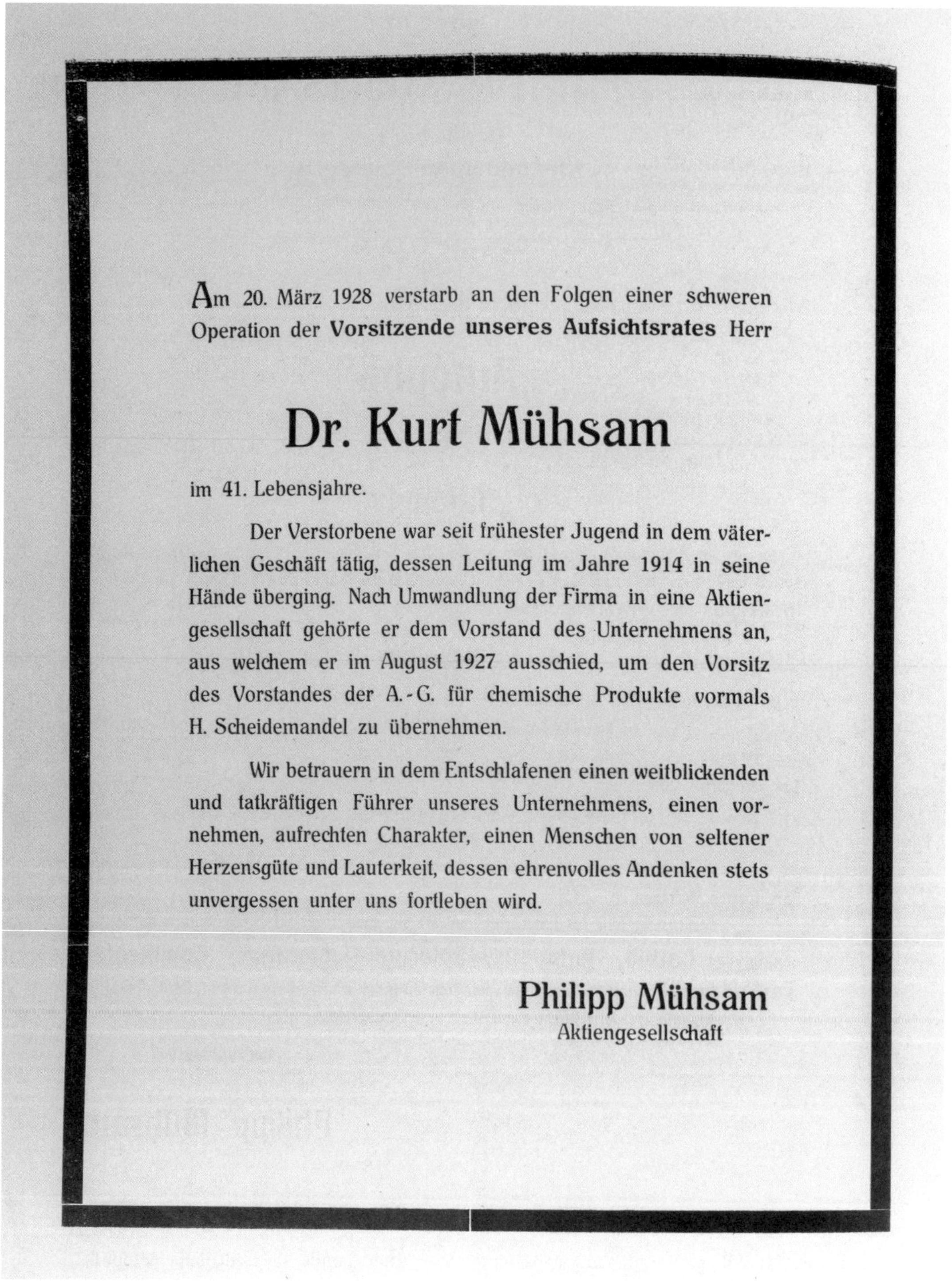

Am 20. März 1928 verstarb an den Folgen einer schweren Operation der **Vorsitzende unseres Aufsichtsrates** Herr

Dr. Kurt Mühsam

im 41. Lebensjahre.

Der Verstorbene war seit frühester Jugend in dem väterlichen Geschäft tätig, dessen Leitung im Jahre 1914 in seine Hände überging. Nach Umwandlung der Firma in eine Aktiengesellschaft gehörte er dem Vorstand des Unternehmens an, aus welchem er im August 1927 ausschied, um den Vorsitz des Vorstandes der A.-G. für chemische Produkte vormals H. Scheidemandel zu übernehmen.

Wir betrauern in dem Entschlafenen einen weitblickenden und tatkräftigen Führer unseres Unternehmens, einen vornehmen, aufrechten Charakter, einen Menschen von seltener Herzensgüte und Lauterkeit, dessen ehrenvolles Andenken stets unvergessen unter uns fortleben wird.

Philipp Mühsam
Aktiengesellschaft

Figure 15: The early death of the main owner Dr. Kurt Mühsam on March 20, 1928.

shares, Ellen Mühsam left the supervisory board. Because of the company's good reputation, there was no reason to change the name *Philipp Mühsam AG* after the last Mühsams left the company's boards. Herz also remained the sole manager of the company.

From 1931 onward, *Philipp Mühsam AG* felt the consequences of the global economic crisis, which had profound and lasting effects on the entire economy, as a number of companies and banks had to close, unemployment rose dramatically, and the economy collapsed. A surplus of just under 7,000 RM showed that sales were shrinking and that selling prices and trading margins were falling. The sharp decline in corporate earnings and private household income forced car owners to sell or deregister their vehicles. The dramatic 30 percent decline in economic output affected all German industries, including the chemical trade, and caused the number of unemployed to rise to six million. The development of private motorization came to a standstill during the crisis and was even reversed. Higher tariffs on oil and fuel imports, imposed to protect domestic oil production and the production of synthetic gasoline, made gasoline more expensive and exacerbated the crisis-related decline in motorization. But even at the height of the Great Depression in 1932, which confronted the population with mass unemployment and fears for the future in the aftermath of the global economic crisis, *Philipp Mühsam AG* still reported a profit of almost 13,000 RM.[72] Although the German economy was in a dramatic crisis and shrank by 30 percent from 1929 to 1932, the company's existence was still secured.

---

72 Annual financial statements for 1932 of *Philipp Mühsam AG*.

5

As a Jewish Company Under the Nazi Regime: The Years from 1933 to 1936

The Consequences of the Global Economic Crisis and the Economic Upswing of the National Socialists

As for many other companies, the global economic crisis lasted a long time for *Philipp Mühsam AG*. The overall subdued mood, high unemployment, and the still weak capitalization of the economy also affected the petroleum business and the trade in chemicals. In 1933, the year the National Socialists came to power, the company was no longer able to avoid restructuring as a result of the long and severe economic crisis. Out of caution, Herz took high depreciation on the buildings and land, which he financed by reducing the share capital from one million to 872,000 RM.[73] Due to the lack of additional documents, it cannot be determined whether his caution was based on negative expectations of National Socialist rule. However, several pieces of evidence speak against this assumption. The mineral oil business of *Philipp Mühsam AG* benefited from the abolition of the motor vehicle tax for new cars by the National Socialist government in March 1933.[74] The owners of used cars were also able to replace the motor vehicle tax with a cheap one-off payment, and sales of gasoline and lubricating oils increased because many car owners reregistered their decommissioned vehicles. *Philipp Mühsam AG's* gross profit from the sale of goods rose from 834,000 to 900,000 RM in 1933.

Regrettably, from the few documents that have survived, it is also impossible to reconstruct how Herz and Ellen Mühsam viewed the future after the National Socialist takeover. In March 1933, just six weeks after Hitler was appointed Chancellor, the NSDAP called for a boycott day against Jewish businesses, but this was not initially followed by a systematic boycott of these businesses. Since *Philipp Mühsam AG* sold primarily to loyal commercial customers and not to government agencies, the risk for the firm of an anti-Semitic boycott was comparatively low at that time. National Socialist activists in Berlin and

---

73   Annual financial statements for 1933 of Philipp Mühsam AG.

74   Christopher Kopper, *Handel und Verkehr im 20. Jahrhundert*, Munich 2002.

Brandenburg had no way of knowing whether the gas stations purchased gasoline and mineral oils from a Jewish or a non-Jewish wholesaler. Customers were also unable to draw any conclusions about a Jewish company from the brand names Benzophil and Autophil.

The positive business development of *Philipp Mühsam AG* continued in 1934. With prices largely stable, gross profit from the sale of goods rose by 7.5 percent compared to 1933. Because of the growing sales, additional employees were even hired.[75] In the following financial year, 1935, the ordinary annual surplus jumped to 46,000 RM, to which an unspecified extraordinary income of 78,000 RM was added.[76] From 1934 onward, the company paid out a dividend of 6 percent of its share capital for the first time in a long while;[77] however, already by the end of 1932, the economy had started moving out of the deep depression. The National Socialist-led government promoted economic recovery through tax incentives for investments and comprehensive job creation measures, which, from 1934 onward, led to the accelerated and initially secret rearmament of the Reichswehr. Fuel traders like *Philipp Mühsam AG* benefited primarily from the regime's motorization-friendly policy. Due to the increasing demand for fuel, Berlin's most modern tank storage company expanded its underground sites, which corresponded to the latest storage technology.

Even if the business of *Philipp Mühsam AG* was not yet affected by the anti-Jewish sentiment in Germany, it can be assumed that the highly discriminatory conditions against Jewish citizens were personally felt by the Mühsam and Herz families. The "Nuremberg Laws" of September 1935 degraded all Jewish residents with more than two Jewish grandparents to second-class citizens with limited civil rights. After the ban on marriages to non-Jewish people, Jewish Germans had to reckon with further restrictions on their rights and increasing discrimination in both professional and everyday life. Between 1933 and 1935, ten members of the extended Mühsam family had already left Germany. On July 10, 1934, members of the SS guards in the Oranienburg concentration camp murdered the well-known anarchist writer Erich Mühsam, a distant cousin of Kurt Mühsam and a participant in that large family gathering in 1911. It can be assumed that these developments affected Ellen Mühsam and her family and, by the end of 1935, forced her to emigrate to Chile with her daughters. She and her mother-in-law Berta Mühsam left no letters or memoirs from which their decision could be

75   Annual financial statements for 1934 of Philipp Mühsam AG.
76   Annual financial statements for 1935 of Philipp Mühsam AG.
77   Annual report 1935 of Philipp Mühsam AG, May 1936.

directly reconstructed. Presumably, Ellen Mühsam wanted to spare her daughters the experience of growing up under discriminatory conditions.[78]

Ellen remarried and left her home country of Germany forever on March 1, 1936, with her second husband Ernst Haase and her daughters.[79] The files of the chief financial president of Berlin and Brandenburg show that she had to leave a significant part of her assets behind. These included the Mühsam family's home at Budapester Strasse 14 in a prime location opposite the Berlin Zoo, an apartment building, and shares in other apartment buildings in Charlottenburg and Neukölln.[80] The rental income flowed into a so-called emigrant blocked account, the receipts of which she could only access to a very limited extent and only with the consent of the tax authorities and the foreign exchange office. Due to increasing German restrictions on cross-border currency transactions, she was only able to transfer a small portion of her rental income to Chile.

Because of the low exchange rate of the Reichsmark in free foreign exchange trading and the priority of using foreign currency for imports important for armaments, Jewish emigrants were only able to exchange their financial assets into freely available foreign currency under very unfavorable conditions. Presumably for this reason, Ellen Haase decided against selling her real estate. She paid the so-called "Reich Flight Tax" (Reichsfluchtsteuer) of 25 percent on assets transferred abroad from her financial reserves. Her assets that remained in Germany ultimately fell victim to the gradual and then total expropriation of Jewish property. In November 1941, due to the Reich Interior Minister's 11th Ordinance on the Reich Citizenship Act, like all emigrated and deported Jews, she lost all the assets that she had involuntarily left behind.[81] In 1942, the Gestapo confiscated a package containing jewelry worth 14,000 RM, which Ellen Haase had previously not been allowed to export and had given to a relative for safekeeping.[82] The state police sold the jewelry to a jewelry dealer and collected the proceeds for the benefit of the Reich. The Mühsam family's house by the zoo was also irretrievably lost: On the night of November 22, 1943, it was completely destroyed in a bomb attack.[83]

---

78 About Jewish life in Germany before and after 1935, see Saul Friedländer, *Nazi Germany and the Jews. The years of persecution 1933–1939*, New York 1997.

79 According to information from the Gestapo files, Ellen Mühsam and Ernst Haase's marriage ended in divorce in 1938.

80 Brandenburgisches Hauptstaatsarchiv Potsdam, quoted hereafter as BLHA, Rep. 36 A (Bundesfinanzpräsident Berlin-Brandenburg), No. 13387, tax file Ellen Haase; ibid., No. 27541, tax file Andrea Mühsam.

81 Reichsgesetzblatt I, 1941, Verordnung zum Reichsbürgergesetz of September 15, 1935, November 25, 1941.

82 BLHA, Rep. 36 A, No. 27542.

83 This emerges from the file on Ellen Haase from the chief finance president of Berlin-Brandenburg.

Figure 16: Philipp and Berta Mühsam's gravestone at the Jewish cemetery Schönhauser Allee in Berlin.

In 1936, at the age of 37, Ellen Haase was not yet too old for a new start in a foreign country. For her mother-in-law Berta Mühsam, however, emigration was no longer an option due to her advanced age of 79. She had to suffer the increasing persecution of Jewish Germans and the pogrom night on November 9, 1938, and died of natural causes in Berlin on March 7, 1939.[84] Her daughter Eva Kantorowicz and her husband, Dr. Franz Kantorowicz, emigrated to Great Britain in time. After the war, they moved to the United States, where Eva Kantorowicz died in 1971 at the age of 89. Her daughter Vera (1907–1994) also emigrated to the USA.[85]

Of the 46 members of the extensive Mühsam family, 32 were able to emigrate to a safe country. Nine relatives were deported and murdered, three committed suicide before the impending deportation, and two survived the persecution by going underground and in hiding.[86]

---

84   Date of death according to www.geni.com [last accessed September 19, 2023].

85   One of Eva Kantorowicz's two sons died in England in 1933. The fate of the second son could not be clarified.

86   Hamann, *Die Mühsams*, 240 f.

6.

"Aryanization": The Sale of Philipp Mühsam AG to the Stinnes Family

Since Ellen Mühsam had already sold her shares in *Philipp Mühsam AG* to Julius Herz after her husband's death, her emigration had no impact on the future of the company. Herz, who was also Jewish, owned 76 percent of the voting rights and 91 percent of the share capital and did not have to take into account a blocking minority.[87] It can be assumed that he found himself compelled to sell the company in view of the increasing legal and social discrimination against Jewish Germans. Research into potential buyers led him to the Stinnes family of entrepreneurs in Mülheim an der Ruhr, to whom he made a sales offer on Christmas Eve 1936.[88]

His negotiating partners were the sons of the legendary industrialist Hugo Stinnes (1870–1924), who had bought up a huge conglomerate of companies during the inflationary period and was at times considered the largest and most powerful entrepreneur in Germany. But just one year after his death, the economic empire was on the verge of bankruptcy. During the inflationary period, Stinnes financed his company purchases with loans from German, British, and American banks, which his sons and his widow were no longer able to repay due to high interest rates and the sluggish economy. The Stinnes family had to sell most of their company as part of the restructuring process. In return for a large American debt restructuring loan, the family transferred part of their companies to the American holding company *Hugo Stinnes Corporation*, in which they had a 54 percent stake. Some mining companies and the *Hugo Stinnes oHG* for the ore, coal, and mining trade were owned and operated by the sons Hugo Hermann (1897–1982) and Otto Stinnes (1903–1983), as well as his widow Cläre (1872–1973). Thus, after Hugo Stinnes' death in 1924, management by the family continued.[89]

Philipp Mühsam AG was a welcome opportunity for the Stinnes family to expand the business circle of their company. The brothers probably knew Herz's plight as a Jewish entrepreneur and suspected that he wanted to emigrate from

---

87 Balance sheet book of Philipp Mühsam AG 1935.

88 LA NRW, Rep. 176, No. 5710, letter from Julius Hart, formerly Julius Herz, to the trustee of the American, British, and French zones for forcibly transferred assets, June 20, 1949.

89 Gerald D. Feldman, *Hugo Stinnes*, Munich 1997, 932–955.

Figure 17: The new co-owner Hugo Hermann Stinnes.

Germany as soon as possible. A business letter from 1947 from Hugo Hermann, who was also called Hugo Stinnes jr., to his director shows that he was aware of the "sound, solid foundation" of *Philipp Mühsam AG.*[90]

Herz estimated the value of *Philipp Mühsam AG* at three million RM and made the brothers a sales offer of 2.5 million RM. Hugo and Otto Stinnes rejected his offer and persuaded him to present them with a lower offer on February 6, 1937.[91] It can be assumed that Herz was unable to find any other solvent potential buyers. Although he lowered his sales offer to 1.6 million RM, an agreement was not initially reached. However, the negotiations continued, and according to information provided by Herz as part of the restitution proceedings, the brothers reduced the purchase price to 1.475 million RM at the last moment. On February 20, 1937, the sale of all shares in *Philipp Mühsam AG* was finally contractually sealed.[92] The behavior of Hugo and Otto Stinnes was quite typical of the buyers of Jewish companies who consciously and purposefully profited from the plight of the previous Jewish owners.

Due to the lack of surviving files from the Berlin Chamber of Industry and Commerce and the Berlin NSDAP district leadership, it cannot be determined whether the Chamber or the economic advisor of the Nazi Party intervened in the sales negotiations, as was usual in the sales of larger Jewish companies. Seminal, empirically based studies on the more or less involuntary sale of Jewish companies to non-Jewish new owners ("Aryanization") show that the district economic advisors (NSDSAP-Gauwirtschaftsberater) approved the non-Jewish

---

90 Archive for Christian Democratic Politics St. Augustin (hereafter: ACDP), 1-220-0338, letter from Hugo Stinnes to his director Bruno Hartung, December 29, 1947.

91 LA NRW, Rep. 176, No. 5710; Günter Buchstab, *Die Stinnes Gruppe 1933–1945*, Rheinbach 1999, 54–59.

92 Ibid.

prospective buyers and, in some cases, intervened in the negotiations on behalf of National Socialist entrepreneurs.[93]

Since there is no evidence of competing potential buyers, the intervention of the district economic advisor in the case of *Philipp Mühsam AG* is very unlikely. From the perspective of the district leadership, there would have been no reason to intervene against the Stinnes family. Hugo Stinnes jr. was viewed by National Socialist officials as politically harmless, despite his external distance from the NSDAP. He had belonged to the nationalist and anti-republican "Stahlhelm" organization until 1933 and joined the SA in the same year.[94] Unlike his brother Otto, he did not become a member of the NSDAP but was considered loyal among Nazi officials.[95] Consequently, the National Socialist mayor of his hometown Mülheim an der Ruhr appointed him city councilman.[96] Even if this voluntary position was exclusively associated with advisory tasks and Hugo Stinnes jr. owed his appointment primarily to his reputation as an entrepreneur, it was an indication of his good reputation in National Socialist circles.

Philipp Mühsam AG's strong foothold in the mineral oil and chemicals trade offered the Stinnes family an opportunity to invest in two business areas with growth potential. Because of the business focus in Berlin and Brandenburg, the Stinnes companies, which were primarily active in the Ruhr area and along the Rhine, were also able to noticeably expand their geographical business circle.

The sale took a long time to complete, which is why Herz was only able to emigrate to the USA on September 22, 1937. Since he was already 55 years old, starting a new career in emigration proved to be very difficult. Herz settled in New York because he hoped to be able to make contact with other Germans more easily and establish business connections more quickly.[97] To be more readily accepted, he changed his name to Julius Hart. Like all other Jewish emigrants, he was only able to save a small part of his fortune as start-up capital abroad. The Gestapo forced him to pledge a claim to the tax authorities against the *Dresdner Bank* amounting to 156,000 RM as security for possible tax debts. He had to pay the "Reich Flight Tax" of 25 percent of his capital transfer abroad to the German state. The greatest loss of assets arose from the very low exchange rate of the Reichsmark (Sperrmark, i.e., blocked marks in emigrants' frozen accounts)

93   Frank Bajohr, *"Arisierung" in Hamburg*, Hamburg 1997, 173–188.

94   Staatsarchiv Hamburg, hereafter: StAHH, 221-11, No. I CC 650, Otto Stinnes' denazification file. Otto Stinnes joined the NSDAP in May 1933.

95   StAHH, 221-11, No. I CC 650, Otto Stinnes denazification file.

96   LA NRWDuisburg, Abt. Rheinland, NW 1000, No. 10165, denazification file of Hugo Stinnes jr.

97   BLHA, Rep. 36 A, No. 14775.

when exporting capital. For *Philipp Mühsam AG's* sales proceeds of 1.475 million RM, he ultimately received an amount of a mere $ 49,500.[98]

In 1937, Hugo and Otto Stinnes certainly did not expect that taking advantage of Herz would have repercussions. But on September 17, 1949, Julius Hart submitted an application for compensation for his financial loss to the British Zone's Central Office for Reparation. Hart could have asked for the sale to be canceled but instead sought an appropriate additional payment on top of the low selling price. His request for restitution put the Stinnes family in a difficult position: The Allied military governments in Berlin and North Rhine-Westphalia placed *Philipp Mühsam AG*, now renamed *Brenntag,* under custodianship and removed it from the unrestricted control of its owners. Hugo and Otto Stinnes were therefore under pressure to reach a settlement with Hart. Their lawyers signed a settlement agreement on September 1, 1950, according to which Hart received 720,000 D-Mark to settle his claim for reparation.[99]

The takeover of *Philipp Mühsam AG* was not the only "Aryanization" in which the Stinnes brothers and their employees were involved. After purchasing and renaming the company, *Brenntag* took over a gas station at Kurfürstenstrasse 41 in Berlin that belonged to Julius Stahl, Lore Lippmann, and Lotte Herzfeld, who had managed to escape to Palestine and America. In 1952, they reached a settlement with *Brenntag* and an additional payment of 5,000 D-Mark.[100]

---

98   LA NRW Abt. Rheinland, BR 336, No. 20799.

99   Ibid.

100 Settlement protocol 84 WGA 1410/51 of the Berlin Restitution Office.

7

Brenntag as Part of the Stinnes Group
Before and During the War

In 1937, the new owners Cläre, Hugo, and Otto Stinnes left the four remaining board members of *Philipp Mühsam AG*, all of whom were not Jewish, in office and only appointed their manager Leo Drees as the new chairman of the board. At an annual general meeting on July 14, five months after the purchase, they changed the name of the company to *"Brennstoff-, Chemikalien- und Transport Aktiengesellschaft,"* or *Brenntag* for short.[101] It was not until 1939 that the "Aryanized" companies were obliged to operate under a new and unambiguously non-Jewish name. However, the renaming was intended to erase the memory of the old owners as quickly as possible, to disguise the "Aryanization", and to emphasize the "Aryan" character. This semantic "Aryanization" was also part of the Nazi policy to expel Jews from German economic life, not only personally and directly but also by means of erasing the consciousness and memory of them.

The "t" in *Brenntag* stood for commercial transport on behalf of other companies, a business area the new owners developed quickly and determinedly. Shortly after purchasing the company, they commissioned two ocean-going motor freight ships, each with a carrying capacity of 8,000 tons, from the *Flensburger Schiffbau-Gesellschaft*, which they stationed in the port of Hamburg. The two ships, each with 5,350 gross tons, were named "Mülheim-Ruhr" and "Mathias Stinnes."[102] They had a balance sheet value of 2.4 million RM each and caused *Brenntag AG's* fixed assets to increase several times over.[103] The purchase was financed partly through ship mortgages and partly through a capital increase from 872,000 to 1,500,000 RM. Compared to the two ships, the expansion of the tank facilities from 1938 to 1940 was almost insignificant in the balance sheets.[104]

The transport business was, however, not particularly successful. The annual report for 1940 simply mentioned that "our shipping department has developed satisfactorily."[105] According to the audit report for 1943, *Brenntag* generated 85

---

101 StaHH, 231-7B 1995-2, Vol. 1, annual report of Brenntag AG 1937; Notarized minutes of the general meeting on July 14, 1937. The name translates as fuel, chemicals, and transport corporation.

102 Matthias Stinnes (1790–1845) was the founder of the Stinnes company and the entrepreneurial dynasty of the same name.

103 Technical information on the ships in the StAHH, "War Damages Office for Maritime Shipping" (Kriegsschädenamt für die Seeschiffahrt), No. D 25-1 and D 25-2.

104 Annual report of Brenntag AG 1938; Balance sheet of Brenntag AG 1940.

105 LA NRW, Gerichte, Rep. 283, No. 58, Vol. 2, Report of the Board of Directors on the 1940 fiscal year, July 1941.

Treibstoffe
Schmieröle
Lösungsmittel · Chemikalien

Brennſtoff-Chemikalien-u.Transport-AG

(vormals Philipp Mühſam AG) Berlin SW 68

688

Figure 18: The advertisement shows how mineral oils were bottled and acids stored in 1938. At the same time, Brenntag informed its customers about the "Aryanization" of the company name.

percent of its income (11.1 of 13.0 million RM) in its core business, trading in petroleum products and chemicals, and in the further processing of mineral oil but only just under 7 percent in the shipping business.[106]

Because of its corporate purpose, which included the storage and transport of fuels, *Brenntag AG* was considered important in terms of armaments policy. Without a corresponding certificate from Hermann Göring's Office of the Four-Year Plan, the Reich Ministry of Economics would have refused to approve the capital increase.[107] Even before the war began on September 1, 1939, *Brenntag* benefited significantly from the increasing demand for fuel and the growing transport needs of the war economy. Unfortunately, no lists of suppliers and customers have been preserved from this time that could provide information about its role in the war economy. There is no evidence that *Brenntag* supplied lethal chemicals to the SS concentration and extermination camps. The camps obtained the deadly crystalline hydrogen cyanide (Zyklon B) directly from the manufacturer Degesch (*Deutsche Gesellschaft für Schädlingsbekämpfung GmbH,* based in Frankfurt am Main) and not from chemical traders.

From 1937 to 1938, *Brenntag's* profits rose significantly from 25,000 to 142,000 RM and remained at this level until 1942. However, the profits were not unusually high in relation to the greatly increased equity capital. They allowed *Brenntag* to distribute the legally stipulated maximum dividend of 6 percent of the share capital to the owners and to continue to value its assets conservatively. *Brenntag's* earnings did not suffer from the war-related rationing of gasoline and diesel. The Reich Department for Mineral Oils in Hermann Göring's Office of the Four-Year Plan decided on the principles for the distribution of mineral oils to the Wehrmacht, armaments producers, utility companies, and all other allottees. The Central Bureau for Mineral Oil, which was subordinate to the Department, administered and implemented rationing and distribution and allocated the quantities of fuel to petroleum dealers that they were allowed to give to recipients of gasoline stamps.[108] Although unlike during the First World War, purchase prices and retail prices were frozen and regulated by the state through a price freeze, *Brenntag* still made a decent profit. In addition to gasoline and diesel, the company also sold propellants to replace gasoline.

---

106 Audit report for 1943 (with comparative figures for 1942).

107 Letter from Hugo Stinnes to Leo Drees, August 9, 1937.

108 Karlsch/Stokes, *Faktor Öl,* 184, 203.

In 1942, *Brenntag* increased its share capital to two million RM, which was financed through free reserves and its retained earnings.[109] Since *Brenntag* was sufficiently capitalized, the capital increase was primarily intended to enable a higher profit distribution to the Stinnes family. In 1943, *Brenntag* even doubled its share capital to four million RM through capital contributions from Cläre, Hugo, and Otto Stinnes and increased the profit distribution from 120,000 to 200,000 RM.[110]

Due to the lack of written and oral sources, the question remains open as to whether – and to what extent – *Brenntag* used forced labor during the war. Since *Brenntag* had 81 employees and only 53 workers in 1938,[111] and the fuel and chemicals business did not grow dramatically during the war, the number of possible forced laborers was certainly small in relation to the large number of forced laborers in the *Stinnes Group's* mines. However, the auditor's report on the 1943 annual accounts contains a note that *Brenntag* had spent 17,000 RM

Figure 19: Brenntag share from 1942 for 1,000 Reichsmark.

109 LA NRW, Gerichte, Rep. 283, No. 58, Vol. 2, Report of the Board of Directors on the 1941 financial year, October 1942.

110 Ibid., notarial minutes of the Brenntag general meeting on April 29, 1943.

111 Buchstab, *Der Stinnes-Konzern*, 57.

on setting up barracks for foreign workers. Due to the situation at the time, it is likely that these were forced laborers.[112]

In 1943, the majority of Western European workers in Germany no longer worked voluntarily but under duress. The numerically dominant workers from Eastern Europe were for the most part deported to the Reich. After the war, a denazification committee collected numerous witness statements about the treatment of forced laborers in the *Stinnes Group's* mines. In contrast, the treatment of possible forced laborers at *Brenntag* was never investigated because of their comparatively small number and because there was no initial suspicion of mistreatment.[113]

Due to the company's relatively small size, it was not divided into business lines. However, *Brenntag's* shipping business was controlled from the Hamburg branch founded in 1937. In 1943, *Brenntag AG* moved its administrative headquarters from Berlin to Mülheim an der Ruhr. Since the very brief annual reports do not provide any information, only factually based conjectures about the reasons are possible. Because of the increasingly difficult traffic conditions caused by the war, it made sense to relocate the *Brenntag* administration to the headquarters of the Stinnes group of companies in Mülheim.

At *Brenntag,* the damage caused by bombings was considerable. In 1943 and 1944, bombs fell on the facilities in Britz and caused damage totaling 150,000 RM. While the storage buildings and tank facilities in Britz suffered comparatively little damage, most of the vehicle fleet was lost. It was either destroyed by bomb damage or requisitioned by the Wehrmacht and destroyed during the war. At the end of the war, a large number of the tank cars were badly damaged or could not be found due to the interrupted communication routes. In contrast to the underground tank systems, which remained undamaged, the refining and bottling systems suffered some damage, but this was repairable after spare parts were delivered. But *Brenntag's* administration building on Berlin's Alexandrinenstrasse was completely destroyed by bombs on February 3, 1945.[114]

By far the greatest war damage was caused by the loss of the two ocean-going ships "MS Mathias Stinnes" and "MS Mülheim-Ruhr." *Brenntag's* high seas fleet survived the war without damage but, like the entire German merchant fleet, had to be handed over to the victorious powers. *Brenntag* ceded the MS Mülheim-

---

112 The auditor's report on the annual financial statements for 1943. Unfortunately, no further documents about the employment of forced laborers could be found.

113 LA NRW, NW 1000, No. 10165, denazification file Hugo Stinnes jr.

114 ACDP, No. 1-220-1099, Brenntag AG overview of war damage, as of December 31, 1945.

Ruhr to the Norwegian government in April 1946, while it had to hand over the MS Mathias Stinnes to Great Britain already in July 1945.[115] Since then, *Brenntag's* fleet consisted of only two inland waterway vessels, the engineless freight barge Brenntag I, and a tanker with the prosaic name Ruhröl. In the 1945

GERMAN ARMED MERCHANTMEN ARE BROUGHT FROM ENEMY PORTS TO BRITAIN : They were sailed across the North Sea by German crews, but under a guard of Royal Marines. The "Mathias Stinnes" is one of the most modern of this fleet of ex-enemy cargo vessels—*Drawing by Wm. McDowell*

The drawing above shows the arrival of the *Mathias Stinnes* in the Firth of Forth. She is a modern cargo-liner of the type that could be of great value in helping to replace those lost during the past five years. She appears to be all-welded, and well armed with anti-aircraft guns. Note the individual electric cranes to each hatch, which replace the usual derricks and ensure rapid handling of cargo, and the imposing superstructure and bridge. Being empty, she rides high in the water, showing clearly the welded laps of her hull. In the foreground, a harbour-master's launch gives her directions where to moor, and in the background are other German craft already at anchor

—AND HERE IS AN ACTUAL PHOTOGRAPH OF THE VESSEL SHOWN IN THE DRAWING ABOVE : It was taken from a naval plane as the merchant fleet sailed from Kiel under British escort. The vessels came to anchor off Methil, on the north shore of the Firth of Forth

Figure 20: "Weekly Magazine" report on the transfer of the MS Mathias Stinnes to Great Britain on August 18, 1945.

115 StAHH, Kriegsschädenamt für die Seeschiffahrt, No. D 25-1 and D 25-2.

financial year, *Brenntag* posted a loss of one million RM, of which 700,000 RM were attributable to unrecoverable receivables, primarily from the no longer existing German Reich.[116] The day of liberation on May 8, 1945, did not mean a new beginning for *Brenntag* but rather a continuation under difficult material conditions.

For Hugo Stinnes personally, however, the American army's invasion of Mülheim on April 11, 1945, brought a significant turning point. Because of his honorary title as military economic leader (Wehrwirtschaftsführer) and his position as a mining entrepreneur, he was suspected of having been an economic and political supporter of the National Socialist regime. The Stinnes brothers were on the U.S. Army wanted list, but this only had consequences for Hugo Stinnes.[117] The British occupying forces in North Rhine-Westphalia interned him until August 1946. After his release, the denazification committee of the city of Mülheim classified him as a "lesser offender" within the meaning of the denazification law of the Allied occupying powers. However, the comparatively harmless-sounding classification as "lesser offender" had drastic consequences for him. The law now prohibited him from "holding a position of a managerial or supervisory nature" and from running his company himself until further notice.[118]

Hugo Stinnes appealed the ruling and benefited from the growing disposition toward closure regarding wartime losses in German society. Contemporaries characterized the disproportionate leniency toward former National Socialists as "mercy fever." The documents of the denazification committee show that Hugo Stinnes and his colleagues obtained a considerable number of positive character references to prove their supposed innocence, which common parlance gave the figurative and sarcastic name "Persilscheine," referring to a common brand of laundry detergent to express the whitewashing of reputations.[119]

In the appeal proceedings, the denazification committee in Düsseldorf followed the defendant's argument to the letter; namely, that he had only accepted the office of Chairman of the Association of Industrialists "hesitantly and with reluctance" and had prohibited the mistreatment of forced laborers in the Stinnes mines. The committee's decision to appeal turned the political offender, henchman, and profiteer of National Socialist rule into a man who

---

116 ACDP, 1-220-1099, 1945 financial statements.

117 Central Registry of War Criminals and Security Suspects, Wanted List, Part II, printed in: Gerd Sudholt (ed.), *Wanted. Die Fahndungsliste der US-Amerikaner 1945*, Stegen 2002.

118 LA NRW, NW 1000, No. 10165, the decision of the denazification panel, December 9, 1947; see Buchstab, *Der Stinnes-Konzern*, 98–104.

119 LA NRW, NW 1000, No. 10165, the decision of the denazification committee, June 16, 1948.

allegedly "opposed the goals of the NSDAP."[120] The denazification committee also took into account the statement of Stinnes director Wilhelm Unger, "Mr. Stinnes did not take part in the so-called Aryanizations." Unger did not conceal the purchase of *Philipp Mühsam AG* but claimed that Julius Herz had received a fair price for the sale of his shares in 1937.

Nevertheless, it was in any case an "Aryanization." Despite this, Hugo Stinnes was able to officially take over the management of his company again in June 1948 due to his classification as "exonerated," after he had previously withdrawn from the company management and left the external representation of the company to his loyal directors.

Owing to the lack of fuel and chemicals, business took off very slowly after the end of the war. Due to low fuel sales, the lack of a filling station at the West German locations in Mülheim and Duisburg was not yet significant. Although *Brenntag* was able to make a considerable profit of 263,000 RM from the beginning of 1948 to June 20, 1948 (the date of the currency reform), it attributed the profit almost exclusively to extraordinary income from receivables that had previously been written off and now regained their value and to the sales of severely damaged or completely destroyed assets.[121] The low inventory of only 21,000 RM and a gross surplus from services and goods sales of 366,000 RM testified to the slow restart of business. But reconstruction did not begin with the date of the currency reform. In the last six months before the currency reform, *Brenntag* was able to procure 15 freight wagons, six tank wagons that were ready for scrap, a truck, and a car and had its crane repaired in the port of Duisburg. The company had sufficient means of transportation for the expected increase in business after the introduction of the D-Mark.

Brenntag tried to compensate for the loss of sales due to the shortage of fuel and chemicals by improvising its product range, such as selling gasoline substitutes. Its Mülheim branch sold wood on a large scale to vehicle owners who had converted their vehicles to run on wood gas due to a lack of gasoline.

---

120 Ibid.

121 Reichsmark final balance as of June 20, 1948.

8.

The New Beginning in Mülheim an der Ruhr

At this point in time, it was still difficult to estimate what *Brenntag's* future structures would look like – the primary aim was simply to respond to the most urgent needs. Looking back, Otto Stinnes said: "We kept going for now, even if in a vacuum."[122] The board in 1946/47 included Wilhelm Unger, primarily responsible for Mülheim, and Richard Kießling, who managed the business in Berlin.[123] The chairman of the supervisory board was Hugo Stinnes jr.

The problems of the immediate post-war period were reflected in the few letters between Mülheim and Berlin that have survived from those years. "We will not let ourselves be defeated," wrote Hugo Stinnes jr. at the end of 1946 in Berlin-Britz to Richard Kießling, who was one of the longest-serving *Brenntag* executives.[124] "Difficulties are there to be dealt with" must now be the principle. Kießling was confident: "You just have to give us the opportunity to work."[125]

As early as 1947, management noticed the first signs of a cautious recovery. The 1947 financial year was "not unsatisfactory," according to the AG's annual report.[126] The facilities had been restored to such an extent that technical operations were functioning again. Nevertheless, the business focus around 1947 was still in Berlin. Here they delivered mainly to local customers.

Around 1948, as in other sectors of the economy, the fuel and chemical wholesale trade was still far from resuming operations under normal economic conditions. The established transport routes no longer existed. Destroyed road networks and transport connections, limited communication options, and the division into occupation zones made it more difficult to restore the broken business connections. Given the significant restraints on postal and telephone connections, it was difficult to maintain communication between *Brenntag* in the western part of Berlin and the company's headquarters in Mülheim an der Ruhr. In addition, part of *Brenntag's* fixed assets were now located in the Soviet

---

122 Quoted from: *Der Spiegel* 24/1957 from June 11, 1957, "Industrie/Stinnes-Konzern. Die Aktien vom Delaware."

123 Report of the Board of Directors of Brenntag AG on the 1947 financial year, in: StAHH, 371, 7B, 1995-2, Vol. 3, 107.

124 Hugo Stinnes to Kießling on December 9, 1946, in: ACDP, 01-220-A0338.

125 Kießling to Hugo Stinnes, December 23, 1946, in: ACDP, 01-220-A0338.

126 Sales for the Britz trading department had almost doubled, and the balance sheet showed a profit of around 760,000 RM – after deducting the losses from the previous year, there was a net profit of around 355,000 RM Report of the Board of Directors of "Brenntag" Fuel, Chemicals and Transport *Aktiengesellschaft*, Mülheim a. d. Ruhr, about the 1947 financial year, StAHH 371-7-B-1995-2, 147. See also LA NRW, Gerichte Rep. 283, No. 58, Vol. 4.

occupation zone or in the eastern sector of Berlin – for example, a number of railway tank cars, which were now considered lost assets.[127]

The Bottleneck Economy and the Currency Reform

Given the severe shortages of important raw materials and everyday goods and the now dysfunctional Reichsmark currency, barter and compensation transactions played a crucial role in the continuation of economic activities. The Brenntag board remembered the first months of 1948 as a phase of "most unhealthy economic conditions." The progressive devaluation of money and the increasing procurement difficulties were faulted as the basic problems of this period.[128] The need for a currency reform now became increasingly urgent: As a result of National Socialist armaments financing, the domestic national debt had reached a level that created considerable inflationary pressure, so that the Reichsmark hardly functioned as a medium of exchange anymore. It was only the official quantity and price regulations that had so far prevented inflation from becoming rampant.[129] While the reform plans of US and German financial experts gradually took shape,[130] traders increasingly anticipated the day when they would be able to offer their products and goods in a stable currency again. "Once the currency reform comes," said Otto Stinnes, "every system must be ready immediately to work productively again."[131]

The starting signal for the long-awaited reform was finally given in June 1948: The D-Mark replaced the now defunct Reichsmark. In the western occupation zones, citizens were allowed to exchange a quota of 60 D-Mark each at the local

127 Archive Brenntag Berlin, collection folder Berlin 1948 – documents and lists for the preparation of the Reichsmark closing balance or D-Mark opening balance as of June 21, 1948; see here the list "Kurzlebige Wirtschaftsgüter, Maschinen und maschinelle Anlagen" from June 20, 1948.

128 See report from the board of directors on the short financial year from January 1 – June 20, 1948, in: StAHH, 371-7 B 1995-2 Vol. 3, fol. 109 f.

129 On war financing, see Willi Boelcke, *Die Kosten von Hitlers Krieg. Kriegsfinanzierung und finanzielles Kriegserbe in Deutschland 1933–1948*, Paderborn 1985; Mark Spoerer/Jochen Streb, *Neue deutsche Wirtschaftsgeschichte des 20. Jahrhunderts*, Munich 2013, 156–207 or relevant literature references there; see also Tim Schanetzky, *Wirtschaft und Konsum im Dritten Reich*, Munich 2015, 193 ff.; Karl-Heinrich Hansmeyer/Rolf Cäsar, *Kriegswirtschaft und Inflation (1936–1948)*, in: Deutsche Bundesbank (ed.), Währung und Wirtschaft in Deutschland 1876–1975, Frankfurt 1975, 367–429.

130 For the currency reform, see, e.g., Christoph Buchheim, *Die Errichtung der Bank deutscher Länder und die Währungsreform in Westdeutschland*, in: Deutsche Bundesbank (ed.), Fünfzig Jahre Deutsche Mark, Notenbank und Währung in Deutschland seit 1948, Munich 1998, 91–138; ibid., *Die Währungsreform 1948 in Westdeutschland*, in: Vierteljahrshefte für Zeitgeschichte 36, 1988, 189–231; Dieter Lindenlaub, *Die Errichtung der Bank deutscher Länder und die Währungsreform von 1948*, in: ibid., Carsten Burhop/Joachim Scholtyseck, *Schlüsselereignisse der deutschen Bankengeschichte*, Stuttgart 2013, 297–319. Hans Möller, *Die westdeutsche Währungsreform von 1948*, in: Deutsche Bundesbank (ed.), Währung und Wirtschaft in Deutschland 1876–1975, Frankfurt 1975, 433–483.

131 Otto Stinnes said in retrospect that that had been his principle. Quoted from: *Der Spiegel* 24/1957 from June 11, 1957, "Industrie/Stinnes-Konzern. Die Aktien vom Delaware."

exchange points, 40 D-Mark on the day of the currency reform, and a further 20 D-Mark within the following two months. In order to create a currency with purchasing power, the reform legislation moved more than 93 percent of the old money stocks out of circulation, so that balances in Reichsmark only amounted to 6.5 percent of their previous value. For 10 Reichsmark, 0.65 D-Mark ultimately remained.[132] The fact that on the day of the currency reform there were suddenly full shop windows in the shopping streets, where there had been shortages just before, surprised many contemporaries and seemed to promise a favorable start for the D-Mark.

However, the reformed currency was not the only important prerequisite for the gradual return to market economy conditions, but so was the liberalization of prices. This took place with the "Guidelines Act" (Leitsätzegesetz), which came into force a few days after the currency reform. With this law, Ludwig Erhard, Director of the Economic Administration of the United Economic Area of the three western occupation zones, released many commercial products from rationing control and lifted their fixed prices.[133]

The Berlin Blockade

With the currency and conversion laws, the Western Allies had made a clear cut for the shift in currency for the occupation zones they administered. However, the city of Berlin, *Brenntag's* most important location at this time, was initially to remain exempt from the reform regulations. Under the omen of the beginning of the Cold War, the currency issue harbored political explosives – the monetary policy decision reinforced the fact that Germany would also be divided as an economic area in the future.[134] The Soviet military administration had also made arrangements for a currency reform in its economic area and, after the

---

132 Rents, prices, and wages were changed at a ratio of 1:1. In addition to the bounty, other credits were gradually converted. The so-called "Fixed Accounts Act" (Festkontengesetz) of October 1948 played a decisive role in the final exchange ratio. For the currency reform, see, e.g., Christoph Buchheim, *Die Errichtung der Bank deutscher Länder und die Währungsreform in Westdeutschland*, in: Deutsche Bundesbank (ed.), Fünfzig Jahre Deutsche Mark, Notenbank und Währung in Deutschland seit 1948, Munich 1998, 91–138. Id., *Die Währungsreform 1948 in Westdeutschland*, in: Vierteljahrshefte für Zeitgeschichte 36, 1988, 189–231; Dieter Lindenlaub, Die Errichtung der Bank deutscher Länder und die Währungsreform von 1948, in: ibid./ Carsten Burhop/ Joachim Scholtyseck, *Schlüsselereignisse der deutschen Bankengeschichte*, Stuttgart 2013, 297–319. Hans Möller, *Die westdeutsche Währungsreform von 1948*, in: Deutsche Bundesbank (ed.), Währung und Wirtschaft in Deutschland 1876–1975, Frankfurt 1975, 433–483.

133 "Law on principles for management and price policy after the monetary reform" (Gesetz über Leitsätze für die Bewirtschaftung und Preispolitik nach der Geldreform), June 24, 1948. For price developments, see Irmgard Zündorf, *Der Preis der Marktwirtschaft: Staatliche Preispolitik und Lebensstandard in Westdeutschland 1948 bis 1963*, Stuttgart 2006.

134 For the Soviet plans for a pan-German currency and the "currency duel", see Werner Abelshauser, *Deutsche Wirtschaftsgeschichte seit 1945*, Munich 2004, 123–128.

reform in the western zones, reacted immediately with emergency measures for the currency area it administered. In order to curb the increasing flow of worthless Reichsmark notes into the Soviet occupation zone, adhesive stamps, so-called coupons, were stuck on the old banknotes for the first exchanges of cash, since new banknotes were not yet available. At the same time, the Soviet zone administration demanded that the new currency of the Soviet occupation zone be introduced throughout Berlin. However, the Western Allies rejected the introduction of the so-called "Kupon Mark" in the western zones of the city and instead introduced the new western D-Mark, marked with the letter "B" for "Berlin."[135] The Soviet military administration reacted with massive sanctions: Soviet troops blocked the access routes to the western zones of Berlin, and the East Berlin large power plant – the main energy supplier for the entire city – interrupted the supply of gas and electricity to the western parts of the city.

Residents of the city, but also companies that, like *Brenntag*, had a location in the western districts, now found themselves largely isolated in Berlin's unique island location, because the blockade affected all transport routes to the city by land and water. Only the air corridors remained open.[136] The Western Allies set up an airlift and continued to supply Berlin's population with food, fuel, and other goods from the air, even after the end of the blockade in May 1949. The blockade situation made it extremely difficult for many local companies to resume normal business operations. *Brenntag* complained about price drops in Berlin; with some products, they found themselves in an "embarrassing situation." In a distressed customer sector, the company recorded outstanding debts in the six-figure range.[137]

However, as a law of April 7, 1949, suggested, companies could apply for support and claim "direct" and "indirect" additional blockade costs as part of an application for blockade aid.[138] *Brenntag* in Berlin-Britz took advantage of this opportunity and listed in its application a number of additional expenses that had resulted from the blockade. For example, transporting many products by plane required more complex packaging – *Brenntag* now had to ship fatty acids in iron barrels, for example, whereas simple transport drums made from less high-quality materials would have been sufficient by land or water. *Brenntag*

---

135 Ibid., 125 ff.

136 On the Berlin blockade, see Helmut Trotnow/Bernd von Kostka (eds.), *Die Berliner Luftbrücke. Ereignis und Erinnerung*, Berlin 2010.

137 For example, over 150,000 D-Mark for the soap industry. See documents on the application for blockade aid from July 20, 1949, Brenntag Berlin archive, file folder, still unsigned.

138 See "Law on Blockade Aid in the Western Sectors of Greater Berlin from April 7, 1949", e.g., Landesarchiv Berlin, Abteilung Zeitgeschichte (ed.), *Berlin: Ringen um Einheit und Wiederaufbau 1948–1951*, Berlin 1962, 151, 223.

now brought in soda ash in tin drums instead of in bags as usual; and for some products that were otherwise delivered in tank wagons, high-quality iron barrels with lids were purchased, since all of the existing iron barrels had been set aside for the soap industry and were full "due to known conditions" and thus unavailable. There were also costs for airlift insurance, for registering transport bags, and for transport from the airport to the company premises, which had a railway siding, so that transport by rail would have been significantly cheaper.[139] All in all, the additional expenses calculated by the *Brenntag* company amounted to around 22,000 D-Mark, an amount that corresponded to around 3 percent of *Brenntag's* West Berlin-based sales in the first quarter of 1949.[140] "As one of the oldest Berlin wholesale companies," as was stated in *Brenntag's* application to the Blockade Aid Committee, "we were particularly committed to supplying Berlin's industry with raw materials – within the scope of our area of interest – during the years of deprivation."[141]

At this point, *Brenntag's* Berlin branch employed about 40 people, around 20 manual workers and 20 white-collar workers, with the number of workers gradually declining during the blockade months – from 21 to 14.[142] Sales in Berlin also fell. Nevertheless, Britz was considered the most important source of revenue for *Brenntag AG*. Given the circumstances, the management found the course of business quite acceptable, even though the balance sheet for the 1948/49 financial year showed losses.[143]

Like all companies in the petroleum industry, *Brenntag* was a member of the Berlin Mineral Oil Industry Association (ABM), which, together with the Berlin magistrate, distributed the scarce fuel according to quotas.[144] Not only in Berlin, but throughout the entire territory of what later became the Federal Republic of Germany, fuels were subject to regulatory controls until the Mineral Oil Act of March 1951 abolished central distribution. The establishment of a fuel distribution organization showed continuities with the wartime organization of sales.[145]

---

139 Documents for the application for blockade aid from July 20, 1949, Brenntag Berlin archive, file folder, still unsigned.

140 Ibid.

141 Ibid.

142 Ibid.

143 See report of the board of directors of "Brenntag" Brennstoff, Chemikalien und Transport Aktiengesellschaft, Mülheim a. d. Ruhr, about the 1948/49 financial year, StA HH 371-7-B-1995-3, fol. 134 ff.

144 See Ibid.

145 During wartime, a report by an oil expert recommended an Allied control center for the distribution of fuels for the German post-war economy, which was intended to continue the functions of the "Zentralbüro für Mineralöl GmbH" founded at the beginning of the war, and was implemented in 1945 in the form of the North German Oil Control. The "Central Office" continued its activity until 1951. The Berlin working group fulfilled this function for the Berlin market until the early 1950s. Regarding the mineral oil industry during the war and the immediate post-war period, see Fren Förster, *Geschichte der Deutschen BP 1904–1979*, Hamburg 1979, 211 f. as well as 223 f.

Reconstruction and Investment

Despite the crisis situation in Berlin, *Brenntag's* management continued to push ahead with investments in other areas of the company. The company built a handling facility with a five-ton gantry crane and a chippings production facility on the site of the decommissioned *Diergardt* coal mine in the parallel port in Duisburg. The idea was to use building rubble to produce brick chippings for the construction industry. The plant also produced brick-shaped stones from the resulting crushed sand.[146]

For the Mülheim activities, *Brenntag AG* had already set up a chemicals department in the spring of 1948, whose business got off to a cautious start.[147] The oil and wood fuel business also continued "within moderate limits" in Mülheim.[148] *Brenntag's* fleet was continually expanded and, by mid-1948, included, among other things, a Daimler-Benz tanker, a DKW delivery van, a motorcycle, and 15 railway freight cars. The operating facilities in Berlin-Britz in 1948 included, among other things, an expanded tank system, a liquid gas filling system, a mixing system, and a defrosting chamber for tank cars.[149] A number of *Brenntag* tank cars were on loan with other companies toward the end of the 1940s. The management now wanted to change this and use the transport vehicles primarily for their own businesses. The tank car stocks were considered a particularly valuable item in the late 1940s, not least because gases were being produced at an increased rate in some production areas of the industry that were now beginning to operate again. However, sales were often difficult for the companies due to a lack of means of transport, such as gas cylinders and pressure tank wagons. In these cases, *Brenntag* was able to offer itself as a distribution partner.[150]

In view of the general production and delivery bottlenecks, compensation transactions still took place after the currency reform, i.e., transactions in which goods were delivered in exchange for goods. This was particularly true for trade with the Soviet occupation zone or with the GDR, in which counter-deliveries of goods developed into a common practice in the long term.

---

146 ACDP, 01-220-1003.

147 See report of the board of directors of "Brenntag" Brennstoff, Chemikalien und Transport Aktiengesellschaft, Mülheim a. d. Ruhr, about the 1948/49 financial year, StA HH 371-7-B-1995-3, fol. 134 ff. (see also fiscal year 1947 and short fiscal year 1948), ibid.

148 See report of the board of directors of "Brenntag" Brennstoff, Chemikalien und Transport Aktiengesellschaft, Mülheim a. d. Ruhr, about the short financial year January 1 – June 20, 1948, StA HH 371-7-B-1995-3, fol. 108.

149 Brenntag AG, Mülheim-Ruhr, comparison of Reichsmark final balance – D-Mark opening balance, Brenntag Berlin archive, file folder 20.6.48/21.6.48, unsigned. See also, with certain variances, Brenntag AG, balance sheet as of December 31, 1949, in: ACDP, 01-220-1099.

150 ACDP, 01-220-949, various notes from Hugo Stinnes to Kießling in March 1949.

In order to initiate new business for *Brenntag*, the business contacts in Hugo Stinnes jr.'s network seemed to play an important role.[151] *Brenntag* was supposed to organize sales in the East for *Feldmühle* – a large paper manufacturer that was part of the sphere of influence of the group of companies that emerged around Hugo Stinnes jr.[152] At times, he wanted *Brenntag* to be involved as a trading partner when it came to finding suitable buyers for by-products from other industries. For example, *Brenntag* was supposed to get involved in the oil business in order to find buyers in neighboring countries for the heating oil produced during coal-tar distillation since there was still no demand for heating oil in the late 1940s in what later became the Federal Republic of Germany.[153] In fact, interested customers for German brown coal and hard coal tar oil were found in Switzerland. A little later, *Brenntag* tried to import gas oil from Switzerland through a German-Swiss clearing business – which was an attractive option given the controlled regulation of fuel sales in the Federal Republic of Germany's economy.[154]

At this time, international trade was still significantly affected by balance of payments difficulties in a number of European countries and the shortage of convertible means of payment, especially US dollars. A number of European currencies devalued in 1949, which did not eliminate the existing "dollar gap" but mitigated it. The Marshall Plan aid also had a stimulating effect on European trade, as did the European Payments Union from 1950 onward, which created a kind of clearinghouse that facilitated the payment transactions of its members and thus ensured that European countries traded with each other, despite the shortage of foreign currency and limited convertibility of the D-Mark and most other European currencies.[155]

One of the central goals that the Allies had already formulated at the Potsdam Conference was the break-up ("decartelization" or "deconcentration") of the large corporations in the German arms industry. For the chemical trade, the splitting-up of the chemical giant *IG Farben AG* after 1945 potentially presented new business opportunities, as the successor plants reorganized their own sales after the unbundling. Hugo Stinnes jr.'s contacts were intended to bring the managing director of *Brenntag* together with the sales people of *Farben's* successor plants.

---

151 A few file notes have survived about Hugo Stinnes' activities in this direction, while a comparable record about Otto Stinnes is missing.

152 Hugo Stinnes jr. to Richard Kießling on September 16, 1949, in: ACDP 01-220-949.

153 See notes for Mr. Kießling from April 2, 1949, and May 2, 1949, in: ACDP 01-220-949.

154 For the German-Swiss business, see notes by Hugo Stinnes from September 8, 1949, and October 1, 1949, in: ACDP, 01-220-949.

155 See Richard Tilly, *Geld und Kredit in der Wirtschaftsgeschichte*, Stuttgart 2003, 187 f.; Barry Eichengreen, *The European Economy since 1945*, Princeton 2007, 77–83; ibid., *Vom Goldstandard zum Euro. Die Geschichte des internationalen Währungssystems*, Berlin 1996, 149 ff.

Richard Kießling was to "personally" devote his "utmost attention" to this issue, according to a note written with great urgency by Hugo Stinnes jr. for the management of *Brenntag*.[156]

Changes at the Stinnes Corporation

If you look at the organizational framework in which *Brenntag AG* was operating at this time, some important decisions were made at this juncture. The *Hugo Stinnes OHG* was of particular importance for the reconstruction of the Stinnes family's activities in West Germany. This had something to do with the recent developments surrounding the US-based *Hugo Stinnes Corporation* because, in the meantime, Cläre Stinnes-Wagenknecht had lost her shares in the corporation, which had been confiscated through expropriation by the US as alien property.[157] In 1948, at the request of the US authorities, all members of the Stinnes family had to resign from the management of *Hugo Stinnes GmbH* – the holding company of the Stinnes activities in Germany which were part of the corporation.[158] The German manager Heinz Kemper now acted as trustee for the Americans, while the brothers Hugo Stinnes jr. and Otto Stinnes pursued their business activities with other companies to rebuild their traditional areas of activity in the coal and steel business and in logistics and shipping.[159] For *Brenntag*, the ties to *Hugo Stinnes OHG* became increasingly important.

Brenntag management also wanted to advance oil trading in the Ruhr area, although it still lacked the necessary infrastructure to be able to store and reload goods. For Hugo Stinnes, the establishment of a fuel depot in the parallel port of Duisburg was seen as an "indispensable prerequisite" that was to be pursued "as quickly as possible" starting in the fall of 1949.[160] He considered it crucial to have a "certain level of sales" in the oil business as soon as the regulatory

---

156 ACDP, 01-220-949, Hugo Stinnes on March 21, 1949.

157 Hugo Stinnes GmbH was the corporation's most important subsidiary. On the structures, see Office of Alien Property, Department of Justice, Annual Report for the Fiscal Year ended June 30, 1947, 48 ff.; Office of Alien Property, Department of Justice, Annual Report for the Fiscal Year ended June 30, 1948, 50 ff.; see also an information report about Hugo Stinnes GmbH in the documents of the Central German Commission for Sequestration and Confiscation in the Soviet Occupation Zone Federal Archives (Bundesarchiv, quoted in the following as BArch), Do 3/314, letter dated December 4, 1946, Fasz. 40 f.

158 See Bernhard-Michael Domberg/Klaus Rathje, *Die Stinnes. Vom Rhein in die Welt. Geschichte einer Unternehmerfamilie*, Vienna 2009, 181 ff.

159 See "Industrie/Stinnes-Konzern. Die Aktien vom Delaware" in: *Der Spiegel*, June 11, 1957.

160 Hugo Stinnes to Richard Kießling, October 1, 1949, in: ACDP 01-220-0949.

control measures in the industry fell. However, many steps and activities still had to be completed to achieve this goal. In addition, near the Stinnes family's traditional Mülheim business building, there was a filling station, "Auf dem Dudel," which so far had been restricted for internal use. But gas stations with a concession for public use also seemed important and were also high on the list of "vigorously" pursued approaches. "The Dudel is the first gas station that will be followed by others in the surrounding area," wrote Hugo Stinnes to the *Brenntag* management. "I already have very specific places in mind, and I also believe that, in connection with our building materials business, we have considerable opportunities to attract customers."[161]

A Second Brenntag

The struggle for new structures was also expressed in another company called "Brenntag". On November 19, 1948, *Hugo Stinnes Verwaltung Gesellschaft* (management company), led by Hugo Stinnes jr. and Otto Stinnes, founded *Brenntag GmbH* with its headquarters in Duisburg and a share capital of 300,000 D-Mark.[162] The purpose of the company was defined in similarly broad terms as that of *Brenntag AG* and included the wholesale trade in chemicals of all kinds, the trade in fuels and mining products, and the trade in raw products. In addition to trade, the company was entitled to "extract and process the above products itself and to participate in similar ventures" and "to operate sea and river shipping."[163]

With the founding of the GmbH, the *Brenntag* activities received an additional aegis. For about a decade, the AG and GmbH businesses existed in parallel, with both companies initially being managed largely by the same people.[164] By the early 1950s, a division of labor had emerged between *Brenntag AG* and the GmbH: While the AG mainly operated the mineral oil business in Berlin, the GmbH's initial focus was on the trading of chemicals. Added to this were,

---

161 Ibid.

162 "Brenntag," Brennstoff-, Chemikalien- und Transport GmbH, partnership agreement, No. 550 of the roll of documents for 1948, negotiated in Mülheim a. d. R. on November 19, 1948, in: ACDP, 01-220-815; see also ACDP, 01-220-925.

163 See the certified copy from the handout for the commercial register of the Duisburg District Court (Amtsgericht Duisburg) Dept. B No. 2541, in: ACDP, 1-220-815.

164 At the same time, the records became more confusing. It is noticeable that some of the AG's assets were recorded as deficits in the books at this time, although this cannot be clearly retraced due to the GmbH's limited reporting obligations.

among other things, scrap recycling, the chips and stone factory, trade in coal, and various export activities.[165]

Restarting the Books

Inflation and currency reform had, in some cases, radically changed the financial situation of companies. Against the background of an increasingly dysfunctional currency, the annual balance sheets lost their informative value in that they could no longer provide a clear, unambiguous picture of the assets of the reporting companies.[166]

However, after the currency reform of June 21, 1948, the companies also made a new beginning in terms of accounting. The legislature created this possibility with the corresponding accounting regulations.[167] The preparation of a Reichsmark closing balance sheet as of June 20, 1948, included an inventory of the companies' assets using old valuation principles. The D-Mark opening balance sheet as of June 21, 1948, did not simply continue the old balance sheet, converted to the new currency, but was based on a completely new assessment of the assets and liabilities of the respective company. For example, a lower share capital could create more scope for action, e.g., for higher dividends, for the option of later capital increases, but also to dedicate funds for the company's self-financing by retaining profits.[168]

At *Brenntag AG*, the losses from the war were taken into account with a share capital reduced to 3.6 million D-Mark. The auditors at *Brenntag AG* held that the aim was to give the company a "healthy start" and to "clean up the balance sheet from dubious assets left over from the war and post-war period."[169] With the new valuation approaches, *Brenntag AG's* capital structure had an improved ratio of equity to debt.[170]

---

165 See annual reports of Brenntag AG 1950-55 in: StAHH, 371-7 B 1995-2, Vol. 3; see also ACDP 1-220-1099; for the GmbH 1948–1954 see ACDP 1-220-1217 and the auditor's reports 1948–1955 in ACDP 1-220-1100.

166 For the following considerations, see also Folkmar Königs, *Die stille Gesellschaft*, Berlin 1961, 213.

167 For example, with the D-Mark Balance Sheet Act ("Gesetz über die Eröffnungsbilanz in Deutscher Mark und die Kapitalneufestsetzung vom 21.8.1949") or the implementing regulations for the conversion laws.

168 See Herbert Möhle, *Bilanzieren heute – gestern – morgen*, Wiesbaden 1973, 82.

169 Bericht der Treuhand-Vereinigung Aktiengesellschaft Wirtschaftsprüfungsgesellschaft Zweigniederlassung Köln über die Prüfung der Reichsmark-Schlußbilanz zum 20. Juni 1948, der DM-Eröffnungsbilanz zum 21. Juni 1948 und der Vorschläge für die Neufestsetzung der Kapitalverhältnisse, in: Archive Brenntag Berlin, auditor reports, unsigned.

170 In the opening D-Mark balance sheet, equity and reserves on the liabilities side amounted to 85.6% and liabilities to 14.4%, while in the Reichsmark closing balance sheet, equity amounted to 53.1% and debt capital amounted to around 46.9% of the balance sheet total.

An Old Shell Company with New Meaning

In the post-war period, the *Brenntag* businesses remained closely linked to the activities of Hugo and Otto Stinnes, with Otto Stinnes' influence becoming increasingly important as the 1950s progressed. Due to the interconnections and overlapping responsibilities between *Brenntag AG, Brenntag GmbH,* and the closely associated *Hugo Stinnes OHG*, it is sometimes difficult to get a clearly defined picture, especially since the company structures of the later parent company, *Hugo Stinnes OHG*, changed dramatically after the Second World War. *Hugo Stinnes OHG* was a shell company founded in 1928 by Cläre Stinnes[171] – emerging from the sole proprietorship Hugo Stinnes founded in 1892. The OHG had hardly any commercial significance until 1948 because its practical importance did not lie in operational business but primarily in giving a second signature to the commercial bills of *Hugo Stinnes GmbH* and acting as a "family clearinghouse".[172] Nevertheless, this shell company was an important point of reference for the rest of *Brenntag's* history because Cläre, Otto, and Hugo Stinnes, in their capacity as shareholders of the OHG, had acquired the shares of *Philipp Mühsam AG* in 1937 and later those of *ETAG, ILAG, Aglukon,* and *Weissensee-Guß*.[173] Since the "Aryanization" of *Philipp Mühsam AG* by the Stinnes family, the chemicals and mineral oil trading company based in Berlin operated as "Brenntag" and was part of the Stinnes family group of companies. However, *Brenntag* and its subsidiaries were not integrated into the widely branched *Hugo Stinnes GmbH* but remained family-owned via the OHG. This was relevant for the rest of *Brenntag's* history, insofar as the balance of power in the former Stinnes empire had shifted further over the course of the war. As early as the mid-1920s, when the *Stinnes Group* was heavily indebted after the death of Hugo Stinnes senior, the company heiress Cläre Stinnes had to transfer a large part of the industrial assets to another company as part of the restructuring efforts, namely to the newly founded *Hugo Stinnes Corporation*, in which US banks

---

171 Otto Stinnes states that Cläre Stinnes-Wagenknecht added Otto Stinnes as a personally liable partner in the resulting OHG in 1928 and Hugo jr. in 1933. In the archive for Christian-Social Politics' finding aid, the founding date of Hugo Stinnes OHG is given as 1892 (the founding date of the sole proprietorship Hugo Stinnes). The GmbH was founded in 1904.

172 See Otto Stinnes, Begründung der Vergleichsvorschläge, 4a, in: Archiv für Diakonie und Entwicklung (in the following quoted as Archive Diakonie), ADW HgSt 8308. For the description as a "clearinghouse," see also "Industrie/Stinnes-Konzern. Die Aktien vom Delaware" in: *Der Spiegel*, June 11, 1957.

173 See Otto Stinnes, Begründung der Vergleichsvorschläge, 4a, in: Archive Diakonie, ADW HgSt 8308.

and Cläre Stinnes each held half of the shares. During the course of the war, the assets held by Cläre and her trustees in US shares were confiscated by the USA and controlled by the US Office of Alien Property.[174] As a result of the expropriation, all members of the Stinnes family had to leave the management of *Hugo Stinnes GmbH* in 1948,[175] and in this context, *Hugo Stinnes OHG* was given a new task in 1948. It formed the basis on which Cläre Stinnes and her two sons Otto and Hugo rebuilt their activities in the coal and steel trade and in shipping from 1948 onward.[176] Soon afterward, conflicts between Cläre and Otto Stinnes on the one hand and Hugo Stinnes jr. on the other led to a rift within the entrepreneurial family, such that Cläre Stinnes terminated Hugo Stinnes jr.'s connection to the company at the end of 1952. The controversies, which also related to corporate strategy issues surrounding *Hugo Stinnes OHG* and *Brenntag*, affected *Brenntag's* history in the 1950s, and it would take until the end of the decade before the legal disputes between both parties came to an end.

---

174 Hugo Stinnes GmbH was the corporation's most important subsidiary. On the structures, see Office of Alien Property, Department of Justice, Annual Report for the Fiscal Year ended June 30, 1947, 48 ff.; Office of Alien Property, Department of Justice, Annual Report for the Fiscal Year ended June 30, 1948, 50 ff.; see also an information report about Hugo Stinnes GmbH in the documents of the Central German Commission for Sequestration and Confiscation in the Soviet Occupation Zone Federal Archives (Zentrale Deutsche Kommission für Sequestrierung und Beschlagnahme in der Sowjetischen Besatzungszone), Do 3/314, letter dated December 4, 1946, Fasz. 40 f.

175 Otto Stinnes, Begründung der Vergleichsvorschläge, 5 in: *Archive Diakonie*, ADW HgSt 8308.

176 Otto Stinnes, Begründung der Vergleichsvorschläge, 6 in: *Archive Diakonie*, ADW HgSt 8308.

9.

The Mineral Oil Company Brenntag in the Motorization Boom

In the 1950s, the German economy was on a growth path. Rapidly rising industrial production figures produced a powerful upswing. Since 1951/52, foreign trade had received noticeable growth impulses and indicated that export-oriented industries were regaining a foothold on world markets.[177] From 1948 to 1960, gross domestic product per capita grew by an average of around 9 percent annually, and in the following decade by around 3.5 percent per year.[178] The domestic economy also picked up again, driven by expanding housing construction and rising consumer demand. In view of the dynamic boom, contemporary observers soon spoke of the "economic miracle." In retrospect, the currency reform was often seen – and sometimes romanticized – as the "birth of the economic miracle."[179] However, many factors actually drove the boom phase forward. This included, on the one hand, the reconstruction after the destruction caused by the war and the laying of the foundation for the market economy. However, in the wake of the Korean War, demand from abroad for capital goods soon also increased, which promoted the reintegration of West German suppliers into the world market. In addition, new technologies, often imported from the USA, were introduced in many industrial sectors. At the same time, a long-term structural change took place, in the course of which the productive industrial and service sectors gained more weight compared to the stagnating agricultural sphere.[180]

Looking back to this period, *Brenntag* also exhibited signs of growth. In the decade between 1948 and 1958, *Brenntag AG's* total assets had grown more than sevenfold and in 1958 amounted to around 32.5 million D-Mark. Sales in the

---

177 On economic history after 1945 see, among others, H. Giersch et al. *The Fading Miracle. Four Decades of Market Economy in Germany*, Cambridge 1992, 101–105; Abelshauser, *Wirtschaftsgeschichte*, 154 ff.; Michael von Prollius, *Deutsche Wirtschaftsgeschichte nach 1945*, Göttingen 2006, 88–91.

178 Spoerer/Streb, *Wirtschaft*, 219; see also Prollius, *Wirtschaftsgeschichte*, 89 ff.

179 For the formulation, see Harald Wixforth, *Bielefeld und seine Sparkassen*, 315, with a critical classification of the "legend."

180 Barry Eichengreen/Albrecht Ritschl, "Understanding West German Economic Growth in the 1950s," in: *Cliometrica 3*, 2009, 191–219; Tamás Vonyó, "Post War Reconstruction and the Golden Ages of Economic Growth," in: *European Review of Economic History 12*, 2008, 234 ff.; Werner Abelshauser, *Deutsche Wirtschaftsgeschichte seit 1945*, Munich 2004, 275 ff.; H. Giersch et al., *The Fading Miracle. Four Decades of Market Economy in Germany*, Cambridge 1992; Ludger Lindlar, *Das mißverstandene Wirtschaftswunder. Westdeutschland und die westeuropäische Nachkriegsprosperität*, Tübingen 1997; Mark Spoerer/Jochen Streb, *Neue deutsche Wirtschaftsgeschichte des 20. Jahrhunderts*, Munich 2013.

Figure 21: Brenntag advertisement from 1952.[181]

trading department in Berlin-Britz had quadrupled.[182] But not all of the lines of business in which *Brenntag* had been involved since the late 1940s developed successfully in the long term. Over the course of the 1950s, it became clear which areas of the partly improvised new beginning of the company also promised prospects for the future.

Brenntag as a Shipping Company

One of the most valuable assets that *Brenntag AG* owned at the end of the 1940s was a tanker called "Brenntag," which had its home port in Hamburg.[183] Here, *Brenntag AG* operated the shipping business in partnership with the Hamburg branch of *Hugo Stinnes OHG*.[184] In the early 1950s, *Brenntag's* management wanted to expand the shipping business; the old ships were sold, shares were acquired in shipping companies, and millions were invested in new ships. "We [can] report a welcome expansion of our shipping interests," declared the board of directors for 1954. At a shipyard in Emden, a new 13,000-ton vessel was being built on behalf of the AG as well as a 950-ton inland freight ship. The project was financed through a reconstruction loan – "long-term and cheap," the supervisory board found.[185] With these investments, *Brenntag* sought to gain a foothold in the international shipping business. *Brenntag GmbH's* fleet

---

181 Firmenhandbuch Chemische Industrie in der Bundesrepublik und in West-Berlin, 1952, 68.

182 ACDP, 01-220-1099, 01-220-A0265; StA HH 371-7-B – 1995-2. Vol. 3.

183 For the ship's articles of the German tanker ship Brenntag from 1947 cf., StA HH 373-10-1078. See annual report of Brenntag AG 1951, in: StA HH 371-7-B – 1995-2. Vol. 3, fol. 143 ff.

184 StA HH 371-7-B – 1995-2. Vol. 3, 190.

185 See the report of the board of directors on the 1954 financial year and the minutes of the constituent supervisory board meeting of Brenntag AG on June 6, 1955, in: StAHH, 371-7-B-1995-2, Vol. 3; see also annual reports 1951–52, ibid.

also grew steadily. The *Frankfurter Allgemeine Zeitung* declared the "age of the tanker" and in this context reported on the test voyage of the Stinnes-Brenntag freighter Westfalen, which was to be used on routes to the West Indies.[186] The ships' routes may have been the first signs of *Brenntag's* intended global reach, although it can be assumed that *Brenntag* did not transport its own commercial goods on these routes.

Figure 22: The Brenntag logo with the flag of the shipping company Hugo Stinnes Zweignie-derlassung, Brennstoff-, Eisen- und Schiffahrts-gesellschaft Hamburg (mid-1950s).[187]

It took until 1954 for *Brenntag GmbH* to set up its own maritime shipping department. At the end of the year, it had ships worth 13.9 million D-Mark on its books.[188] Business had been going so well since 1948 that shipping was at times even the company's driving force. The table below makes this clear in detail: Until the mid-1950s, the inland shipping and maritime shipping departments together generated the highest results for the company – before depreciation, even more than the chemicals and petroleum departments combined. In contrast, activities in the scrap trade, with the chips and stone factory and with selected export activities, were now rather stagnant and resulted in losses.[189]

In 1955, due to high depreciation, almost all of the GmbH's seagoing vessels were only recorded at a scrap value.[190] This move fit with the general framework for corporate finance in the 1950s. The capital market was not yet efficient in the first years of the young Federal Republic, and the loan interest rates were comparatively high.[191]

---

186 *Die neuen Schiffe*, in: *Frankfurter Allgemeine Zeitung*, December 20, 1952, BuZ 1.

187 Cf. also Esso AG, Deutsche Reedereien und ihre Erkennungszeichen, n. p. 1960, 7.

188 Previously, the shipping business was not assigned to a separate department. See Brenntag GmbH business documents for 1954 and 1955, ACDP, 1-220-382.

189 The shipping divisions generated around two-thirds of the department's income. Overall, however, the company made losses from 1948 to 1955, ACDP, 01-220-1100 (Report by *Treuhand Aktiengesellschaft Wirtschaftsprüfungsgesellschaft Köln* on a special audit at Brenntag GmbH, 10).

190 See the overviews for December 31, 1955, in ACDP, 01-220-382. See also ACDP, 01-220-1100, 3, 31 f.

191 Hans Möller, "Die westdeutsche Währungsreform von 1948," in: *Währung und Wirtschaft in Deutschland 1876–1975*, Frankfurt 1975, 433–483, here 477.

Table 1: Outcomes of the Departments of Brenntag GmbH 1948–1955, in D-Mark (rounded).[192]

Department	excluding depreciation	including depreciation
Chemicals and Mineral Oil	8,778,200	7,175,000
Export	−1,066,000	−1,083,800
Scrap Trade	−1,070,500	−1,206,600
Transshipment/Handling	−592,300	−999,700
Chips and Stone Factory	−160,600	−528,600
Coal	50,600	50,600
Colmonoy[193]	−58,800	−63,600
Inland Shipping	409,200	188,900
Maritime Shipping	12,066,500	4,045,500
Headquarters	−21,378,400	−10,083,600
Ilag GmbH	2,026,700	2,026,700
Aglukon GmbH	−935,500	−935,500
Betonwerk GmbH	283,600	−225,100
Parten Shipping Company Württemberg	−248,400	−248,400
Other Investments	−127,800	−127,800
Frankfurt Scrap Facility	8,000	500
Total	**−2,015,500**	**−2,015,500**

From a tax perspective, it was attractive for companies at this point to take advantage of the generous depreciation options offered by the state.[194] However, this practice also carried certain risks. Economists at the time criticized that, given this option, companies' balance sheets lost their informative value and transparency during this phase. They could contain high hidden reserves if

---

192 Cf. ACDP, 01-220-1100, Bericht der Treuhand Wirtschaftsprüfungsgesellschaft Köln über eine Sonderprüfung bei der Brenntag GmbH.

193 This was a deal Hugo Stinnes had initiated, evidently without notice to Otto Stinnes. When faced with the losses, Otto's verdict was that there was a "no apparent reason for Brenntag to deal with these problems at all." File note Otto Stinnes to Mr. Unger regarding Brenntag GmbH dated 20.8.1952, p. 3, in: ACDP 01-220-1003.

194 Patrick Kresse, *Finanzierungsstrukturen in der deutschen Automobilindustrie: Bayerische Motorenwerke, Daimler Benz und Volkswagenwerk 1948–1965*, Berlin 2018; see also Richard Tilly, *Willy H. Schlieker. Aufstieg und Fall eines Unternehmers (1914–1980)*, Berlin 2008, 131, 138.

the depreciation did not adequately reflect the degree of wear and tear.[195] At *Brenntag*, the balance depreciation actually reached an excessive level.[196] In addition, it exacerbated the latent discrepancy between capital resources and the growing scope of business, as the company's share capital had only been increased slightly. By the mid-1950s, the company's losses totaled many times its share capital.[197]

Yield Problems in the 1950s

Despite the dynamic development in some lines of business, *Brenntag* definitely struggled with earnings problems in the mid-1950s. Looking at the period from the currency reform to the middle of the decade, the GmbH was only in the black in 1951 and 1952, while the AG only reported profits in 1953 and 1955.[198]

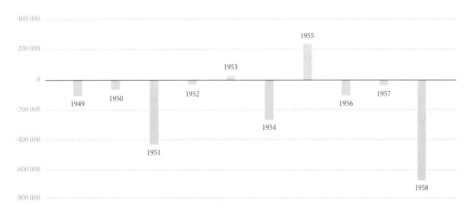

Chart 1: Brenntag AG, profit and loss in the financial years 1949–1958 (in D-Mark).[199]

At Brenntag GmbH, initially only the chemical and mineral oil trade and the shipping departments made profits. A particular problem child was the concrete plant built in the Duisburg parallel port, which had been added to the chips plant since the early 1950s and supplemented *Brenntag's* building material portfolio with large-format, high-quality components.[200] While the market for building

---

195 For contemporary criticism of the depreciation options, see Kresse, *Finanzierungsstrukturen*, 41 f.

196 See the overviews for December 31, 1955 in ACDP, 01-220-382. See also ACDP, 01-220-1100, 3, 31 f.

197 See the auditor's reports in ACDP 01-220-1100.

198 ACDP 01-220-1100; see also the annual reports of the AG 1948–1955, in: StA HH, 371-7-B-1995-2, Vol. 3.

199 Information for the respective financial year, without taking into account profit or loss carryforwards from the previous year. Compiled following StaHH, 371-7-B-1995-2, Vol. 3, Berichte des Vorstands der "Brenntag" AG für die Geschäftsjahre 1949–1958.

200 ACDP, 01-220-811; ACDP 01-220-1003.

materials still offered promising prospects at the end of the 1940s, it became more differentiated in the early 1950s. As new processes, product requirements, and suppliers became established in the ups and downs of the construction economy, the *Brenntag* systems in the Duisburg parallel port increasingly proved to be uneconomical with their high fixed costs, relatively limited storage capacity, and comparatively small production volume.[201]

Overall, *Brenntag's* area of activity during this time focused on the trade in chemicals, mineral oil, and scrap, the production of building materials, and water transport services. For its business in Berlin-Britz, *Brenntag* initially focused on expanding its commercial lines of business. The company now also traded in plastics and in the AG and GmbH sold not only fuels, lubricants, mineral oil, and heating oil but also oil burner systems.[202]

Shipbuilding Boom and Overinvestment

For the time being, however, shipping remained an important pillar in the AG's portfolio. In 1956, the cargo ship "Cläre Hugo Stinnes," designed for transatlantic routes, was launched, and the board had great hopes for it because of its modern, economic engine systems. "We believe that even in times of poor freight profitability, a ship of this type can still operate positively," the annual report stated.[203] In addition, further ships were ordered, which were to be operated from Duisburg-Ruhrort and were intended largely for Rhine traffic.[204] The newly built ships "Brenntag 5" and "Brenntag 6" were ready for service by the summer of 1957. Over the next year, the river freighters "Brenntag 7," "Brenntag 8," and "Brenntag 9" were added to *Brenntag's* inland shipping fleet.[205]

However, the management soon realized that the expectations associated with the investments in the shipping line were not being fulfilled. Worldwide demand for cargo space was declining, although it had recently shown great momentum due to a boom in the economy and had resulted in rising prices for shipping space. This had given an enormous boost to investments in cargo ships – in the Federal Republic of Germany, such investments were supported

---

201 *Betonwerk, Brenntag GmbH/Rhein Ruhr Baustoff und Beton GmbH*, report on the years 1949–1954, February 15, 1955, in: ACDP 01-220-1003.

202 Report of the Board of Directors on the 1956 financial year, StAHH, 371-7-B-1995-2, Vol. 3.

203 Report of the Board of Directors for Fiscal Year 1956, ACDP 1-220-1081.

204 Ibid.

205 Report of the Board of Directors for Fiscal Year 1957, 3 in ACDP 1-220-A0815.

by high depreciation and cheap reconstruction loans, which made it attractive to reinvest the profits in new projects.[206] In the second half of the 1950s, however, excess freight space capacity met falling demand, which put pressure on freight rates and significantly reduced the earnings prospects in shipping.[207]

Brenntag had invested significantly in expanding its shipping fleet during the phase of high freight rates. Nevertheless, their ships were not large enough to compete long-term internationally with the large bulk carriers. The modern ship "Cläre Hugo Stinnes" proved to be "economically more resilient," as it was described internally, but the output of the shipping division of *Brenntag AG* and the shipping company investments remained unsatisfactory overall. At the beginning of 1958, for example, the MS Concordia had to rest in port for several months.[208] Difficult conditions also manifested themselves with inland shipping. At the annual general meeting in the summer of 1958, the *Brenntag* supervisory board chairman Otto Stinnes answered the censorious question about the conditions under which the inland waterway vessels had been commissioned "with a certain embarrassment," according to internal notes.[209] The report by the board of directors of *Brenntag AG* admitted that there were no "signs of an imminent improvement" in the shipping industry, although the company management still hoped that for the time being, the use of the ships for *Hugo Stinnes OHG* would make them more "immune" against the cyclical risks in shipping.[210]

Despite the negative market signals, it still took some time before *Brenntag's* management began a learning process toward an investment preference that would characterize distribution in later years: keeping investments in their own means of transport as low as possible and instead using the existing structures and networks more flexibly and at less cost.

---

206 See Tilly, Schlieker, 124 ff. The loan conditions were designed in such a way that there was an incentive to reinvest profits from the new buildings because the repayment obligation only began with the profits. See also: "Opfer des Schweinezyklus," *Der Spiegel* 7/1958 from February 11, 1958.

207 Tilly, Schlieker, 126.

208 Brenntag AG was the correspondent shipping company for the partner shipping company Concordia. The Concordia (approx. 1366 gross registered tons) was jointly owned by Brenntag AG and many individuals, mainly senior employees of Hugo Stinnes OHG, Brenntag AG, Brenntag GmbH, and other companies close to the brothers Otto and Hugo Stinnes (including Feldmühle AG and Atlas-Werke Bremen), see ACDP 01-220-1019. For the ship's articles see StAHH, 373-10-1569.

209 See note for Mr. Hugo Stinnes from July 24, 1958, from Werner Best as well as questions to be asked at the general meeting of Brenntag AG on July 24, 1958 ("Fragen, die in der Hauptversammlung der Brenntag AG am 24.7.1958 zu stellen sind") in: ACDP, 1-220-1081.

210 Report of the Board of Directors for Fiscal Year 1957, ACDP 1-220-A0815.

Motorization and Petrochemistry

While *Brenntag's* management gradually had to abandon the expectation that the shipping division would continue to serve as a "cash cow" – as it had in previous years – trading in chemicals and petroleum products remained a cornerstone of *Brenntag's* business. After the war, fundamental processes of change began in both industries, influencing and reinforcing each other. In fact, the structures and priorities began to change dramatically in both the petroleum and the chemical industry.

Over the course of the 1950s, the demand for mineral oil products in the German economy increased to an impressive degree. "The entire post-war period was an era of unprecedented growth in the West German oil industry," commented economic historian Raymond Stokes, adding that the industry also changed its character "profoundly."[211]

Motorization was an important driving force for the increased demand for mineral oil. In the Federal Republic of Germany in the 1950s, the use of motorized vehicles was still lagging behind compared to Great Britain, France, and the USA, but picked up noticeably in the course of the boom.[212] Between 1951 and 1955, the number of passenger cars in the Federal Republic grew by around one million vehicles, and the number of motorcycles by more than 1.5 million.[213]

From the mid-1950s onward, the pace at which cars took over road traffic increased – in 1955, for the first time, more passenger cars were newly registered than motorcycles. In the 1960s, average incomes reached a level that enabled a breakthrough toward mass motorization. As early as 1963, the "Federal Motor Transport Authority" (Kraftfahrtbundesamt) recorded more than twice as many cars as in 1959. The inventory now amounted to around 6.8 million vehicles.[214] With ever new production records, the automobile industry was seen

---

211 Rainer Karlsch/Raymond Stokes, *Faktor Öl. Die Mineralölwirtschaft in Deutschland*, Munich 2003, 323.

212 See Nils Beckmann, *Käfer, Goggos, Heckflossen. Eine retrospektive Studie über die westdeutschen Automobilmärkte in den Jahren der beginnenden Massenmotorisierung*, Vaihingen 2006, 92 ff.

213 On July 1, 1951, the number of cars including ambulances amounted to 444,894 and motorcycles to 877,373 vehicles; on July 1, 1955, to 1,596,694 (cars) and 2,432,559 (motorcycles), see *Statistisches Jahrbuch der Bundesrepublik 1953*, 381 f. and *Statistisches Jahrbuch der Bundesrepublik 1956*, 326 f. On motorization in the Federal Republic see Beckmann, *Käfer*, 89 ff.; see also Stephanie Tilly/Florian Triebel, *Automobilindustrie 1945–2000*, Munich 2013, 2 ff.

214 The number of passenger cars (including ambulances) amounted to 3,337,576 on July 1, 1959, and 6,847,894 on July 1, 1963, see *Statistisches Jahrbuch der Bundesrepublik 1953*, 381 f. and *Statistisches Jahrbuch der Bundesrepublik 1964*, 355. On the importance of the used car market for mass motorization, see Christopher Kopper, "Der Durchbruch des PKW zum Massenkonsumgut 1950–1964," in: Stephanie Tilly/Dieter Ziegler (eds.), "Automobilwirtschaft nach 1945. Vom Verkäufer- zum Käufermarkt?", in: *Jahrbuch für Wirtschaftsgeschichte 2010/1*, 19–36.

as the pacesetter of post-war prosperity, and the car, especially the popular Volkswagen Beetle, became a symbol of the economic miracle.[215]

With the increased volume of traffic, the need for fuel for motorized road transport increased significantly. The changed conditions were reflected in the oil industry, which tried to meet this increasing demand.[216] Imports of finished refined products declined, while the importance of domestic petroleum processing increased. In keeping with its commitment to free trade, German economic policy focused on liberalizing the market. After management and price controls in the German mineral oil industry were phased out in 1951, the new mineral oil tax law in 1953 provided a tailwind for investments in the exploration and production of crude oil in the Federal Republic. Production began on 39 new oil fields between 1953 and 1955.[217] In addition, the refinery capacities in the federal territory were expanded significantly, with the Rhenish-Westphalian industrial area playing an important role, as it converted three hydrogenation plants to crude oil.[218] After the petroleum tariff was reduced in 1956, crude oil imports increased noticeably. Starting in the middle of the decade, the traditional route of transporting crude oil by water or rail was supplemented by a network of pipelines that grew rapidly well into the 1960s. In 1958, the pipelines for transporting crude oil had an operating length of 46 kilometers, but by 1960, this had increased to 455 kilometers. Accordingly, the amount transported rose from 1.468 million tons to 13.318 million tons between 1958 and 1960.[219] In the early 1960s, a pipeline network connected the North Sea port of Wilhelmshaven with the Rhenish refinery site of Wesseling.

Figure 23: Brenntag oil cabinet from the 1950s.

---

215 In 1955, the one millionth Volkswagen Beetle rolled off the assembly line, see Manfred Grieger/Markus Lupa, *Vom Käfer zum Weltkonzern. Die Volkswagen-Chronik*, Wolfsburg 2015, 68.

216 See Raymond Stokes, *Faktor Öl*, 286–290.

217 See Ibid.

218 Stokes, *Faktor Öl*, 291.

219 *Statistisches Jahrbuch der Bundesrepublik Deutschland 1962*, 382 (containing information for the federal territory, excluding Berlin).

In 1960, Wesseling was connected to the Rotterdam-Rhine pipeline. Other important routes followed in 1964 with the Southern European Pipeline, which created a connection from the Mediterranean to southern Germany.[220]

As an alternative to coal, oil also became increasingly important as a raw material for the chemical industry, as it increased the economic efficiency of manufacturing many new products.[221] In the summer of 1953, the first German petrochemical production plant was founded, based on a joint venture between *BASF* and *Shell* to produce the plastic Lupolene near the Wesseling refinery site.[222] This was an early example of a reorientation of chemistry that would significantly reshape the industry over the course of the decade.

While in the chemical industry at the beginning of the 1950s, one might initially have envisaged a coexistence of traditional, coal-based technology and new processes,[223] there was soon a brisk increase in demand on the market for plastics that were produced on a petrochemical basis, such as polyethylene. Already at the beginning of the 1960s, around 90 percent of the basic chemicals for chemical production were petrochemicals.[224] At *Brenntag*, this change was reflected in the portfolio of traded products in the medium term.

Oil also gradually began to compete with the traditional energy source coal when it came to supplying energy to private households and companies. Heating oil was produced as a byproduct of fuel production in refineries. Since the beginning of the 1950s, there had been an increase in demand for heating oil, which intensified over the course of the decade. Experts predicted an increase in heating oil consumption in the Federal Republic of around one million tons to around 16–17 million tons from the mid-1950s to the mid-1960s.[225] *Brenntag* also gradually expanded its heating oil business. The company's own department

---

220 Stokes, *Faktor Öl*, 320 f.

221 Rainer Karlsch, "Wie Phönix aus der Asche?" Rekonstruktion und Strukturwandel in der chemischen Industrie in beiden deutschen Staaten bis Mitte der sechziger Jahre, in: Lothar Baar/Dietmar Petzina (eds.), Deutsch-deutsche Wirtschaft 1945 bis 1990. Strukturveränderungen, Innovationen und regionaler Wandel. Ein Vergleich, St. Katharinen 1999, 262–303, here 289.

222 Werner Abelshauser, *Die BASF. Eine Unternehmensgeschichte*, Munich 2002, 444–452.

223 Stokes, *Faktor Öl*, 295 f.

224 Karlsch, "Phönix," 289.

225 Stokes, *Faktor Öl*, 291 and 279. In the summer of 1956, tariffs on the import of heating oil fell for a few years. This step was necessary, as a State Secretary of the Federal Ministry of Economics put it in advance, "in order to promote heating oil as a real supplementary factor for the energy balance of the federal territory," said State Secretary Westrick on February 10, 1956; see minutes of the 129th meeting of the 2nd German Bundestag, Bundestags-Plenarprotokoll (hereafter quoted as BT-Plenarprotokoll) 02/129, 6734. For the forecasts see Schriftlicher Bericht des 3. Sonderausschusses Gemeinsamer Markt, Bundestags-Drucksache (hereafter quoted as BT-Drucksache) 02/3660 of June 28, 1957, 49. See also, with slightly different figures, Fren Förster, *Geschichte der Deutschen BP 1904–1979*, Hamburg 1979, 269.

for "Oil Firing and Heating Oil," which was set up at the end of the 1950s, grew and generated increasing profits.[226]

In the late 1950s, growing piles of millions of tons of unsold Ruhr coal revealed the woes and pressures of adaptation facing the West German coal industry. In the first year of the coal crisis that began in 1958, the share of oil in the industry's fuel consumption had almost doubled.[227] In the medium term, coal's "energy monopoly" began to erode.[228]

Changing Framework for Business: From the Founding of the EEC to the Construction of the Berlin Wall

At the same time, economic policy changes took place in the late 1950s, which, from the perspective of some contemporary observers, marked the end of the post-war period.[229] It was to prove promising for trade beyond German borders that France, the Benelux states, and Italy, together with the Federal Republic of Germany, announced their intention to found the European Economic Community in the Treaty of Rome in the spring of 1957. In addition, shortly afterward, the D-Mark joined the ranks of those currencies that had full international convertibility. Given the economic growth, unemployment fell sharply and reached a rate of less than one percent in 1961. At the beginning of the 1960s, the economic circumstances had changed compared to the previous decade: Empty labor markets, a reformed pension system that "dynamized" pensions and allowed pensioners to participate in rising wage levels, and a new competition policy framework with the "Law against Restraints of Competition" (Gesetz gegen Wettbewerbsbeschränkungen), increased incomes that had higher "disposable" income shares available for non-essential consumption purposes – these were all developments that pointed to a changed overall situation for the West German economy.[230]

Meanwhile, the East-West conflict had escalated further since 1958 in the second Berlin crisis. The Soviet demand that the Allies withdraw from Berlin was followed by negotiations and a commitment by US President John F. Kennedy to West Berlin and to the presence of the Western Allies in the city.

---

226 ACDP, 01-220-404; see also ACDP, 01-220-421.

227 Werner Abelshauser, *Deutsche Wirtschaftsgeschichte seit 1945*, Munich 2004, 203–206, here 204.

228 Abelshauser, BASF, 448.

229 See, for example, Ludwig Erhard's assessment of the "end of the post-war period." For a compilation of the aspects, see also Holtfrerich, *Deutsche Bank*, 543f.

230 See, among others, H. Giersch et al., *The Fading Miracle. Four Decades of Market Economy in Germany*, Cambridge 1992, 101–105.

The construction of the Berlin Wall along the sector border on August 13, 1961, marked the end of this crisis and demonstrated emphatically the division of the city and the isolation of West Berlin.[231]

Trading in Heating Oil and Chemicals

The *Brenntag* branch in Berlin was firmly established again in this island location over the course of the 1950s. The special situation of the city's economy was partly reflected in *Brenntag's* books. When it was decided in West Berlin in 1953 to expand the Berlin Senate's stocks in the event of another blockade, *Brenntag* used state funds to set up appropriate reserve stocks. The Senate storage warehouses built in 1953/54 and 1959 contained a total of around 790,000 kilograms of chemicals.[232]

Toward the end of the 1950s, *Brenntag's* management in Berlin grappled with the fact that the political tensions surrounding the Berlin question would have an impact on their current business. "So far, we have only felt the impact of the Berlin crisis in the oil burner department, where placed orders were temporarily withdrawn or postponed until the crisis was resolved," the Berlin management wrote to Mülheim in the spring of 1959. However, it was considered questionable whether the upturn in business that had been registered at the start of the year could be sustained over the next few months.[233] Although this uncertainty remained during the next year, the Berlin branch was also able to report "welcome" increases in sales for 1960. However, from 1961 onward, prices fell, so sales revenue did not increase despite increased petroleum sales. Nevertheless, other lines of business compensated for this: The trade in oil-fired heating systems in Berlin, which began in 1955, developed very positively. Since 1956, *Brenntag* had sold over 700 oil burners in Berlin, more than doubling sales in this segment and thereby boosting heating oil sales. In the meantime, it also provided customer service for the oil-fired heating systems.[234]

---

231 For background, see, e.g., Heinrich-August Winkler, *Der lange Weg nach Westen II. Deutsche Geschichte 1933–1990*, Bonn 2004, 195–205.

232 See auditor's report of *Treuhand-Vereinigung AG* on Brenntag GmbH, Berlin branch, dated December 31, 1962, and partial financial statements 1962, in: Brenntag Archive Berlin, auditor's reports (still unsigned); see also Peter Auer, *Die Verhältnisse zwingen zur Bewirtschaftung ... STRENG GEHEIM: Die zweite Blockade, die es nie gab*, 2nd ed. Berlin 1998.

233 Brenntag Archive Berlin, file folder Entwürfe Vorstandsbericht, still unsigned, containing documents for the board of directors' report on the 1958 financial year of Brenntag AG, Berlin, dated April 29, 1959.

234 Brenntag Archive Berlin, file folder Entwürfe Vorstandsbericht, still unsigned, containing documents for the board reports 1958–1961.

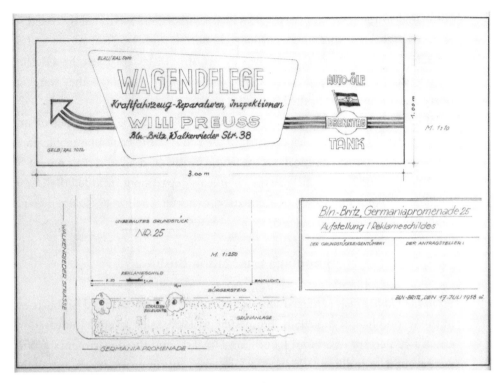

Figure 24: Plans for the erection of a billboard in Berlin-Britz, 1958.

In Mülheim, too, it became clear early on that the sale of oil-fired systems was lucrative and generated increasing profits.[235] The oil burner department of *Brenntag GmbH* had experienced an "extraordinary upswing" and quadrupled its sales just one year after its launch.[236]

Growth opportunities were also expected from *Brenntag's* chemical trade. In fact, the list of chemicals in stock was growing longer and longer – at the end of 1958, there were around 85 items in the alphabetical list of *Brenntag's* stocks, from acetone to xylene to zinc white. The most important hub for chemical transport was the location in Duisburg. Smaller stocks were stored in the *Brenntag* warehouses in Antwerp (the only base outside the Federal Republic of Germany), Frankfurt, Stuttgart, and Erlangen. In 1958, the chemistry department generated sales revenue of around 21 million D-Mark in drop-delivery-shipping and almost 13 million D-Mark in warehouse business – with a departmental profit of around 1.55 million D-Mark, which had increased by almost 60 percent

---

235 See ACDP 01-220-404.

236 See note for Mr. Unger on April 12, 1957 (Wirtschaftsbericht für die Landeszentralbank), in: ACDP 01-220-1003.

compared to the previous year.[237] The business partners were mainly based in Germany as well as in various European countries and the USA: At the end of 1958, for example, goods were on the way to or from Paris, Brussels, East Berlin, Rotterdam, New York, and San Francisco on behalf of *Brenntag* – they were "in transit," as it was stated in the books.[238]

While *Philipp Mühsam OHG* had been purchasing crude oil and petroleum products from the USA since the turn of the century, the transatlantic business connections in the chemical sector were probably a new development.[239] *Brenntag's* important suppliers in the chemicals department included the *Union Carbide Corporation* (UCC), the chemical exporter *Steuber & Company*, and *California Chemical International*.[240]

Brenntag's Gas Station Business

Brenntag GmbH also achieved large sales volumes in the mineral oil business in the second half of the 1950s. From 1956 to 1957, sales revenue increased by around 40 percent to around 63 million D-Mark, and the department's profits were around one million D-Mark.[241] Regrettably, only fragmentary records of the business development of the mineral oil division have survived. Nevertheless, they reflected – at least to some extent – the dynamic development of the mineral oil industry and motorization in the 1950s. For example, from *Brenntag's* perspective, the boom can be captured in the number of gas stations listed in the documents. In 1951 there were still only eight gas station managers listed by name, but in 1954 the number rose to 36, while in 1957 there were over 80 names of leaseholders in the gas station directory, and in 1958 there were already over 100 – with locations mainly in North Rhine-Westphalia. Since 1952, *Brenntag* had also operated a gas station on the autobahn near Opladen.[242]

The Berlin gas stations must have been run by *Brenntag AG* until the end of the 1950s, as they do not appear in the GmbH's business documents. Even the gas station, which *Brenntag* operated on a property on Kurfürstenstrasse in Berlin and which had been acquired from a Jewish owner through "Aryanization" in the

---

237 ACDP 01-220-421.

238 Ibid.

239 See above, Christopher Kopper in this volume. There is no evidence that Brenntag (or Philipp Mühsam OHG or Philipp Mühsam AG) purchased chemical products from the USA before 1945.

240 ACDP 01-220-421. California Chemical International, Inc. was a subsidiary of Standard Oil that marketed petrochemicals internationally.

241 ACDP, 01-220-376.

242 Vertrag Brenntag und Deutsche Total GmbH vom 21.12. 1962 zur Autobahntankstelle Opladen, in: HAC 500-4771-2002.MS.

Figure 25: Brenntag filling station, probably 1950s.

1930s, was apparently still part of the *Brenntag* portfolio in the 1960s, as invoices for construction work document.[243]

The fact that *Brenntag* operated more and more gas stations over the course of the 1950s was in keeping with the general trend. In West Berlin, around 330 gas stations were statistically recorded at the end of 1951, while at the end of 1958, there were 705.[244] Across the country, the number of gas stations was around 18,000 at the beginning of the 1950s and rose continuously to around 46,000 in 1970.[245] Along with the number of gas stations, the number of customers that *Brenntag* supplied rose as well. The most important suppliers in the gas station business were *Aral* and *Shell*.[246]

In relation to the book value, *Brenntag's* gas station business was considered extremely profitable. At the same time, *Hugo Stinnes OHG*, which had long been closely linked to *Brenntag* and had acted directly as the parent company since 1959, had a keen interest in increasing its liquidity. Against this background, the idea arose to bring the lucrative business area around gas stations into a joint venture with another company in order to optimize utilization and be able to valorize it as a short-term liquidity injection. At the end of 1962, *Brenntag GmbH* concluded a cooperation agreement for West German gas stations

---

243 Brenntag Archive Berlin, correspondence Btg. Mülheim 1965–1966, still unsigned. In it: Invoices to Brenntag GmbH, Mülheim for paving work for the Brenntag gas station on Kurfürstenstrasse. Cf. also chapter 6.

244 Statistisches Jahrbuch für Berlin 1960, 213.

245 See *Statista, Industrie und Märkte: Tankstellenmarkt*, Hamburg 2021, 4.

246 See Brenntag GmbH, Mineral Oil Department, December 31, 1958, in: ACDP 01-220-0370; Brenntag GmbH, mineral oil department, December 31, 1957 in: ACDP 01-220-0366. For 1951–1954, see also ACDP 01-220-502.

Figure 26: Brenntag filling station in Mülheim an der Ruhr, 1962.

with *Deutsche Total Treibstoff GmbH*, the German subsidiary of *Compagnie Française des Pétroles* (CFP). *Brenntag* brought parts of its fuel business into a new company, *Brenntag Kraft- und Schmierstoff GmbH & Co. KG*, in which *Brenntag* and *Deutsche Total* each held a 50 percent stake.[247] The cooperation included *Brenntag* leasing a large part of its gas station network to *Deutsche Total GmbH* in return for an annual lease guarantee and a fixed severance indemnity payment of six million D-Mark. In the meantime, *Brenntag's* gas station network had grown to around 130 stations. The exceptions were the Berlin gas stations and the autobahn gas stations, for which separate agreements were made.[248]

247 See *Erdöl und Kohle, Erdgas, Petrochemie*, Vol. 15, December 1962, No. 12. See also *Zusammenarbeit Deutsche Total – Brenntag*, in: *Frankfurter Allgemeine Zeitung*, November 24, 1962, 9 and Otto Stinnes, Begründung der Vergleichsvorschläge, in: Archive Diakonie, ADW HgSt 8308, 10 and 21.

248 Contract dated October 3, 1962, between Brenntag GmbH and Deutsche Total GmbH, in: HAC 500-4771-2002.MS. Information on the number of petrol stations varies.

Financing Problems at Brenntag GmbH

The leasing of the gas stations was the end point of a development that began in the early 1950s and was related to the liquidity problems in which *Brenntag GmbH* and its closely associated company, *Hugo Stinnes OHG*, found themselves at times. How did *Brenntag's* financial situation develop in the decade of post-war prosperity? During the 1950s, *Brenntag GmbH* had booming business sectors alongside those that were not generating any income. In this context, *Brenntag GmbH's* debt increased noticeably over the years. Progressively, partner companies, especially *Hugo Stinnes OHG* and *Brenntag AG*, were made responsible for *Brenntag GmbH's* commitments. As early as February 1952, Otto Stinnes wrote to the managing director of *Brenntag GmbH* Wilhelm Unger "that *Brenntag GmbH* needs to think about how it [...] covers its debts." The message was that the Hugo Stinnes company should not be "pumped for credit so heavily."[249] Despite this knowledge, little seemed to change in principle in this practice. In November 1956, Otto Stinnes wrote to *Brenntag GmbH* – on the letterhead of *Hugo Stinnes OHG* – that the "burden of financing" had recently "rested entirely on our shoulders." The GmbH had made efforts to repay the liabilities, but the debts had now reached a considerable amount – almost 10 million D-Mark.[250] In consideration of the low equity capital, this was a considerable sum.[251] In order to make *Brenntag GmbH's* bills discountable, the letter went on to state, *Brenntag AG* was also forced to stand surety for an unlimited amount. In this difficult situation, it was hard for *Brenntag* management to raise new funds for investments.[252] With this in mind, the management developed a number of activities in the second half of the 1950s to improve the company's financial situation through debt restructuring. In this context, the *Bank für Gemeinwirtschaft* granted *Brenntag GmbH* a loan of five million D-Mark with a term of three years, secured by ship mortgages. At the same time, it released the company *Hugo Stinnes OHG* from responsibility for other loans that *Brenntag GmbH* had taken out from the *Bank für Gemeinwirtschaft*.[253]

---

249 Otto Stinnes to Wilhelm Unger on February 21, 1952, in: ACDP 01-220-1199.

250 Otto Stinnes to the management of Brenntag GmbH on November 5, 1956, in: ACDP, 01-220-1226.

251 See Brenntag GmbH, balance sheet and profit and loss statement as of December 31, 1956, in: ACDP 01-220-313.

252 Otto Stinnes to the management of Brenntag GmbH on November 5, 1956, in: ACDP, 01-220-1226. At this point, he made the provision of further funds for investments conditional on the other shareholder, Hugo Stinnes Verwaltungs GmbH, run by his brother Hugo, giving half.

253 These amounted to six million D-Mark; see Brenntag GmbH to Verwaltung und Abwicklung GmbH on June 25, 1957, in: ACDP 01-220-0815.

What were the causes of *Brenntag's* earnings problems? The fragmentary business documents offer some clues to possible explanations. The difficulties had a long history, some of them going back to the early 1950s. The first thing that stands out is the large number of activities that *Brenntag* promoted during the reconstruction era. In the first years after the currency reform, *Brenntag* management tried to exploit its business opportunities on the broadest possible basis, especially in developing export business, and in doing so, also initiated business that did not fit with *Brenntag's* previous core strangths.[254] Hugo Stinnes jr. consequently soon demanded more focus: "We have neither the space nor the people nor the grounds to process every request in all areas from all corners of the world," he said in a letter to the export department in 1951. "Our work will not achieve results if we do not impose wise restrictions on the areas we work in and the products we work on."[255]

In the early phase, it was also sometimes problematic that the departments in Mülheim and Berlin were sometimes run by the same people. This balancing act soon became almost impossible to uphold for managing director Richard Kießling.[256]

Stinnes Against Stinnes

The transition from an improvised restart to established corporate structures had already caused certain problems. In the long term, however, the structural aspect was far more important: The sheer framework in which *Brenntag's* business took place contained the potential for management problems or disruptions to operational routines. With Otto Stinnes and *Hugo Stinnes Verwaltungs GmbH*, *Brenntag GmbH* had shareholders who initially pursued the common goal of rebuilding *Brenntag's* traditional businesses. However, the basis for their cooperation was fragile. In the course of the reconstruction activities, lines of conflict soon became apparent between the brothers, which became so acute within a few years that the senior partner Cläre Stinnes-Wagenknecht withdrew her trust in her son Hugo as a partner in *Hugo Stinnes OHG* and established an

---

254 Among other things, there are indications of business with iron-rolled products and machines with Brazil, business with pumps in Venezuela, and the initiation of connections with business partners in Saudi Arabia. However, in the early export activities, the boundaries between the activities of Hugo Stinnes OHG and Brenntag cannot always be clearly drawn, as became clear in retrospect in conflicts between Hugo and Otto Stinnes. ACDP-01-220-0949; ACDP 01-220-1003 (including file note for Mr. Unger on August 20, 1952; note to Masling on April 24, 1956); ACDP 01-220-925 (file note from Otto Stinnes dated March 26, 1953).

255 Note from Hugo Stinnes jr. to Iron Export Department, Brenntag Export Department on October 12, 1951, in: ACDP 01-220-949.

256 See Hugo Stinnes jr. to Richard Kießling on October 1, 1949, in: ACDP-01-220-949.

arbitration panel to resolve the differences.[257] "We hereby cancel all loans to the companies close to you – with the exception of the 250,000 DM loan for shares in *Brenntag GmbH*," Cläre wrote to her son. "Your actions have forced us to take these measures in the interests of the company." The accusation made by Cläre and Otto Stinnes against Hugo Stinnes jr. was, among other things, that he had misused funds from the OHG for his own investment projects and violated the declared wishes of the other managing partner.[258] The dispute between the brothers was also related to *Brenntag's* business activities. From the perspective of Hugo Stinnes jr., *Brenntag* suffered economic losses due to Otto Stinnes' management of the firm's ships.[259] However, the auditors who examined *Brenntag's* business since 1948 for the points considered to be controversial in 1956 did not see this accusation borne out by the performance recorded in the books.[260]

But even without gauging in retrospect which criticisms the two partners voiced were true to what extent, it seems obvious that the brotherly dispute blocked important decisions at *Brenntag GmbH* at times and forced to the surface latent governance problems. For example, a required capital increase at *Brenntag GmbH* was not implemented because the brothers could not agree on the modalities and passed the buck to each other for the failure.[261] It also often took a while until the necessary investment funds were available for *Brenntag GmbH* because the partners fought over the procedure.[262] In addition, they held different views with regard to business policy decisions.[263] The disputes at Stinnes did sometimes also lead to conflicts of loyalty among members of *Brenntag's* management.[264] Furthermore, both shareholding partners complained about a

---

257 Personal letter to Hugo Stinnes dated June 7, 1951, in: ACDP 01-220-1199. When Cläre Stinnes terminated the company on December 31, 1952, the deletion from the commercial register was initially waived; this took place after another termination on December 31, 1955, in 1956, see ACDP 01-220-649. For Otto's view of the points of conflict, see Otto Stinnes, Begründung der Vergleichsvorschläge, in: Archiv Diakonie, ADW HgSt 8308. With reference to Brenntag, see also a letter from Hugo Stinnes OHG to Hugo Stinnes Verwaltungs GmbH dated February 22, 1954, and Otto Stinnes to Wilhelm Unger on February 21, 1952, in: ACDP 01-220-1199. For Hugo Stinnes' view, see Hugo Stinnes to the management of Brenntag GmbH on January 23, 1953 (4 pages, first page dated January 21, 1952), in: ACDP 01-220-1199.

258 See letter to Hugo Stinnes OH, Finance Department (Mr. Unger) and personal letter to Hugo Stinnes personally, both dated June 7, 1951, in ACDP 01-220-1199. For the conflict between Otto and Hugo Stinnes, see also Domberg/Rathje, *Stinnes*, 188 f.

259 See, for example, Hugo Stinnes to the management of Brenntag GmbH on August 16, 1956, in: ACDP 01-220-1003.

260 See ACDP, 01-220-1100, Prüfbericht über eine Sonderprüfung der Brenntag GmbH 1948–1955, 71 ff.

261 See various documents in ACDP 01-220-925, e.g., an excerpt from a letter from Mr. RA Dr. Söller from December 13, 1956, and an excerpt from a letter from Hugo Stinnes to the management of Brenntag GmbH dated July 20, 1955.

262 See, for example, Otto Stinnes to the management of Brenntag GmbH on November 5, 1956, in: ACDP, 01-220-1226.

263 Hugo Stinnes was critical of Otto Stinnes' investments in shipbuilding and was quite right in this point of criticism – viewed ex post. For Hugo's criticism, see, e.g., ACDP, 01-220-1081 (questions about the general meeting) and various documents in ACDP 01-220-925 and ACDP 01-220-1199.

264 See, for example, note for Mr. Stinnes dated February 12, 1957, with Wilhelm Unger's request to destroy a note that provides information about his involvement in a Hugo transaction, ACDP 012-220-925. After the settlement between Hugo and Otto Stinnes in 1959, there were also senior employees who resigned from their duties at Brenntag.

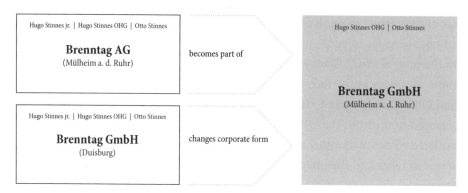

Chart 2: Simplified representation of the transformation of Brenntag in 1959.

lack of transparency in some *Brenntag* transactions.[265] The disagreement among the partners may also be a reason why the company did not take consistent and timely action on problem areas that had long been recognized by all shareholders as potential loss-makers – such as the poorly performing concrete plant – but instead allowed the problems to persist for the time being. As long as the conflict between Cläre and Otto Stinnes on the one hand and Hugo Stinnes jr. on the other simmered, the confusing and sometimes disadvantageous structures of *Brenntag* that had emerged from the coexistence of the AG and the GmbH remained in place. Nevertheless, it initially did not appear to be advantageous for *Hugo Stinnes OHG* to force the brothers to separate prematurely. "The situation of the company would not at present or in the near future bear an open dispute or a breakup visible from the outside," the lawyers of Hugo and Cläre Stinnes explained in May 1953. "Mr. Hugo Stinnes and Mr. Otto Stinnes must stay together for the time being, each in his very own interest."[266] In order to reduce the "friction" to a "tolerable level," the responsibilities in their common areas of activity were partially redistributed.[267] Nonetheless, as the examples showed, Otto and Hugo Stinnes retained enough opportunities to use their veto to prevent changes. These forces of inertia could only fade after the conflict was resolved at the end of the decade and were then to give way to a new, uniform organizational framework for *Brenntag's* business. The arbitration proceedings to settle the differences between the conflicting parties ended in 1959 with a settlement in which Hugo Stinnes jr. made repayments to Cläre and Otto Stinnes,

---

265 See, for example, Otto Stinnes to the management of Brenntag on June 28, 1951, and file note for Mr. Unger.

266 Copy of a letter to Hugo and Otto Stinnes dated May 28, 1953, in: ACDP, 01-220-649.

267 However, for Brenntag GmbH and AG, no need was seen for this, as Otto and Hugo Stinnes could only conduct formal business here with the agreement of the management; see copy of a letter to Hugo and Otto Stinnes dated May 28, 1953, in: ACDP, 01-220-649.

among other things in the form of shares in *Brenntag AG* and the 50 percent partner share he held in *Brenntag GmbH*.[268] Since all shares in *Brenntag* were now brought together again in one hand, both companies could be merged and organizationally streamlined: In November 1959, after being transformed into a GmbH, *Brenntag AG* absorbed the previous GmbH and – somewhat confusingly – started operating under the name *Brenntag GmbH neu*.[269] The new GmbH was based in Mülheim an der Ruhr and, like the AG, had a share capital of 3.6 million D-Mark.[270] The shareholding partners were now Hugo Stinnes OHG and Otto Stinnes. A few weeks later, the company changed its name: Instead of "Brenntag – Brennstoff, Chemikalien- und Transport-Gesellschaft mit beschränkter Haftung," it was now called "Brenntag – Brennstoff, Chemikalien- und Schiffahrts-Gesellschaft mit beschränkter Haftung"[271] – the change in the name thus merely specifying the "transport" line as "shipping."

The New Brenntag GmbH

With the new corporate organization, there was now a uniform, clear framework for *Brenntag's* business. The operation under corporate law eliminated unnecessary, confusing double structures and thus created a new, streamlined basis for its further development. *Brenntag* continued on its previous course. Nevertheless, even after this streamlining, certain imbalances remained within the company, since despite the formal reorganization, the coexistence between the historically more established weight of the Berlin location and the headquarters in Mülheim continued to exist in practice. Due to its special market situation, the Berlin branch seemed to continue to maintain a certain independence and special status. For larger investment projects at the beginning of the 1960s, such as new elevated tanks, pipelines, and pumps, especially for the heating oil business, *Brenntag* was able to use investment allowances within

---

268 See Otto Stinnes, Begründung der Vergleichsvorschläge, 7, in: Archiv Diakonie, ADW HgSt 8308. At the beginning of the 1950s, Hugo Stinnes OHG held 38.3% of the shares, Cläre Stinnes 28.7%, Hugo Stinnes jr. 16%, Otto Stinnes 11%, Nora Hermann 6%; see ACDP, 01-220-841 ("Distribution of Brenntag AG shares," June 29, 1951). In the summer of 1958, Hugo Stinnes OHG held 76% of the share capital, Otto Stinnes 1.4%, Hugo Stinnes jr. 10.375%, Hugo Stinnes Transozean Schiffahrt GmbH 5.55%, Nora Hermann 6.2%, see StAHH, 371-B-1995-2, Vol. 3 (list of shareholders represented at the general meeting on July 24, 1958).

269 At times, three Brenntag companies existed side by side: the GmbH based in Duisburg, the AG, and the new GmbH based in Mülheim. For the snapshot from 1959, see Kurt Pritzkoleit, *Männer, Mächte, Monopole. Hinter den Türen der westdeutschen Wirtschaft*, Düsseldorf 1963, 349.

270 LA NRW, Gerichte, Rep. 439, No. 23, notarial documents from November 28, 1959.

271 LA NRW, Gerichte, Rep. 439, No. 23, fol. 28 (letter from Wilhelm Unger dated December 21, 1959).

Figure 27: In the Brenntag tank farm, 1950s.

the framework of the Berlin Act of 1962, as the Berlin management reported to Mülheim.[272]

Some fragments that have been preserved from the correspondence between the Berlin branch and the Mülheim headquarters also highlight the fact that the management of the Berlin location certainly had the potential to create friction. For example, the headquarters in Mülheim found it problematic that Berlin had its own accounting department, so they thought about centralizing this task in Mülheim in the future. Difficulties arose from time to time, especially when monitoring the Berlin gas station accounts, and after the spin-off of a large part of the *Brenntag* gas station business, efforts were made to resolve these difficulties.[273] Berlin and Mülheim also still had to come to an agreement on the new allocation of administrative costs after leasing some of the gas stations.[274]

---

272 Report from the Berlin management dated May 29, 1963, in: Brenntag Archive Berlin, Btg. correspondence Mülheim 1962–1964.

273 See, for example, file note about the visit to Berlin by Mr. Stiepermann and Mr. Buch in May 1963, in: Brenntag Archive Berlin, Btg. correspondence Mülheim 1962–1964.

274 File note about the redistribution of costs from April 8, 1963, and file note about the visit to Berlin by Mr. Stiepermann and Mr. Buch in May 1963, in: Brenntag Archive Berlin, Btg. correspondence Mülheim 1962–1964.

Breaches in the Boom

Even during the economic miracle years, the signs at Brenntag were not pointing solely toward growth. Rather, certain developments since the early 1950s had been characterized by ambivalence. While the West German economy achieved extraordinary, sometimes double-digit growth rates, *Brenntag* also grew rapidly again after the war but, at the same time, struggled with earnings problems, internal difficulties, and weaknesses in financing. Organizational inefficiencies due to the confusing corporate structure, family disputes, and some unfavorable investment decisions had, at times, created a situation in which the company did not fully realize its potential.

However, the structural problems in the 1950s did not mean that there was a standstill at *Brenntag* over the course of this decade. Rather, some business areas developed particularly dynamically in the second half of the 1950s, and some new lines of business and locations were added. *Brenntag GmbH* now had departments for oil burners and heating oil, mineral oil, inland and maritime shipping, freight forwarding, scrap trading, and the concrete plant. Around 1958, apart from Duisburg and Mülheim, warehouses for chemicals and oil were located in Stuttgart, Erlangen, Neuss, and Antwerp.[275] In 1959, merged into the

Figure 28: Brenntag tank truck, probably around the 1950s.

275 See ACDP 01-220-366; ACDP 01-220-370; ACDP 01-220-376; ACDP 01-220-421.

new GmbH, Brenntag had branches in Berlin, Bremen, Hamburg, Frankfurt, and Stuttgart.[276]

While shipping can be seen as the driving force of development in the early 1950s, trade in mineral oil, heating oil, and chemicals developed a particular dynamic beginning from the mid-1950s.

Brenntag in German-German Trade Until 1963

At that time, *Brenntag* was a company whose business focus was on the domestic market. In addition, *Brenntag* had long-term business connections with trading partners in the GDR – not least due to its location in Berlin.

The first evidence of intra-German goods transactions can be found as early as the end of the 1940s. There is also evidence of *Brenntag* doing business with chemical and mineral oil companies in the GDR in the late 1950s and early 1960s. Nevertheless, the documentation is too fragmentary to be able to trace the continuous development of *Brenntag's* intra-German goods business since 1949.

But what were the general conditions in which *Brenntag's* GDR business took place? To what extent did German-German trade stand out from other cross-border trade transactions?

From the Federal Government's perspective, trade with the GDR had a special character that distinguished it from other foreign trade relationships. Beyond the narrower economic function, the movement of goods and capital to and from the GDR had a political dimension, as the Federal Republic initially had no official relations with the GDR and did not recognize it as a sovereign state. The East-West contrast was reflected in inter-German trade relations. Even after the two German states were constituted, the exchange of goods between the Federal Republic and the GDR initially continued to be called "interzone trade" in Bonn, but since the last third of the 1960s, people spoke of intra-German or German-German trade. Key legal provisions were made in the Military Government Act No. 53 of 1949, which regulated the intra-German exchange of goods until reunification in 1990.[277] The Foreign Trade Act of 1961 did not

---

276 LA NRW Gerichte, Rep. 439, No. 23, fol. 32 ff.

277 For intra-German trade see Peter Fäßler, *Durch den "Eisernen Vorhang". Die deutsch-deutschen Wirtschaftsbeziehungen 1949–1969*, Cologne 2006; Peter Krewer, *Geschäfte mit dem Klassenfeind. Die DDR im innerdeutschen Handel 1949 bis 1989*, Trier 2008; and Michael Kruse, *Politik und deutsch-deutsche Wirtschaftsbeziehungen von 1945 bis 1989*, Berlin 2005; see also Abschlussbericht des 1. Untersuchungsausschusses des 12. Deutschen Bundestages. Der Bereich Kommerzielle Koordinierung und Alexander Schalck-Golodkowski, BT-Drucksache 12/7600, 1994, 82 ff. André Steiner, "Ostgeschäfte: Westliche Unternehmen in der DDR," in: *Zeitschrift für Unternehmensgeschichte 2018*, 62/2, 221–234, introduces the state of research on the GDR business of West German companies.

apply to business with trading partners in the GDR. In principle, all transactions across the German-German border required approval from the appropriate authorities. On the Federal Republic's side, this fell under the responsibility of the Federal Ministry of Economics and the Deutsche Bundesbank, which monitored payment-related issues and managed the clearing accounts.[278] The contractual framework was created by the Berlin Agreement of 1951, which established annual lists of goods and circumvented the official recognition of the East German state by naming the areas of application "currency area of the DM-West or DM-East." On the GDR side, the Ministry for Foreign Trade and Inner-German Trade (Ministerium für Außenhandel und Innerdeutschen Handel, abbr. MAI) was in charge. The settlement of the bilateral trade transactions was carried out via accounts at the two central banks using a specially constructed calculation unit, the so-called "accounting unit" (Verrechnungseinheit, abbr. VE), which mathematically equated the DM-West and DM-East but in practice corresponded to the DM-West. The GDR had to spend the income generated from exports to the Federal Republic on imports from it, because the accounting unit did not represent a freely convertible currency.[279]

In bilateral clearing, the balances of the trading partners were supposed to correspond, but if they did not, they could be equalized with the so-called "swing" mechanism, which was, in fact, equivalent to an interest-free account overdraft option that the GDR regularly used. The so-called "country of origin bond" stipulated that only goods that were manufactured in the GDR or the Federal Republic were allowed to be exchanged, while products from abroad – such as oil – required a special permit. For their business transactions, the trading partners had to take into account a number of administrative requirements and to present purchase permits and notes to accompany the traded goods.[280]

Some favorable special regulations underlined the unique character of intra-German trade: West German companies that purchased goods from the GDR were able to realize tax refund claims. Purchases of goods from the GDR were also exempt from customs duties. After the founding of the Federal Republic and the GDR, intra-German trade was on a growth path: Between 1950 and 1960, the volume of business grew from around 670 million accounting units to around two billion accounting units. Despite these periods of significant growth, however, it remained behind the dynamics of foreign trade, both in the Federal

278 See BT-Drucksache 12/7600, 83.

279 See ibid.

280 Krewer, *Geschäfte*; Kruse, *Politik*.

Republic and the GDR.[281] The Federal Republic primarily supplied products from the electrical engineering and mechanical engineering industries as well as base materials and intermediate products, including chemical products. Initially, an important trading commodity from the GDR to the Federal Republic in the 1950s was lignite coal, but during this same time period, mineral oil and mineral oil products were already in second place. A large part of the GDR's deliveries to the Federal Republic consisted mostly of base materials, chemical products, and steel and iron.[282]

This rough sketch of the trading structure already suggests that *Brenntag*, with its focus on chemicals and mineral oil trading and its Berlin location, had the necessary prerequisites to be able to develop into a permanent fixture in goods traffic across the German-German border. At the end of the 1950s, the GDR adopted a seven-year plan that formulated ambitious economic goals and also attached great importance to the energy and chemical industries.[283] A chemistry program announced in the fall of 1958 in the GDR focused on the raw material crude oil: "Chemistry gives bread, prosperity, beauty" was the motto of the programmatic announcement.[284] Among other things the program called for building a refinery in Schwedt and expanding the chemical plant in Leuna for polyethylene and petrochemical production. It included the planned oil pipeline from the Soviet Union to the GDR in its scope. At the end of 1958, the Council for Mutual Economic Assistance also decided on the project for an oil pipeline that could supply Hungary, Poland, the CSSR, and the GDR with Soviet crude oil.[285] Until the "Friendship" ("Druzhba") pipeline went into operation in December 1963, Soviet oil came by rail or later by sea via the Baltic Sea ports of Wismar or Rostock. The quantities of diesel and carburetor fuel that the GDR delivered to the Federal Republic rose and their value increased from 164 million in 1959 to 191.7 million accounting units in 1963.[286] The export of further processed or refined products was permitted under the trade

281 See overview in Fäßler, *Störfreimachung*, 2, and ibid., 13. See ibid., *Handel*.

282 BT-Drucksache 12/6700, 85.

283 See Fäßler, *Eiserner Vorhang*, 282; Johannes Bähr, *Industrie im geteilten Berlin, Die elektrotechnische Industrie und der Maschinenbau im Ost-West-Vergleich. Branchenentwicklung, Technologien und Handlungsstrukturen*, Munich 2001, 212 f.

284 André Steiner, *Von Plan zu Plan. Eine Wirtschaftsgeschichte der DDR*, Munich 2004, 89; see also W. Mertsching, "Die Entwicklung der Mineralölindustrie in Mitteldeutschland nach 1945," in: *Merseburger Beiträge zur Geschichte der chemischen Industrie Mitteldeutschlands*, Vol. 3/98: "Vom Erdöl zu Kraft- und Schmierstoffen," 5–50, here 24. Carbide chemistry was also expanded until the mid-1960s; see Rainer Karlsch, "Energie und Rohstoffpolitik," in: Dierk Hoffmann (ed.), *Wirtschaftspolitik in Deutschland 1917–1990*, Vol. 3. Die zentrale Wirschaftsverwaltung in der SBZ/DDR. Akteure, Strukturen, Veraltungspraxis, Berlin/Boston 2016, 249–362, here 308.

285 Karlsch, *Energie und Rohstoffpolitik*, 313 ff.

286 However, the percentage of total deliveries remained roughly the same; see Fäßler, *Eiserner Vorhang*, 282.

agreements, while further export of non-processed products ran counter to the agreements under the principle of the country-of-origin bond. Although the share of petroleum products in the entire trade range grew only slowly until 1963, the concept of forced re-export of refined products still concealed a lucrative business idea. Due to the special agreements on internal market status, the tariff surcharge in domestic German trade was eliminated, so that the GDR was able to sell its fuels below the world market price in 1963 but still achieve a high profit margin.[287] During this phase, *Brenntag* was also already trading in GDR mineral oil products. In the early 1960s, for example, it had business connections with *MIEG*, the GDR's mineral oil import and export company.[288] During the 1970s, *Brenntag's* GDR business with mineral oil and mineral oil products was to gain considerable momentum.

The "Church Business"

The churches also took on an important mediating role in economic relations with the GDR. *Brenntag* was involved early on in deliveries of goods organized by the Protestant Church (Evangelische Kirche in Deutschland, abbreviated as EKD). As early as the late 1950s, *Brenntag's* parent company, *Hugo Stinnes OHG*, was one of a small group of companies commissioned with deliveries to GDR foreign trade companies by the Diakonisches Werk, a charitable organization of the EKD. The value of the deliveries was to be allocated to the churches. *Brenntag GmbH* had also been part of this group since the late 1950s. These firms were soon referred to as "trusted companies" by those involved in the transactions.[289]

As of December 31, 1958, a list from the *Brenntag* chemistry department of "goods in transport" registered eight chemical shipments worth a total of 140,000 D-Mark with the destination "Deutscher Innen- und Außenhandel Chemie" (commonly known as DIA Chemie) in East Berlin.[290] Later, in accordance with agreements from spring 1962, as part of a goods transfer initiated by the church, *Brenntag* delivered, for example, textile auxiliary substances, pigments

---

287 See Fäßler, *Eiserner Vorhang*, 282.

288 See, for example, references to a toluene business, Brenntag Berlin to Mr. vom Bruck, Brenntag Mülheim, on October 29, 1963, in: Brenntag Archive Berlin, Btg. Correspondence, Mülheim, January 1, 1962 – December 31, 1964.

289 PA-DBT 3327 12. WP Prot. 132, 1–78, here 14.

290 ACDP 01-220-421, Brenntag GmbH, Chemical Department, list of goods in transit as of December 31, 1958. Although this is proof of the business connection to DIA Chemie in 1958, it remains unclear at this point whether these deliveries were made as part of what was termed "Church Business A" (Kirchengeschäft A); see below in main text. The final report of the Schalck-Golodkowski investigative committee mentions that Brenntag was added in 1959. BT Drucksache 12/7600, 296.

and textile dyes, rubber threads, activated carbon, liquid chlorine, red lead, nickel sulfate, sodium perborate, and cable-insulating compound to the East Berlin companies *DIA Chemie* and *MIEG* worth 2.8 million D-Mark. Added to this were pigments, bone charcoal, and soot – and, the year before, zinc sulfates. The latter were now used more and more frequently to protect ferrous metals from rusting.[291]

But How Did So-Called "Church Business" Work During This Time?
While solidarity measures after the war by the West German established regional churches – e.g., through donations of money and material – for their Protestant equivalents in the GDR began as spontaneous and sometimes improvised relief operations, their activities became permanent and institutionalized over time. This had something to do with church politics in the GDR. When the GDR financial administration stopped collecting church taxes in 1956, the financial resources of the churches in the GDR threatened to dwindle rapidly. Against this background, the aid measures taken by the EKD[292] so far formed the basis for future operation: Since a money transfer was not possible, the Diakonisches Werk agreed to commission selected companies to deliver goods to the GDR. The equivalent value of these deliveries would then be credited to the Protestant Church in the GDR in DM-Ost (from 1968: Mark of the GDR). The funds for these deliveries from the so-called "Church Business A," which averaged around 40 million German marks per year, were raised by the EKD – with "significant" subsidies from the federal government.[293]

In practice, the business was carried out in such a way that the director of the Diakonisches Werk of the EKD, Ludwig Geißel, negotiated with representatives of the GDR Ministry of Commerce (MAI) which goods should be delivered in what quantities and which values should be credited to the churches in the GDR in return. The representative of the EKD Council – Bishop Kunst, who was a

---

291 Archive Diakonie, ADW, HGSt., 7810.

292 The EKD had been founded in Eisenach in 1948, as the official association of the Protestant national churches of both German states, with the purpose of performing joint public tasks for the 28 member churches. Heinz Brunotte, *Die evangelische Kirche in Deutschland. Geschichte, Organisation und Gestalt der EKD,* Gütersloh 1964.

293 BT-Drucksache 12/7600, 86, 296. See also the list in the report by Barthold Witte, ministerial director in the Foreign Office and member of the Council of the Evangelical Church; Barthold Witte, *Bericht über kirchliche Transferleistungen im evangelischen Bereich in die DDR von 1957 bis 1990,* Bonn 1993. See also Armin Volze, Kirchliche Transferleistungen in die DDR, in: Deutschland-Archiv, 24. Jg., 1991/1, 59 ff.

bank clerk by training – then requested approval and the note ("U," i.e., free of charge) to accompany the goods from the Federal Ministry of Economics and made the necessary coordination with the Ministry of Economics and Transport of North Rhine-Westphalia and the Federal Office for Commercial Business in Eschborn.

Geißel was convinced of the principle of awarding the delivery contracts to West German companies, which in turn would conclude subcontracts with the foreign trade companies in the GDR. "The companies involved must work reliably and absolutely trustworthily," emphasized Geißel. "They must bear the greatest risk, while we are the boss."[294]

Little by little, routines for carrying out the transfer of goods were established. "The ongoing business is being handled quite well," wrote Ludwig Geißel in the summer of 1962 to the representative of the Berlin office of the Internal Mission and the relief organization of the EKD. "Apart from a few remaining deliveries, the essential items have been delivered."[295] Every now and then, it took some time to work out the details of the transaction in advance. In 1962, for example, the price negotiations with *Brenntag* for nickel sulfate dragged on somewhat. "We won't be able to agree there," reported the Berlin observer of the negotiations. "The prices between *DIA Chemie* and *Brenntag* are about DM 120 per ton apart." The plants were out of stock and not willing to offer discounts, he went on. Nickel salts were in high demand during this phase because they were used in the production of premium stainless steel and for various products made thereof.

Difficulties in handling goods transfers initiated by the church also sometimes occurred due to slow processing by the ministerial bureaucracy, which in turn led to dissatisfaction with the negotiating partners in East Berlin. On one occasion, *Brenntag* regretted that they were no longer able to deliver on time in a letter to Ludwig Geißel, dated August 4, 1961. The approval from the Düsseldorf ministry had taken so long, while *Brenntag* itself had initiated the delivery immediately after the clearance. "The first wagons rolled out on July 22, so no time was wasted there, and we are currently trying hard to make up for the delay caused by the licensing holdup."[296]

---

294 Ludwig Geißel, *Unterhändler der Menschlichkeit. Erinnerungen*, Stuttgart 1991, 267 f.

295 Archive Diakonie, AdW, HGSt 7810, Geißel to Menck on August 7, 1962. For the individual deliveries, see ibid.

296 Archive Diakonie, AdW, HGSt 7810, Brenntag to Geißel on August 4, 1961.

In 1962, orders to *Brenntag* in what was called the "Sondergeschäft EKD 1962" totaled around 3.7 million D-Mark.[297] This corresponded to around 3 percent of *Brenntag's* sales in this financial year. In 1963, Brenntag delivered chemical goods worth around four million D-Mark as part of Church Business A. The total volume of Church Business A in that year was 43.49 million D-Mark, plus an additional agreement for the delivery of coal worth two million D-Mark.[298] In addition to *Brenntag*, three other companies were involved in Church Business A as trust companies: the Stuttgart company *Verwi* as a supplier of wool, the *Haniel* company for gas coking coal, and the *Hugo Stinnes* company for various metal goods.[299]

Since the 1960s, the term church business had stood for various business activities that the West German churches carried out to support their sister churches in the GDR. In addition to church business "A" outlined above, there was also church business "C," which included corresponding transfers from the Catholic Church in the West to the Catholic Church in the GDR. Behind the label "B," however, there was a barter trade of a completely different nature: the "purchase" of political prisoners from the GDR prison system, which had been practiced since 1962/63, and their transfer to the Federal Republic of Germany in exchange for deliveries of goods and raw materials to the GDR. [300] *Brenntag* was also regularly involved in these transactions, as will be described in more detail in the following chapters.

For trade with the GDR, the trade fairground in Leipzig was an important place to make contacts, exchange information about developments in the various industries on both sides of the German-German border, and initiate business connections.[301] This also applied to church business, which the involved parties got to talking about in Leipzig. Since the construction of the Berlin Wall, visiting the GDR had become more difficult. However, traveling for business purposes, such as visiting a trade fair in Leipzig, was possible. Several thousand people

---

297 See list from December 5, 1962, in Archive Diakonie, AdW, HGSt 7810.

298 Geißel's note to Kunst about the Leipzig Autumn Fair, September 6, 1963, in: Archive Diakonie, AdW, HGSt 7811.

299 See the list from March 22, 1963, for deliveries with a volume of around 34 million D-Marks, Archive Diakonie, AdW, HGSt 7811.

300 On the prisoner release program, see Jan Philipp Wölbern, *Der Häftlingsfreikauf aus der DDR 1962/3–1989. Zwischen Menschenhandel und humanitären Aktionen*, Göttingen 2014, and Alexander Koch, *Der Häftlingsfreikauf. Eine deutsch-deutsche Beziehungsgeschichte*, Munich 2014.

301 On the function of the trade fairs, see Christiane Fritsche, *Schaufenster des "Wirtschaftswunders" und Brückenschlag nach Osten. Westdeutsche Industriemessen und Messebeteiligungen im Kalten Krieg (1946–1973)*, Munich 2008, 301 ff.; see also Karsten Rudolph/Jana Wüstenhagen, *Große Politik. Kleine Begegnungen. Die Leipziger Messe im Ost-West-Konflikt*, Berlin 2006.

from the Federal Republic usually came to the spring and fall fairs in Leipzig.[302] For *Brenntag*, Hermann vom Bruck, who, at the beginning of 1963, ran *Brenntag's* business together with Heinz Bohlen, usually traveled to Leipzig in order to devote himself intensively to business contacts there.[303]

---

302 Fritsche, *Schaufenster*, 309.

303 Internal mission and relief organization of the Evangelical Church in Germany, Berliner Stelle on March 8, 1963, to Ludwig Geißel, in: AdW HGST 7811.

10.

The Crisis of the Stinnes Group of Companies and the Sale of Brenntag

In the early 1960s, *Brenntag's* parent company, *Hugo Stinnes OHG*, found itself in existential distress.[304] Because the parent and subsidiary businesses were closely intertwined, *Brenntag* also briefly plunged into extremely turbulent waters. For about three weeks from mid-October 1963, it was completely uncertain what the future development of the chemical trading company would look like.

But how did the crisis in the parent company come about? In the post-war period, *Hugo Stinnes OHG* had resumed the traditional business activities of the former *Stinnes Group* at the Mülheim location and had now grown into a trading company with around 1,600 employees that maintained a number of branches – including in Berlin, Hamburg, Bremen, Hanover, Duisburg-Ruhrort, Andernach, Braunschweig, Düsseldorf, Siegen, Frankfurt, Mannheim, Stuttgart, Nuremberg, and Munich. It was involved in sea and inland shipping, traded in steel, iron, coal, and other fuels, and exported machinery. In addition, *Hugo Stinnes OHG* also got into banking, with a focus on financing export and import activities as well as transactions with associated companies within the group of companies.[305] It had received the permit for this arrangement from the Allies. Due to the increased demand for German steel products with the start of the Korean War, the company was able to realize lucrative export orders in the early 1950s by selling steel products from the Ruhr area – made with US-imported coal – to North America.[306] In banking circles, the Stinnes Bank was not considered a bank in the strict sense but rather as a speculative trading company.[307] This meant that *Brenntag* belonged to a parent company whose business model was based on a quite risky business policy approach.

---

304 On the crisis at Hugo Stinnes OHG, see Commerzbank Historical Archives (HAC), 500 4771-2002; HAC 500 4772-2002; Otto Stinnes, Begründung der Vergleichsvorschläge, in: Archive Diakonie, ADW HgSt 8308. See also "Medio in Moll," in: *Der Spiegel* 44/1963 on October 29, 1963 (https://www.spiegel.de/politik/medio-in-moll-a-1b55f5d3-0002-0001-0000-000046172546, last accessed February 10, 2023).

305 See Otto Stinnes, Begründung der Vergleichsvorschläge, 5 in: Archive Diakonie, ADW, HgSt 8308. For a short profile, see also Kurt Pritzkoleit, *Männer, Mächte, Monopole. Hinter den Türen der westdeutschen Wirtschaft*, Düsseldorf, 324 f. Employee numbers from "Medio in Moll," in: *Der Spiegel* 44/1963 on October 29, 1963.

306 On the "steel-coal business," see Richard Tilly, Willy Schlieker, *Aufstieg und Fall eines Unternehmers*, Berlin 2008, 80–92. See also "Die Aktien vom Delaware," in: *Der Spiegel* 24/1957, June 11, 1957 (https://www.spiegel.de/politik/die-aktien-vom-delaware-a-6c39dea5-0002-0001-0000-000041757691, last accessed February 10, 2023).

307 See *Zeitschrift für das gesamte Kreditwesen*, issue 23, 1963, 1085.

Hugo Stinnes OHG in a Crisis of Trust

The sales volume of *Hugo Stinnes OHG* in 1960 was around 679 million D-Mark. Even without its subsidiaries, company owner Otto Stinnes found its "earning power" to be "quite satisfactory" in the crisis year of 1963.[308] Nevertheless, there was an open flank that tended to increase with the expansion of business: the company's insufficient capital resources. When the family-owned business had started again in 1948, it was supported by only a small capital base. This disproportion between equity capital and business volume became more pronounced in the boom years because the capital increases that had taken place in the meantime were not sufficient to substantially increase the firm's self-financing power.[309] The company often had to draw on short-term credit reserves between the middle of the month and the end of the month in order to meet the payment obligations from the trading transactions. These bridging loans reached a volume of 40 million D-Mark but were mostly covered by incoming payments toward the end of the month. This practice worked well as long as customers, suppliers, and banks trusted the company's security. However, a crisis of trust could have devastating consequences. If "those depositors who had held balances for years refrained from making new deposits out of precaution," explained Otto Stinnes, the company's liquidity would be seriously threatened.[310]

Such a worst-case scenario had been apparent since the late summer of 1963 when the group of companies owned by Hugo Stinnes jr. stumbled, and the press reported on the difficulties of this other Stinnes group.[311] Both brothers had relied on the goodwill of their father's name and also battled about the disputes over naming law issues in court. Although Hugo Stinnes jr.'s ailing company – with the two main companies *Hugo Stinnes Industrie und Handel GmbH* (Hustinhand) and *Hugo Stinnes persönlich GmbH* – had nothing at all to do with the *Hugo Stinnes OHG* run by Otto Stinnes, the similarity of the names caused serious uncertainty among the depositors of *Hugo Stinnes OHG*. Stinnes

---

308 Otto Stinnes, Begründung der Vergleichsvorschläge, 40, in: Archive Diakonie, ADW, HGSt., 8308.

309 As of December 31, 1961, their own funds amounting to 9.5 million D-Mark were offset by liabilities amounting to 159.841 million D-Mark, according to Otto Stinnes, cf. Archive Diakonie, ADW, HGSt., 8308, 29.

310 Otto Stinnes, Begründung der Vergleichsvorschläge, 31, in: Archive Diakonie, ADW, HGSt., 8308. To bridge the gap, Otto Stinnes had repeatedly resorted to euro-dollar loans; see "Zweite Welle," in: *Der Spiegel* 51/1963 on December 17, 1963 (https://www.spiegel.de/politik/zweite-welle-a-30f46b1a-0002-0001-0000-000046173110?context=issue, last accessed February 11, 2023).

311 See also "Plus Minus Null," in: *Der Spiegel* 40/1963 on October 1, 1963 (https://www.spiegel.de/politik/plus-minus-null-a-dab9e718-0002-0001-0000-000046172129?context=issue, last accessed February 10, 2023).

Bank customers withdrew their funds and refrained from making new deposits into their accounts. The Stinnes Bank general representative Franz von Papen explained: "Although they knew that we had nothing in common with Hugo Stinnes, they declared that out of caution, they would not work with our bank for six weeks."[312]

Although Otto Stinnes emphasized the confusion with his elder brother as the trigger for the crisis, it should not be overlooked that the withdrawal of depositors' funds coincided with homemade problems that made it difficult for management to free up cash on short notice in this crisis situation. During the boom years, the company owner all too often relied on investing profits in founding companies or acquiring investments instead of building up reserves. Due to high losses from the revaluation of the D-Mark in 1961, the management postponed the capital increase. Other banks saw the conditions for company financing at the OHG and their banking business as risky in any case.[313]

In addition, some of *Hugo Stinnes OHG's* customers were in difficulties, while internal governance problems had also slowed down the rapid reversal of course following a bad investment and poor handling of a large oil import deal. In addition to the unexpected and persistent cash loss in September 1963, there were outstanding debts due to frozen customer receivables, which totaled over ten million D-Mark. In mid-October, Otto Stinnes was forced to admit that his liquidity was no longer sufficient to continue business.[314] From Monday, October 14, 1963, the company stopped making payments and decided to apply for judicial settlement proceedings.[315] As the news magazine *Der Spiegel* reported, on the afternoon of the same day, Wilhelm Unger, head of the Stinnes Bank and long-time board member of the former *Brenntag AG*, attempted suicide and jumped into the Ruhr but was saved by passersby.[316]

Concern for Brenntag's Future

Of the dozens of subsidiaries of *Hugo Stinnes OHG*, *Brenntag Mineralöl, Chemikalien- und Schiffahrtsgesellschaft mbH* stood out as the most valuable

---

312 Quoted from "Medio in Moll," in: *Der Spiegel* 44/1963 on October 29, 1963.

313 From a banking perspective, the transactions were considered too speculative. People spoke of the bank in quotation marks ("Epilog zum Fall Stinnes-'Bank'"), and in retrospect there was talk of "abuse of the bank letterhead for corporate financing on unusual terms"; *Zeitschrift für das gesamte Kreditwesen*, issue 23, 1963, 1085.

314 Stinnes, Begründung der Vergleichsvorschläge, 32 ff., in: Archive Diakonie, ADW, HGSt., 8308.

315 Stinnes, Begründung der Vergleichsvorschläge, 41, in: Archive Diakonie, ADW, HGSt., 8308.

316 "Medio in Moll," in: *Der Spiegel* 44/1963 on October 29, 1963.

associate company. Two-thirds of *Brenntag's* share capital of 3.6 million D-Mark were pledged to *Dresdner Bank* as loan security. The *Rheinische Girozentrale*, the region's central giro institution, also had liens.[317]

Dresdner Bank estimated *Brenntag's* earning power at around three million D-Mark annually.[318] According to the credit institution, *Brenntag* had "significant assets" that were only inadequately reflected in the valuations in the firm's books.[319] The chemical dealer had around a hundred special tank trucks in its fleet, the new purchase value of which was estimated to be around three to four million D-Mark, while the book value of the entire fleet of 130 vehicles was only 700,000 D-Mark.[320] Annual sales between 1960 and 1962 were around 140 million D-Mark.[321]

While the events surrounding Otto and Cläre Stinnes' company had been coming to a head since mid-October 1963, feverish attempts began behind the scenes to sell the *Brenntag* shares in a timely manner. The company owner and his bank agreed that *Brenntag* had to be separated from the ailing *Stinnes Group* as soon as possible and sold at the best possible price. "There is complete agreement because of concerns about the future of *Brenntag*," said Otto Stinnes, summing up a discussion with his lender.[322] Time was of the essence because *Brenntag* also faced payment obligations in the next few weeks that it would not be able to meet due to its close financial ties to the illiquid parent company.

The preservation of *Brenntag* was considered a prerequisite in order to successfully begin the settlement proceedings of *Hugo Stinnes OHG*. It was "vital to the whole," emphasized Otto Stinnes, who described it as the "golden goose that lays the eggs."[323] A quick sale of *Brenntag* would have a positive effect on the bulk of *Hugo Stinnes OHG* because *Brenntag* had liabilities of 24.8 million D-Mark at the Stinnes Bank, which a potential buyer would have to take over.

---

317 Historical archive of Commerzbank (HAC), 500 4771-2002, containing a file note regarding the company Hugo Stinnes, Mülheim a. d. Ruhr, overview of account balances, credit limits and collateral. Nominal 2.46 million D-Marks of the Brenntag shares were pledged to Dresdner Bank. See also note dated October 15, 1963, regarding Hugo Stinnes OHG, pledge realization and the letter from the management of Hugo Stinnes OHG to Dresdner Bank dated October 17, 1963, ibid.

318 See note "Betr. Angelegenheit Brenntag" about a meeting of representatives of Deutsche Total Treibstoff GmbH and Union Carbide in the Dresdner Bank on October 16, 1963, in: HAC, 500 4771-2002.

319 See Dresdner Bank to the Federal Ministry of Finance and to the Finance Minister of North Rhine-Westphalia on October 31, 1963, in: HAC, 500 4771-2002.

320 Note "Betr. Angelegenheit Brenntag" about a meeting of representatives of the German Total group and Union Carbide in the Dresdner Bank on October 16, 1963, in: HAC, 500 4771-2002.

321 Otto Stinnes, Begründung der Vergleichsvorschläge, appendices in: Archive Diakonie, ADW, HGSt., 8308.

322 Letter from Otto Stinnes to Dresdner Bank, October 30, 1963, Brenntag headquarters archive; see also "Notiz betr. Angelegenheit Brenntag" about a meeting at Dresdner Bank (participants included Otto Stinnes, von Papen, Krueger, Stein), in: HAC, 500 4771-2002.

323 Minutes of a meeting of the Brenntag management at Dresdner Bank on October 16, 1963, in: HAC, 500 4771-2002.

There was a broad consensus among the creditors and banks involved that a complete bankruptcy of *Hugo Stinnes OHG* should be avoided. Already at the first meeting of major creditors, a representative of a Dutch credit institution emphasized "in serious words" – as an observer from *Dresdner Bank* described it – what a "bad impression the collapse of a bank would make."[324]

A few days later, in a submission to the North Rhine-Westphalia finance minister, *Dresdner Bank* asked for tax benefits for the possible *Brenntag* sale and reiterated that the effects of bankruptcy would be "particularly serious."[325] Due to the company's status as a bank, a large number of foreign banks (including American, French, Dutch, Swiss, and English) were involved, so there were fears of the consequences that a complete collapse of the *Hugo Stinnes OHG* would have "for the reputation of the entire German economy in the international sphere."[326] It was therefore important to move toward a settlement with the highest possible outcome and to prevent major negative consequences.[327]

Although the creditors had a "calm and constructive attitude," as an employee at *Dresdner Bank* noted,[328] the situation was complicated given *Brenntag's* narrow window of opportunity timewise and its confusing financial situation. Precise figures on the status were not yet available and were only compiled in the course of the process. On the one hand, this was due to the peculiarities of *Brenntag's* booking system, but on the other hand, it had something to do with the fact that *Brenntag* had outsourced the majority of its gas station operations to the oil and gas station company *Deutsche Total Treibstoff GmbH* on January 1, 1963, which now made the overview more difficult.[329] In addition, Otto Stinnes considered making the sale of *Brenntag* easier by allowing "dispensable assets" to be separated out beforehand and transferred to the parent company. The two ocean-going vessels were considered as well as the investments in the *Partenreederei Württemberg* and *Doehler Gußwerke*.[330]

---

324 Note about a meeting of the major creditors of Hugo Stinnes OHG on October 15, 1963, HAC, 500 4771-2002.

325 Dresdner Bank to the Federal Ministry of Finance and to the Finance Minister of North Rhine-Westphalia on October 31, 1963, in: HAC, 500 4771-2002.

326 Dresdner Bank to the Federal Ministry of Finance or to the Finance Minister of North Rhine-Westphalia on October 31, 1963, in: HAC, 500 4771-2002. The banks included Chase Manhattan Bank, L'union Européenne Paris, Amexco, Hollandsche Bank Unie, and others; see among others *Frankfurter Allgemeine Zeitung*, February 25, 1964, 18 ("Stinnes-Gläubigerversammlung schwach besucht").

327 Some parts of the company were liquidated, and some were leased. In the spring of 1964, the settlement between Otto and Cläre Stinnes and the creditors was concluded. The payout ratio reached around 80 percent; see Archive Diakonie, ADW, HgST, 8308 (internal statements and correspondence on the settlement procedure and the development of the remaining settlement assets); the Diakonisches Werk was able to realize 80 percent of its claims by the 1970s.

328 This was the assessment at a meeting of the Brenntag management at the Dresdner Bank on October 16, 1963, in: HAC, 500 4771-2002.

329 See Stein (Dresdner Bank), "Betr. Angelegenheit Brenntag/Stinnes oHG, Notiz über die Sitzung im Hause der Landeszentralbank am 4. November 1963", in: HAC, 500 4771-2002. Cf. also chapter 9.

330 Letter from Otto Stinnes to Dresdner Bank, October 30, 1963, Brenntag headquarters archive.

With an overdraft, *Dresdner Bank* initially ensured that *Brenntag* could meet its due dates by the end of the month. The valuable tank depot in Berlin-Britz served as security. Meanwhile, both bank representatives and Otto Stinnes held discussions with potential buyers.[331] *Total* – the *Compagnie Francaises des Pétroles* (CFP) and its subsidiary *Deutsche Total* – signaled serious interest. In preliminary discussions, representatives of *Deutsche Total* considered joining forces with two other companies, the US company *Union Carbide* and the French *Societé d'Hydrocarbure de St. Denis*. At this point in time, *Brenntag* had exclusive rights to distribute *Union Carbide* products in the Federal Republic.[332] The US chemical company *AMSCO* (American Mineral Spirits Company), *Preussag*, and a major Dutch corporation were also interested, as was *Hugo Stinnes AG*, which had emerged from the former Stinnes Corporation. In addition, the representatives for the *Brenntag* sale held several discussions with the CEO of *Saarbergwerke AG*.[333]

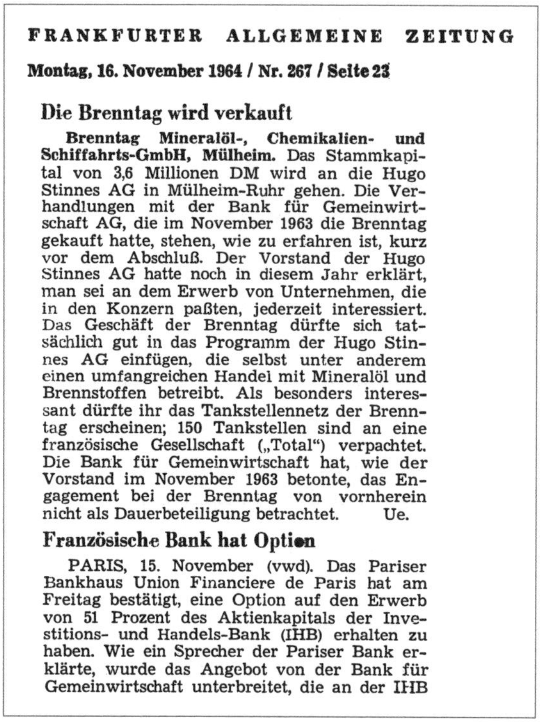
FRANKFURTER ALLGEMEINE ZEITUNG

Montag, 16. November 1964 / Nr. 267 / Seite 23

Die Brenntag wird verkauft

Brenntag Mineralöl-, Chemikalien- und Schiffahrts-GmbH, Mülheim. Das Stammkapital von 3,6 Millionen DM wird an die Hugo Stinnes AG in Mülheim-Ruhr gehen. Die Verhandlungen mit der Bank für Gemeinwirtschaft AG, die im November 1963 die Brenntag gekauft hatte, stehen, wie zu erfahren ist, kurz vor dem Abschluß. Der Vorstand der Hugo Stinnes AG hatte noch in diesem Jahr erklärt, man sei an dem Erwerb von Unternehmen, die in den Konzern paßten, jederzeit interessiert. Das Geschäft der Brenntag dürfte sich tatsächlich gut in das Programm der Hugo Stinnes AG einfügen, die selbst unter anderem einen umfangreichen Handel mit Mineralöl und Brennstoffen betreibt. Als besonders interessant dürfte ihr das Tankstellennetz der Brenntag erscheinen; 150 Tankstellen sind an eine französische Gesellschaft („Total") verpachtet. Die Bank für Gemeinwirtschaft hat, wie der Vorstand im November 1963 betonte, das Engagement bei der Brenntag von vornherein nicht als Dauerbeteiligung betrachtet. Ue.

Französische Bank hat Option

PARIS, 15. November (vwd). Das Pariser Bankhaus Union Financiere de Paris hat am Freitag bestätigt, eine Option auf den Erwerb von 51 Prozent des Aktienkapitals der Investitions- und Handels-Bank (IHB) erhalten zu haben. Wie ein Sprecher der Pariser Bank erklärte, wurde das Angebot von der Bank für Gemeinwirtschaft unterbreitet, die an der IHB

Figure 29: News article on the sale of Brenntag in *Frankfurter Allgemeine Zeitung* of November 16, 1964.

This meant that a whole series of potential buyers had lined up, some of which already had business relationships with *Brenntag*. Since the time window was narrowing in view of the payment terms due in a few days, *Dresdner Bank* initially directed its efforts toward forming a consortium for the takeover in order to be able to "then carry out the final sale in peace," as was stated in retrospect in an internal memo of the *Dresdner Bank*.[334]

331 Note "Betr. Angelegenheit Brenntag" about a conversation with representatives of Deutsche Total on October 16, 1963, HAC, 500 4771-2002.

332 Quoted from the *Frankfurter Allgemeine Zeitung* from October 19, 1963, 9 ("Was wird aus der Brenntag und in ihren Tochtergesellschaften?").

333 For the various exploratory discussions, see file notes in HAC, 500 4771-2002 and, in summary, "Unterrichtung der Filialen zur Verwendung in Gesprächen mit Kunden," dated November 7, 1963.

334 "Unterrichtung der Filialen zur Verwendung in Gesprächen mit Kunden," dated November 7, 1963, in: HAC, 500 4771-2002.

The Sale of Brenntag

On November 4, interested parties met at the state central bank where, among others, the Federal Banking Supervisory Office, *Deutsche Bank AG, Volkswagenwerk AG, Bank für Gemeinwirtschaft AG, Flick KG, Westfalenbank AG, Gelsenkirchener Bergwerks AG*, the *Burchardt Bank,* and the *Rheinische Girozentrale* were present with high-ranking representatives.[335] Although no consortium emerged from this high-profile Monday round, the possibilities for this move were explored, and it was planned to give them more concrete shape a few days later, on Thursday, when other participants would join the meeting. However, that didn't happen: The news was already circulating on Wednesday that *Union Treuhand GmbH*, a subsidiary of the *Bank für Gemeinwirtschaft*, would take over *Brenntag* as the sole buyer. At the end of the week, the purchase agreement of November 8, 1963, confirmed that Otto Stinnes sold *Brenntag Mineralöl-, Chemikalien and Schiffahrtsgesellschaft mbH* to a subsidiary of the *Bank für Gemeinwirtschaft* at a price of 250 percent.[336] The purchase price was, therefore, lower than Otto Stinnes had originally hoped, but given the pressure of the circumstances, it was higher than other parties involved at the time thought was realistic. For example, *Hugo Stinnes AG* had discussed a share price of 60 percent with *Dresdner Bank*.[337]

The *Bank für Gemeinwirtschaft's* solo effort caused astonishment among the others involved and gave rise to speculation as to whether it might have acted on behalf of a third party. Those involved at *Dresdner Bank* seemed surprised and were probably duped by the fait accompli.[338] The employees in the branches were given a letter summarizing the course of events – with the request that this memorandum only be used in oral conversations and not given out in writing.[339] "In the Ruhr area, the events surrounding *Brenntag* are understandably being discussed vigorously," wrote the *Frankfurter Allgemeine Zeitung* in a detailed report that testified to precise knowledge of the previous events.[340]

---

335 Ibid., "Teilnehmer an der Besprechung am 4. November 1963 im Hause der Landeszentralbank in Nordrhein-Westfalen in Düsseldorf" and "Notiz über die Sitzung im Haus der Landeszentralbank am 4. November 1963," in: HAC, 500 4771-2002.

336 Union Treuhand GmbH took over 89.1 percent of Brenntag's shares. 10.1 percent went to the company Nottebohm & Co. KG; see contract for the sale of Brenntag to Union Treuhand GmbH dated November 8, 1963, in: Brenntag headquarters archive. The price summed up to 9 million D-Mark, see ibid.

337 See note "Betr. Angelegenheit Brenntag" about a meeting with Otto Stinnes, von Papen, Dr. Peugin and other participants at the Dresdner Bank (on October 30, 1963), in: HAC, 500 4771-2002.

338 File note "Betr. Entschuldigung der Bank für Gemeinwirtschaft," November 7, 1963, in HAC, 500 4771-2002; see also internal board correspondence on the matter (Hans Rinn to Werner Krueger on November 8, 1963, in HAC, 1089998).

339 "Unterrichtung der Filialen zur Verwendung in Gesprächen mit Kunden", dated November 7, 1963, in: HAC, 500 4771-2002.

340 "Wie es zum Verkauf der Brenntag gekommen ist," *Frankfurter Allgemeine Zeitung*, November 8, 1963, No. 268, 36. See also HAC, 500 4771-2002.

With the sale of Brenntag, the greatest risks to the company's continued existence were averted, as the *Bank für Gemeinwirtschaft* was able to provide the necessary funds on short notice. At the same time, the sale of *Brenntag* significantly improved the position of Cläre and Otto Stinnes. "The *Brenntag* sale secured the Stinnes settlement," said the contemporary business press.[341] However, it remained unclear why the flourishing *Brenntag* was so heavily indebted to its parent company. There was a rumor circulating in the Ruhr area that *Brenntag* had been forced to absorb the Stinnes Bank's losses due to the appreciation of the D-Mark.[342]

The *Bank für Gemeinwirtschaft* thus played an important role in supporting *Brenntag* in the short term. However, it did not plan to undertake a long-term commitment.[343] The next step was to clean up the company's structures and sell off those parts of the firm that no longer fit *Brenntag's* profile. In addition to the shipping activities and *Doehler Gußwerke GmbH*, this included *ILAG*, i.e., *Düsseldorfer Industrie- und Lackwerke GmbH,* with 300 employees, and *Aglukon GmbH*, also based in Düsseldorf, which manufactured plant protection agents. The *Bank für Gemeinwirtschaft* arranged for the *Düsseldorfer Industrie-Lackwerke* to be sold to *Deutsche Solvay-Werke GmbH Solingen-Ohligs.* The 50 percent stake in *Aglukon* went to the Philips subsidiary *Philips Duphar GmbH*, which already owned the other half of the company.[344]

After roughly a year, *Brenntag* changed hands again. And their new parent company again bore the name Stinnes – but this time the group of companies that appeared had no connection with the groups of Otto Stinnes or Hugo Stinnes jr. In November 1964, *Hugo Stinnes AG* acquired the *Brenntag* shares from the *Bank für Gemeinwirtschaft* – i.e., the *Stinnes Group,* which had emerged from the former corporation.

Hugo Stinnes AG had already signaled interest in the *Brenntag* business during the crisis months and the impending liquidity crunch. The buyer's business priorities matched *Brenntag's* profile well. *Hugo Stinnes AG* also traded in petroleum products and fuels, and it had its own gas station network with the Fanal gas stations, which were now supplemented by the 130 operating locations of the *Brenntag* gas stations leased to *Deutsche Total.* This brought

---

341 "Der Brenntag-Verkauf hat den Stinnes-Vergleich gesichert," *Frankfurter Allgemeine Zeitung*, November 11, 1963, 19.

342 Ibid.

343 See also "Die Brenntag wird verkauft," *Frankfurter Allgemeine Zeitung*, November 16, 1964, 23.

344 See Felix Fabian, "Die großen Pleiten: Stinnes-Konzerne – Das verspielte Erbe," in: *Die Zeit* 11/1966, March 11, 1966. See also "Deutsche Solvay kauft Ilag GmbH," *Frankfurter Allgemeine Zeitung*, March 18, 1964, 18.

about a situation that the business press had highlighted just the year before as a strange peculiarity, should a company in the petroleum industry acquire *Brenntag*: In addition to its own gas stations, the new owner would have to maintain a network of gas stations in which a competitor also earned income. For this reason, the *Frankfurter Allgemeine Zeitung* had considered it unlikely in October 1963 that *Hugo Stinnes AG* would buy *Brenntag*.[345]

The management of *Hugo Stinnes AG* saw the potential that Brenntag had, which appeared to be more valuable in the long term than the book value reflected: "We expect the acquisition to significantly expand our sphere of activity, especially in the chemical trading sector," the firm's management stated.[346] At the end of the 1964 financial year, *Hugo Stinnes AG* was able to integrate a new associate company into its broad group of companies. The *Bank für Gemeinwirtschaft* had sold its 90 percent stake in Brenntag to *Hugo Stinnes AG* for almost 11.4 million D-Mark.[347] In the following year, the purchase price was subsequently reduced by 397,000 D-Mark.[348]

As early as mid-November 1964, *Brenntag* managing directors Hans Kempken and Heinz Bohlen were able to inform the Berlin branch of the upcoming changes. They welcomed this step because it promised a continuation of the usual practice: "The takeover of the partner shares by *Hugo Stinnes AG* gives us the guarantee that we will continue the business unchanged and protect our interests within the current framework."[349]

Looking back, the crisis of the former parent company and the subsequent sale of *Brenntag* appear to be important turning points in the company's history. For the continued existence of *Brenntag*, the consensus of those involved was crucial to separating it from the association with the ailing parent company. There was an accelerated cleanup of areas that were no longer viable for the future, such as shipping. On the one hand, the sale of *Brenntag* secured the settlement proceedings of *Hugo Stinnes OHG* and, on the other hand, opened up a new, more independent opportunity for development for *Brenntag* itself.

---

345 "Was wird aus der Brenntag und ihren Tochtergesellschaften?", *Frankfurter Allgemeine Zeitung*, October 19, 1963, 9.

346 Hugo Stinnes AG, annual report 1964, 12.

347 See Hugo Stinnes AG, annual report 1964, 15.

348 The reasons for this reduction are not reported in the files. Hugo Stinnes AG, annual report 1965, 13.

349 Telegram Kempken/Bohlen, November 13, 1964, in: Archive Brenntag Berlin, correspondence Btg. Mülheim 1962–1964.

Brenntag's Church Business After the Hugo Stinnes OHG Settlement Proceedings

During the turbulence surrounding the Stinnes crisis and the sale of *Brenntag*, it was for the most part possible to continue business as usual. How did these events affect the GDR business initiated by the church and in which *Brenntag* was involved?

When it became known that settlement proceedings would begin regarding the assets of *Hugo Stinnes OHG*, several companies from the Ruhr area expressed keen interest in stepping up as new trusted companies and taking on orders in the context of church business. Ludwig Geißel, for his part, emphasized the "special nature of the business."[350] At the same time, the Diakonisches Werk wanted to continue to work, if possible, with the people who had previously been in charge of the business at Stinnes. With this in mind, a joint project came about: The companies *Phoenix Rheinrohr, Deutsche Edelstahlwerke,* and *Thyssen-Hütte* founded an iron trading company, *Essener Stahl- und Metall-Gesellschaft mbH*, based in Essen, with a majority stake from *Simon Bank*. One of the chief executives was a former Stinnes director. The trading company was supposed to take over the orders that Otto Stinnes' company had previously carried out. Nevertheless, it was made clear in advance that there was no connection to the *EKD* nor any "moral or financial obligation" to commission them on the part of the Diakonisches Werk.[351] *Brenntag*, on the other hand, as a former subsidiary of the *Otto Stinnes Group*, remained unaffected by the reallocations and continued to operate as a trusted company of the EKD. Even after the crisis at *Hugo Stinnes OHG*, the inner circle of trusted companies remained limited to a handful of firms.

A New Transaction in the Context of Church Business: The First Ransomed Prisoner Releases

In addition, there were new developments in the transfer of goods organized by the EKD during this time. For the first time, an agreement was reached between the East German SED regime and the federal government on the release of political prisoners, stating that prisoners would be released from the GDR

---

350 Representative of the EKD at the state government in North Rhine-Westphalia to Geißel on December 4, 1963, in: Archive Diakonie, AdW, HGSt 7811.

351 Contact with Phönix Rheinrohr was established by the representative of the Evangelical Church at the state government of North Rhine-Westphalia in Düsseldorf, "Vermerk Sondergeschäft EKD – Stahllieferungen," December 10, 1963, in: Archive Diakonie, AdW, HGSt 7811.

prison system in return for material consideration. The churches' initiatives had again played an important role in advance, so that their connections and well-established procedures were used for future transfers.[352] While cash payments were sometimes made in the first exchanges, goods and raw materials were later delivered exclusively in return for the release of the prisoners, which – as in Church Business A – were processed as a "special order EKD" at the Diakonisches Werk in Stuttgart. The EKD received the funds for the delivery of raw materials from the federal government: The Federal Agency for Pan-German Tasks provided the funds through the representative of the EKD Council at the seat of the federal government.[353] Since the GDR government and the federal government kept the transactions secret, the funds used did not appear in the budget of the Ministry for Pan-German Issues and Intra-German Relations until the 1980s. As the head of the responsible department in the Federal Ministry for Inner-German Relations reported, the sum spent on buying the freedom of political prisoners in 1964 was 37 million D-Mark.[354] As a trusted company of the EKD, *Brenntag* was involved here as well. According to confirmation of the agreed transfers from July 1964, it delivered 3,300 tons of natural rubber as transit goods worth seven million accounting units and 1,600 tons of active carbon black worth 1.14 million accounting units to *DIA Chemie*.[355]

Over the course of the 1960s, the ransoming of prisoners from the GDR – Church Business B – experienced a "gradual consolidation."[356] After various raw materials as well as foodstuffs such as tropical fruits, coffee, and cocoa beans were initially delivered in return, by the early 1970s the range of goods was narrowed down to a few items that could be traded on stock exchanges and therefore easily converted into foreign currency: copper, petroleum, industrial diamonds, and silver.[357] As a result, the goods that *Brenntag* had originally delivered became less important for these specific transactions. Nevertheless, *Brenntag* was to remain active as a trusted company in "Special Business B" in the 1970s, mainly as a supplier of crude oil.

---

352 See also Jan Philipp Wölbern, *Häftlingsfreikauf*, 55 ff.; Koch, *Häftlingsfreikauf*, 98 ff.

353 BT-Drucksache 12/7600, 309.

354 Armin Volze, "Kirchliche Transferleistungen in die DDR," in: *Deutschland-Archiv*, Vol. 24, 1991/1, 59–66, here 63; see also Wölbern, *Häftlingsfreikauf*, 437 f.; 544. Differences in the numbers are due to smaller transactions that were not listed.

355 Agreement between Horst Roigk and Ludwig Geißel on the delivery of various goods from July 31, 1964, in: Deutscher Bundestag (ed.), Bericht des 1. Untersuchungsausschusses des 12. Deutschen Bundestages. Der Bereich Kommerzielle Koordinierung und Alexander Schalck-Golodkowski. Werkzeuge des SED-Regimes, Anlagenband 3, Doc. 670, 2711.

356 Wölbern, *Häftlingsfreikauf*, 496. For the releases in 1963, see ibid., 55 ff.

357 Volze, *Transferleistungen*, 63; BT-Drucksache 12/7600, 310.

11.

Brenntag as a Subsidiary of (Hugo) Stinnes AG in the VEBA Group (1965–1999)

With the purchase of *Brenntag GmbH* by Mülheim-based *Hugo Stinnes AG*, a new period in *Brenntag's* corporate history began. Until the early 21st century, i.e., for almost four decades, *Brenntag's* activities were very closely linked to the development of *Hugo Stinnes AG*. Whether Otto Stinnes and the top management of *Hugo Stinnes AG* had already had the purchase of *Brenntag* by *Hugo Stinnes AG* in mind as a possible scenario for the future when *Brenntag* was bought by the *Bank für Gemeinwirtschaft* in the fall of 1963 remains an open question at this point, but it is certainly conceivable. Up to that point, the AG in Mülheim had had extremely eventful years – and in the autumn of 1963, the process of reorganizing its structures was in full swing.

Hugo Stinnes AG at the Beginning of the 1960s: "Repatriation" and Sale to VEBA

When it acquired *Brenntag*, *Hugo Stinnes AG* had only recently become a German company again. The US Office of Alien Property controlled the *Hugo Stinnes Corporation* until 1957 and, toward the end of the 1940s, authorized the manager Heinz Kemper to run the business instead of Hugo Stinnes jr. When it became apparent in the mid-1950s that the US Department of Justice and the Office of Alien Property wanted to sell the majority shares in the *Hugo Stinnes Corporation*, the procedural regulations initially ruled out the possibility that interested German parties could take part in the bidding process set up by the US Department of Justice. Due to the importance of the *Stinnes Group* for the German economy, Chancellor Adenauer intervened with the American government and ensured that prospective buyers from all countries that participated in the Marshall Plan structure around the Organization of European Economic Cooperation (OEEC) were admitted to the bidding process. This meant that representatives from all OEEC countries were allowed to submit a bid. With the backing of the federal government and the significant commitment of Hermann Josef Abs, the CEO of the recently recentralized *Deutsche Bank*, a banking consortium was formed that aimed to buy back the majority of the corporation's shares.[358] The *Kreditanstalt für Wiederaufbau* and seven private banks were involved in this consortium, while *Deutsche Bank AG* took over the leadership of the consortium. In the summer of 1957, the consortium managed to acquire the majority stake in the *Hugo Stinnes Corporation* from the US Office of Alien Property and private American shareholders, thereby bringing the company back into the hands of German investors.[359] The buyers had largely met the financial requirements for this investment from funds from the federal government, which had provided the *Kreditanstalt für Wiederaufbau* with 101 million D-Mark to take over 75 percent of the acquired shares. As part of a gradual reorganization of the group, in 1962 over 864,000 shares of the corporation were exchanged for *Hugo Stinnes AG* shares.[360] With this transaction, those involved had achieved the first step – the repatriation of the company to the Federal Republic.

The plan for the near future was to sell the company's assets to private parties. The further conversion steps took a rather slow course. This may also have had something to do with the fact that the interests of the various groups involved in the buyback were quite different and changed over time. This also reflected the rapidly changing conditions in the sectors involved – energy and chemicals. At the beginning of the 1960s, the federal government had in mind to combine *Hugo Stinnes AG* or parts of it – the associate company *Steinkohlenbergwerke Mathias Stinnes* was thought of in particular – with the federally owned mining company *Hibernia* and thus give an economization impetus to the mining sector. Significant economic benefits were expected from a merger of activities in the areas of mining, coking plants, and the gas industry as well as their energy suppliers. In addition, a high level of economization potential was also seen in the chemicals division of both companies.[361] Nevertheless, there

---

358 The main participants in the consortium were the Kreditanstalt für Wiederaufbau and Deutsche Bank. "Draft of the consortium agreement between the Kreditanstalt für Wiederaufbau and the Deutsche Bank, also on behalf of a consortium to be formed by it regarding Hugo Stinnes Corporation, USA" (Entwurf des Konsortialvertrages zwischen der Kreditanstalt für Wiederaufbau und der Deutschen Bank zugleich namens eines von ihr zu bildenden Konsortium betreffend Hugo Stinnes Corporation, USA), in: BArch B 102/76064.

359 Raimund Le Viseur, *Die Kaufleute aus Mülheim. 175 Jahre Stinnes. Eine deutsche Firmenchronik*, Düsseldorf 1983, 98 ff.; Bernhard-Michael Domberg/Klaus Rathje, *Die Stinnes*, Vienna 2009, 199 ff. For background information, see correspondence and memoranda from the Federal Ministry of Economics, in: BArch B 102/76064.

360 Deutsche Bank to Kreditanstalt für Wiederaufbau on December 22, 1971, regarding Hugo Stinnes Corporation/Hugo Stinnes AG, in: BArch B 126/77037.

361 A rationalization report presented in the fall of 1962 proposed, among other things, to supply the Stinnes chemical plant Ruhröl with coking oven gas through a connecting line in the planned network and to use its full capacity to produce ammonia in the future, since it produced it more cost-effectively than Hibernia, while Hibernia was to concentrate on the next processing stages. Further advantages were seen in merging sales. See note from October 1, 1962, "Rationalisierungsmöglichkeiten bei einer Zusammenlegung von Stinnes und Hibernia," in: BArch B 126/77036.

was still no consensus among the actors involved with regard to *Hibernia-Stinnes* interlinking. The bank representatives, especially Hermann-Josef Abs for *Deutsche Bank AG*, rejected the idea and called for the original consortium order to privatize the *Stinnes Group*.[362]

In this context, considerations of bringing the Stinnes blocks of shares into *VEBA* gained traction.[363] *VEBA*, short for *Vereinigte Elektrizitäts- und Bergwerks AG* (hereafter *Veba),* was a federally owned energy company and acted as a holding company for various mining companies, including *Hibernia*. The participating ministries thought that by means of a share swap, *Hibernia* would afterward operate as a production group and *Hugo Stinnes AG* as a trading and shipping group within *Veba*.[364] The bank representatives, especially the banker Hermann-Josef Abs, only wanted to support the sale of Stinnes to *Veba* if the federal government made a "binding declaration about privatization,"[365] i.e., if a partial privatization equaled the shareholdings in *Veba*. Share capital would be settled and would correspond to the value of the Stinnes block of shares to be taken over.[366] When *Brenntag* joined the *Stinnes Group* at the end of 1964, the federal cabinet had already made a decision to this effect.[367] Nevertheless, the conditions for cooperation in the chemical division within the group were different compared to the initial assessments.[368] In the long term, however, the Federal Ministry of the Treasury still generally considered it conceivable to promote cooperation in the chemical sector – for example, through a federal AG for the chemical sector, which could take over all federal chemical companies and thus rule out "investing and competing against each other."[369]

Before taking over the shares, *Veba* also wanted a declaration of exemption from the federal government for the risk that members of the Stinnes family could bring recourse claims against them. In the spring of 1965, the consortium

---

362 A summary, for example, in a note dated June 20, 1973, "Hugo Stinnes AG, Repatriierung der shares der Hugo Stinnes Corporation" for Department VIII A 3 in the Federal Ministry of Finance, BArch B 126/77037.

363 When Hugo Stinnes AG bought Brenntag, the share capital of Stinnes-Aktiengesellschaft amounting to almost 98.9 million D-Mark was a majority holding – around 87.4 percent – in the hands of a banking consortium led by Deutsche Bank AG and with the participation of the Kreditanstalt für Wiederaufbau. A further 12.6 percent were in free float.

364 File note regarding Hugo Stinnes AG on January 28, 1963, to State Secretary Westrick, in: BArch, B 126/77036.

365 This was the demand at a consortium meeting at the beginning of 1963; see file note regarding Hugo Stinnes AG on January 28, 1963, to State Secretary Westrick, in BArch, B 126/77036.

366 Deutsche Bank to Veba on March 24, 1965, in: BArch B 126/77037. Abs agreed in the spring of 1963; see also note dated June 20, 1973, "Hugo Stinnes AG, Repatriierung der shares der Hugo Stinnes Corporation," for Department VIII A 3 in the Federal Ministry of Finance, ibid.

367 Cabinet decision of July 31, 1963; see note of June 20, 1973, in: BArch B 126/77037.

368 In the meantime, Ruhröl, for example, had made other contractual agreements, so that the possibilities for cooperation with them appeared to be slim in the short term.

369 Note dated August 10, 1964, in: BArch B 102/76867.

offered its 87.5 percent stake in *Veba's* Stinnes shares for sale for 171.7 million D-Mark, which corresponded to a market value of around 200 percent.[370] In addition, the independent shareholders received a severance payment offer. On this basis, *Hugo Stinnes AG* was ultimately transferred to *Veba,* even before the partial privatization. In August 1965, *Veba* shares were introduced on the stock exchange as "Volksaktien," namely, people's shares.[371]

However, they quickly lost their popularity – the market value could only be maintained through support purchases over the course of the year. Shortly before the IPO, the selling point for the security paper was that *Hugo Stinnes AG* had now joined the group of companies as a profitable company. *Hugo Stinnes AG* has "nothing to do with the Stinnes companies that got into trouble some time ago," said *Deutsche Bank AG's* sales prospectus, as the news magazine *Der Spiegel* reported.[372] In addition, the CEO of *Hugo Stinnes AG*, Heinz Kemper, was considered the designated *Veba* boss a few months after the transition to *Veba.* He stood for a pragmatic approach to increasing the company's profitability from the economies of scope in the three main areas of mining, chemicals, and electricity. At *Hugo Stinnes AG*, he had previously scaled back traditional divisions such as mining and inland shipping in order to strengthen trade in building materials and fertilizers as well as chemicals, glass, oil burners, and tools.[373]

In 1965, the ownership architecture of *Hugo Stinnes AG* was structured as follows: More than 96 percent of the shares were owned by *Veba,* which in turn, even after partial privatization, was a company with relevant federal participation, with around 36 percent of the shares, which increased again in the following years.[374] The acquisition of *Brenntag* by *Hugo Stinnes AG* came at a time in which the group's investment configuration was being restructured.

---

370 Deutsche Bank AG to Veba on March 24, 1965, in: BArch B 126/77037. The market values varied: The private banks in the consortium estimated a sales price of 225 percent, and the federally owned Kreditanstalt für Wiederaufbau (due to the lack of interest expenses) offered a price value of 190 percent. Heiner Radzio mentions a higher purchase price – albeit for the entire acquisition of Hugo Stinnes AG – amounting to 262 million D-Mark. Cf. Heiner Radzio, *Unternehmen mit Energie. Aus der Geschichte der Veba*, Düsseldorf/Wien/New York 1990, 175.

371 On December 18, 1964, the Bundestag approved a partial privatization of Veba; see BT-Drucksache 04/2861.

372 "Volksaktien. Geflüsterter Kurs," in: *Der Spiegel*, April 27, 1965, online at https://www.spiegel.de/politik/gefluesterter-kurs-a-1fd70549-0002-0001-0000-000046272408 [last accessed June 10, 2023].

373 See *Der Spiegel*, December 21, 1965. Veba Kemper. "Wenn es Brei regnet."

374 This was the situation shortly after the IPO, after the federal government had allowed more shares to be sold than originally planned due to strong demand for the paper; see Alfred Hartmann, "Die Privatisierung bundeseigener Unternehmen in der Bundesrepublik Deutschland," in: Jörn Axel Kämmerer (ed.), *Privatisierung. Typologie, Determinanten, Rechtspraxis, Folgen*, Tübingen 2001, 209–228, here 215. Federal participation later increased again and was 43.7 percent at the beginning of the 1980s.

For *Brenntag GmbH*, the basis of its business activities had changed significantly at the beginning of the 1960s. With the acquisition by *Hugo Stinnes AG*, it now belonged to a group of companies with a different size and capital resources than the previous parent company, *Hugo Stinnes OHG*. After a short transition phase in which *Brenntag* had operated without much contact with a parent company close to the industry, such a framework was now within reach again and in a broader and more differentiated form than before. *Brenntag* certainly had a historical connection to the *Stinnes Group* and thus also to *Hugo Stinnes AG*.

From the end of 1964, *Brenntag* found a place within the group of companies that also wanted to expand its international orientation. *Brenntag* had brought chemical trading into the broad-based Stinnes trading and shipping group as a new division, thereby opening up a new business segment. However, in retrospect, *Brenntag's* business activities cannot always be clearly defined, because in the years shortly after the takeover of *Brenntag*, *Hugo Stinnes AG* initially built on its existing trading bases when it came to penetrating foreign chemical and plastics markets.

Brenntag GmbH in Its New Structure

What impact did the sale of *Brenntag* to *Hugo Stinnes AG* have on its business? Was the company actually able to "continue the business unchanged" and pursue its "interests within the previous framework," as formulated by the company management on the occasion of the sale?[375] Based on the documented sources, further clues can only be obtained in partial aspects of these questions. The documents from the Stinnes family's estate, some of which could provide information about *Brenntag's* business from an internal perspective, broke off at the end of the 1950s. For developments from the mid-1960s onward, the findings must now be based on a different type of source. These include, for example, the annual reports of *Hugo Stinnes AG*. In addition, files from ministerial officials who took their seats on the supervisory board of *Hugo Stinnes AG* as part of the required federal participation have also been preserved for a number of years. They reveal relevant investment decisions by *Brenntag* that were also discussed. There is, however, no direct record of *Brenntag's* business operations. Even in

---

375 Telegramm Kempken/Bohlen, November 13, 1964, in: Archive Brenntag Berlin, Korrespondenz Btg. Mülheim 1962–1964. [Corrected lower-case entry].

the *Veba* archive, which only exists in parts, no documents could be found that provide information about *Hugo Stinnes AG* and its control of *Brenntag*. Unfortunately, no documents have been preserved regarding *Veba's* Eastern Committee, which was headed for many years by a Stinnes board member responsible for *Brenntag's* business and whose activities must have been highly relevant to *Brenntag's* trading activities with countries in Eastern Europe and the GDR. On this point, however, the existing fragments of sources can be supplemented with documents that the GDR Ministry for State Security[376] created as they were observing *Brenntag's* trading transactions.

There is some evidence to suggest that *Brenntag's* management was right in its assessment that business could continue to remain largely constant even after the sale to *Hugo Stinnes AG*. The adjustment of *Brenntag's* loss-making divisions had already taken place before their sale to *Hugo Stinnes AG*. In addition, the structures had been thinned out somewhat – for example, the branch in Bremen had already been separated from the firm in the summer of 1964.

When it comes to the question of continuity, however, it was particularly important that the management staff remained constant. This was possible because the generational change among senior employees had already begun before the sale. According to shareholder resolutions, long-time director Richard Kießling withdrew from management in the winter of 1962/63. Heinz Bohlen, Hermann vom Bruck, Heinz Höhn, and Joachim Stiepermann then moved up into the executive ranks and remained in positions of responsibility for *Brenntag's* business for the next decades. A new management team had already emerged before *Brenntag* joined *Hugo Stinnes AG* at the end of 1964. The integration into the newly configured *Stinnes Group* was not accompanied by a noticeable change in *Brenntag's* top management.[377]

Tensions Between Berlin and Mülheim

Typical distributions of tasks also initially remained the same. Even before *Brenntag* joined *Hugo Stinnes AG*, there had been occasional misunderstandings

376 Ministerium für Staatssicherheit, abbreviated "Stasi" or "MfS", was the state security service of GDR.

377 See the Brenntag commercial register file and the entries from autumn 1962. LA NRW, Abt. Rheinland, Gerichte, Rep. 439 No. 23. Heinz Bohlen, Hermann vom Bruck, Hermann Meyer, and Hans Kempken were managing directors of Brenntag GmbH. Meyer was in charge of the oil firing business and left when it was sold. Hans Kempken died in 1975. Vom Bruck and Bohlen were appointed authorized representatives in 1958; see ACDP, 01-220-A0815.

between the headquarters in Mülheim and the Berlin branch. *Brenntag* Berlin had often complained that the Mülheim headquarters sent unjustified payment reminders to Berlin customers, even though they had paid on time. "Every care is taken to ensure that all […] payments are reported to you on the same day," the Berlin branch wrote to the head of the Mülheim accounting department. It was "incomprehensible" that the receipts were not recorded "because, after all, you receive everything already prepared by us." There had already been "the worst rows" with the customers. "Can't your ladies and gentlemen work a little more carefully?" demanded a letter from Berlin to Mülheim on another matter. Some suggestions for improvement or practical advice from Mülheim were viewed as simply "outrageous" in Berlin.[378] With this background in mind, management had been looking for ways to solve problems and optimize business processes with new operational routines for some time. However, it was a long-term process that was delayed by the crisis of the parent company in the autumn of 1963.

As late as the summer of 1964, the Berlin branch of *Brenntag* made suggestions to the headquarters on how to improve the sending and recording of invoices. Those responsible in Berlin also pointed out differences in the yield calculation. "We have absolutely different numbers, even though we have now accepted your numbers through our balance sheet," the Berlin management wrote to the management of *Brenntag GmbH* in Mülheim. At the same time, they called for more speed in profitability calculations. In the past, an "approximate profitability calculation" was made every month in order to gain an indication of real profits, since the corresponding figures from Mülheim arrived "very late." They then decided to halt this procedure but hoped that information on sales and profitability would be provided promptly – because it was an "unpleasant feeling when we don't know how business is actually going for months."[379]

After the sale to *Hugo Stinnes AG*, there seemed initially to be little fundamental change in the potential conflict issues. Nevertheless, the headquarters tried to solve the problems by combining functions in Mülheim. On January 1, 1965, the entire accounting department was transferred from Berlin to Mülheim.[380]

---

378 See correspondence on various smaller events (e.g., November 28, 1963; November 21, 1963; November 26, 1963; February 20, 1964; February 24, 1964; and spring 1964), in: Brenntag Archive Berlin, Korrespondenz Btg. Mülheim 1962–1964.

379 Letter dated August 28, 1964, to the management in Mülheim, in: Brenntag Archive Berlin, Korrespondenz Btg. Mülheim 1962–1964.

380 See documents in the Brenntag Archive Berlin, Korrespondenz 1.1.1965–31.12.1966, and letter dated March 10, 1965, in: Brenntag Archive Berlin, Korrespondenz Btg. Mülheim 1962–1964.

Even after the transition to the new parent company, the coordination of business routines between *Brenntag* Berlin and the headquarters in Mülheim still seemed to cause problems in many respects. The accounting was now centralized in Mülheim, but from a Berlin perspective, this did not represent an immediate improvement. "We are completely floundering because we do not hear of any money transactions from you," wrote *Brenntag* Berlin to the chief controller in Mülheim on June 1, 1965. It happened "very often that we do not know whether the payments we arranged to arrive in Mülheim actually got there. It is imperative that a different system be created here so that we are informed about such incoming payments."[381]

The examples cited above provide an indication of the tensions that arose between the headquarters and the branch. However, since only fragments have survived, no conclusive assessment can be made with regard to the capacity for control of the headquarters in Mülheim. It also seems plausible to consider that some actors in the Berlin branch rejected the idea of having to hand over functions for which they were previously independently responsible and therefore did not hold back with criticism of existing coordination issues or still half-baked processes. What remains clear is that the Berlin location continued to be of great importance.

The Growing Network, First Steps Toward Internationalization, and the Economic Downturn of 1966/67

Since January 1, 1966, *Brenntag* had operated under the shorter company name *Brenntag GmbH*. "We are convinced that we are so well known in the market that we can afford such a simplification without any additions," said a circular that the Mülheim management sent to the *Brenntag* branches and sales offices.[382]

Business had continued to improve since 1964, so a capital increase was carried out from the free reserves in the summer of 1967, and a profit of around 1.99 million D-Mark was also shown.[383] The share capital now amounted to 4.5 million D-Mark, and the sales volume had once again grown significantly and now amounted to over 150 million D-Mark.[384] With seven contact points, the

---

381 Brenntag Berlin archive, Korrespondenz 1.1.1965–31.12.1966.

382 Rundschreiben No. 18 of December 14, 1965, in: Archive Brenntag Berlin, Korrespondenz 1.1.1965–31.12.1966.

383 Brenntag profit and loss statement as of December 31, 1966, in: LA NRW, Abt. Rheinland, Gerichte, Rep. 439 No. 24.

384 Brenntag, balance sheet as of December 31, 1966, and Brenntag profit and loss statement as of December 31, 1966, in: LA NRW, Rhineland Department, Gerichte, Rep. 439 No. 24, fol. 15.

Figure 30: Brenntag Berlin, outdoor advertising "Propane Gas," 1970s.

network of *Brenntag* representative offices was densely connected, especially in North Rhine-Westphalia – there were also sales offices in Hamburg, Frankfurt, Nuremberg, Stuttgart, and the branch in Berlin. In addition, warehouses at various locations in Germany as well as in the Netherlands and Belgium formed central hubs for the transport of goods.[385] By 1966, *Hugo Stinnes AG* had also acquired the remaining 10 percent of the shares in *Brenntag*, the value of which was now on the books at around 12.23 million D-Mark, making it second in the ranking list of *Hugo Stinnes AG's* associate companies.[386]

A new statute of *Brenntag GmbH* from the summer of 1967 focused primarily on trading as the main field of business activity. The company's purpose included "the purchase and sale, […] the forwarding and storage of mineral oil products, products from the mining, metallurgical, and metal industries, the chemical industry and agriculture, as well as the trade in all kinds of goods." According to the statutes, the production and processing of these goods was also part of the company's purpose.[387] Shipping – still item number one of the stated business purpose in one of the last versions of the company statutes from the late 1950s – was no longer mentioned in the revised statutes.[388]

---

385 See, for example, file note August 5, 1964, in: Archive Brenntag Berlin, Brenntag correspondence January 1, 1965 – December 31, 1966.
386 Hugo Stinnes AG, Annual Report 1966, 18. The remaining 10 percent could have been sold by Nottebohm & Co. KG, which in any case had acquired a 10 percent share in Brenntag in November 1963 (see above).
387 LA NRW, Abt. Rheinland, Gerichte, Rep. 439 No. 24, fol. 17.
388 Ibid.

When *Hugo Stinnes AG* was acquired by *Veba, Brenntag* was a medium-sized chemicals and mineral oil dealer. In the previous two decades, the focus of its business activities had been primarily on the domestic market, although *Brenntag* also had international business relationships through various export activities. After the transition to a parent company that already owned numerous affiliates abroad, *Brenntag* also made corresponding investments. Within a decade, it gained in international presence by founding subsidiaries abroad. An early example of this was the Belgian market, where *Brenntag* had been represented since the acquisition of *NV Balder* in Antwerp in 1966. An important chemical production site was being established here, close to the large European port. For example, the chemical company *BASF* decided in 1964 to build a new plant in Antwerp, while the *Bayer* company had had corresponding investment plans for years and laid the foundation stone for the *Bayer* plant there in 1965.[389] *Brenntag* had long had a warehouse location in Antwerp but had now strengthened its local offering by taking over the Belgian company.[390]

Around the middle of the 1960s, the basic tendencies of economic development in the West German economy gradually changed. The boom of the reconstruction years had lost momentum and was gradually ebbing. The economy began to weaken in the summer of 1966, and in the following year, 1967, the national product shrank for the first time in the history of the Federal Republic.[391] At the same time, plant closures in the steel industry and coal mining signaled shrinking trends in traditional economic sectors. Although the economic downturn appeared minor in retrospect, it caused uncertainty and worries about crises among the population, who had become accustomed to economic growth during the long boom phase.

At this time, *Hugo Stinnes AG* was on a growth path and increased its sales, due to the increasing number of affiliates. The recession of 1966/67 was, nevertheless, reflected in a decline in margins and a deterioration in revenues.[392] However, this only affected some business areas. The economic downturn had no impact on the chemical trading division, which essentially consisted of *Brenntag*. A series of new products broadened the portfolio in the expanding chemicals

---

389 For Bayer, see Christian Marx, *Wegbereiter der Globalisierung. Multinationale Unternehmen der westeuropäischen Chemieindustrie in der Zeit nach dem Boom (1960er-2000er Jahre)*, Göttingen 2023, 118 f.; on BASF in Antwerp see Werner Abelshauser, "Die BASF seit der Neugründung von 1952," in: ibid. (ed.), *Die BASF. Eine Unternehmensgeschichte*, Munich 2002, 359–637, here 497 ff.

390 Gerald Scheffels, *125 Jahre Brenntag Stinnes Logistics*, published by Brenntag AG, Essen 1999, 28.

391 Spoerer/Streb, *Wirtschaftsgeschichte*, 219. Nützenadel, *Stunde der Ökonomen*, 296 ff.

392   Hugo Stinnes AG, annual report 1966, 7. As part of consolidation measures, Hugo Stinnes AG acquired, among other things, subsidiaries of Mathias Stinnes GmbH.

Figure 31: Brenntag tanker truck, 1970s.

and plastics trade, especially in exports. The slump in growth of 1966/67 was quickly overcome. Toward the end of the 1960s, the governing bodies of *Hugo Stinnes AG* noted above-average growth in the chemical trade in terms of sales and earnings.[393]

The development of the Northern European markets made rapid progress. Since 1966, the chemicals trading division had traded in Danish petrochemical products as well as pharmaceutical and industrial chemicals. From 1968 onward, a new department for the import and export of chemicals was intended to help coordinate foreign trade activities in the chemicals division and to exploit the "opportunities offered within the group."[394] Steps were taken that resulted in an increasing international orientation of the chemicals trading business. *Brenntag*, together with a Danish Stinnes subsidiary, founded a new chemicals trading company, *4 K/Kemi AS Copenhagen*,[395] which acted as a mainstay for handling the Nordic markets. In Italy, *Brenntag* acquired a majority stake in Milan-based

---

393 See note of the supervisory board meeting Hugo Stinnes AG for ministerial director Lamby from September 26, 1969, in: BArch B 126/34884.

394 Hugo Stinnes AG, annual report 1968, 9.

395 Hugo Stinnes AG, annual report 1968, 10; annual report 1970, 50.

Sochital SpA. This meant that *Brenntag* had bases in both European trading blocs – the European Economic Community (EEC) and the European Free Trade Association (EFTA). Toward the end of the 1960s, the first steps toward liberalizing trade in the European economic area had already been taken: After the eight member states of the EFTA – Great Britain, Switzerland, Austria, Denmark, Sweden, Norway, Portugal, and Finland as an associated member – had reduced tariffs within their free trade zone on January 1, 1967, the European Economic Community implemented the customs union for its member states on July 1, 1968. It dispensed with internal tariffs and introduced a common external tariff. With the accession of Great Britain, Ireland, and Denmark to the EEC in 1973, European markets were finally brought closer together.[396]

At the beginning of the 1970s, the *Stinnes Group* had ambitious plans for the next decade for *Brenntag's* division. The aim was to strengthen the group's

Figure 32: Warehouse in Duisburg in the 1970s.

396 Gerold Ambrosius, *Wirtschaftsraum Europa. Vom Ende der Nationalökonomien*, Frankfurt 1996; see also Christian Franck, "Kleine Freihandelszone – was nun?", in: *Wirtschaftsdienst* Vol. 47, year 1967, issue 1, 18–20.

Figure 33: Opening ceremony of Brenntag Japan Ltd, 1974.

position in the chemicals and plastics market with the "purposeful expansion of the German and international organization," according to the annual report.[397] Domestically, the aim was to keep the contact with the producer geographically close and the route to customers as short as possible. Accordingly, the sales organization and storage capacities in the Federal Republic and West Berlin were expanded. In Duisburg, the largest inland port in Europe, *Brenntag* significantly expanded its storage capacity.[398] In foreign markets, the goal was to be present at central transshipment points for chemicals. A milestone in *Brenntag's* history was the expansion into North America, a region that would become one of their most important markets over the years. Around 1969/1970, a branch of the *Hugo Stinnes Chemical Division* was founded in Houston, Texas, a major location for the US chemical industry, which continued to expand in the following years. The headquarters of the US *Hugo Stinnes Chemical Division* was in New York, which was considered a hinge point for trade between the US and Europe. A one-man sales office started there around 1968. Soon thereafter, however, the headquarters were relocated to Houston.[399] In the following years, *Brenntag* created further

---

397 Hugo Stinnes AG, annual report 1970, 17.

398 See Hugo Stinnes AG, annual report 1972, 17.

399 Overview of Soco, Inc. (1984), in: Brenntag Archive, still unsigned.

pillars for the development of new markets. In 1971, it founded a subsidiary in Great Britain, *Brenntag UK Ltd.*, based in London, took over the Paris-based company *Vandierdonck SA* in 1972, and founded *Brenntag Iberica S. A.* in 1973 in Madrid. What was remarkable was the start of business activities in the Far East, which was carried out since 1974 through *Brenntag Japan Ltd.* based in Tokyo.[400] In order to also be present on the West Coast of the USA, another office was opened in Los Angeles for the *Hugo Stinnes Chemical Division*, which was now known as *Stinnes Oil & Chemical Company*.[401] As the organization expanded, the chemical trading division's sales generated abroad also rose rapidly.[402]

Reorganization of the Stinnes Group

Meanwhile, the parent company also continued to grow and put out feelers into various business areas: Since the end of the 1960s, management began to reorganize the *Stinnes Group* and streamline some business areas. With the main sectors being trade, transport, and services, Stinnes companies operated in the trade of fuels, chemicals, mineral oil, steel, timber, and tires, in shipping, in freight forwarding, in data processing, and in refrigeration and air conditioning technology. *Brenntag* represented the chemical trade and traded in heating oil but also operated in the fuel sector with *Brenntag Kraft- und Schmierstoff GmbH & CO. KG*, in which *Total* still held a 50 percent stake. In the Stinnes "domestic engineering" division, *Brenntag GmbH* also occasionally offered the construction of swimming pools that were manufactured using the concrete spraying method.[403] Since 1971, *Brenntag Schwimmbad GmbH* has been listed in the annual reports as the unit specifically responsible for this line of production.

In 1972, some subsidiaries were converted to *Hugo Stinnes AG* for tax reasons, and the business was transferred to new management companies. At the same time, *Brenntag AG* was founded, whose board members and authorized representatives were identical to those of the previous *Brenntag GmbH*. *Brenntag AG* acted as a representative of the newly founded operating company *Brenntag AG & Co. OHG*, based in Duisburg, which had taken over the business activities

400 Hugo Stinnes AG, annual report 1974, 20.

401 Hugo Stinnes AG, annual report 1974, 20. The year for the name change is dated differently in the internal review to 1976; see Overview of Soco, Inc. (1984), in: Brenntag Archive, still unsigned.

402 Between 1969 and 1975, sales in the chemicals and minerals trading division increased from 19.1 million D-Mark (at then-current prices) to 196.4 million D-Mark, about ten times as much. However, price increases must be taken into account, which accelerated in the first half of the 1970s. Adjusted for prices, foreign sales are likely to have increased sevenfold in the period mentioned.

403 See Hugo Stinnes AG, annual report 1969, 22.

of the converted GmbH and whose total capital amounted to eight million D-Mark.[404] During the conversion, those involved made sure to preserve the well-established name "Brenntag." This reorganization of the legal form law would not change the practical course of the business relationship, *Brenntag* assured business friends in a January 1973 letter.[405]

With a "healthy mix of divisional and regional principles," as the CEO of *Hugo Stinnes AG* explained his measures to the supervisory board, the aim was to develop "company awareness from bottom to top and profit awareness from top to bottom."[406] However, the reorganization measures in this phase did not affect the basic principle of the company's structure, which remained decentralized. The decentralized organization in the *Stinnes Group* was an integral part of the corporate philosophy and shaped the management style, which gave the subsidiaries – like *Brenntag* – great scope of action. The Stinnes corporate umbrella brought together a large number of medium-sized companies that were active in different markets under different names. While critics found the group to be too large and confusing, this management structure was cultivated internally as a traditional success factor of *Hugo Stinnes AG*, part of the core of the historically evolved corporate identity. "The nomarchs have always been strong at Stinnes, and that was a good thing," explained CEO Günter Winkelmann at a company meeting in the 1970s. Diversity was a strength; only a "generous scope for decision-making and clearly defined personal responsibility" could release "those creative forces" on which they depended.[407]

In the first half of the 1970s, the trading company and its subsidiaries faced particular challenges. Fluctuations in exchange rates and prices caused the market to become hectic at times and made market events more confusing. This had to do with changes in the global economic framework: Since the beginning of the decade, the Bretton Woods international monetary order, which was based on fixed exchange rates and the gold convertibility of the US dollar, had faltered in the face of increasing US balance of payments deficits and dollar inflows to other countries, until it finally eroded in the spring of 1973. A few months later, the oil price shock in the fall of 1973 suddenly made it clear to

---

404 Hugo Stinnes AG, annual report 1972, 47. See also the list of consolidated group companies and Hugo Stinnes AG, annual report 1972, 41 ff.

405 Letter from Brenntag GmbH regarding changes to its legal form "an unsere Geschäftsfreunde" from January 1973, in: Brenntag archive, still unsigned.

406 Note from department head F/VIII dated May 24, 1972, for the supervisory board meeting of Hugo Stinnes AG on May 18, 1972, in: BArch B 126/34885.

407 See the keynote speech by CEO Günter Winkelmann at the "Stinnes Forum" group conference on February 6 and 7, 1976, in: BArch B 126/77038.

what extent Western economies depended on oil imports from the Middle East. The reduction in production by OPEC caused a rapid increase in the price of oil, which quadrupled from just under three to around twelve dollars per barrel between January and December 1973.[408]

As the price of oil rose, so did the prices of other important raw materials and energy sources. The realization that "the age of 'cheap' energy [was] a thing of the past" had now been confirmed, summarized *Hugo Stinnes AG* in the 1973 financial year.[409] In view of rising prices and scarce energy, many industrial sectors slipped into a short-term crisis, while in the Federal Republic of Germany's economy, medium-term stagnation tendencies, rising inflation rates, and increasing unemployment rates condensed into the phenomenon of "stagflation." The global economy also stalled due to the oil price shock and currency turbulence. The extraordinary dynamics of the economic miracle years could not be continued. Rather, the complex and changeable developments over the course of the 1970s indicated new challenges and changed economic conditions.

Initially, the chemical industry was one of those sectors that was considered particularly vulnerable to the crisis due to its high energy intensity. However, the key figures for 1974 showed a different picture: The rapidly rising raw material and producer prices inflated the chemical industry's turnover by around a third. But sales also picked up. Due to concerns about future shortages and further price increases, buyers of chemical products sometimes purchased more than they needed and increased their inventories, which temporarily increased demand. Large corporations in particular were initially able to noticeably improve their earnings. For example, the profit at *Hoechst* in the first half of 1974 increased by around 70 percent compared to the corresponding period of the previous year, at *BASF* by almost 37 percent, and at *Bayer* by 31 percent.[410] This meant that the chemical industry – measured in terms of sales – became the largest industrial field in the Federal Republic in the 1974 financial year.[411] The export business offset declines in domestic business and proved to be an important source of

---

408 Jens Hohensee, *Der erste Ölpreisschock 1973/74. Die politischen und gesellschaftlichen Auswirkungen der arabischen Erdölpolitik auf die Bundesrepublik Deutschland und Westeuropa*, Stuttgart 1996, 78. See also Michael von Prollius, *Deutsche Wirtschaftsgeschichte nach 1945*, Göttingen 2006, 183.

409 Hugo Stinnes AG, annual report 1973, 11.

410 Information according to *Der Spiegel* 38/1974, "Chemie-Konzerne, Kräftig zugelangt."

411 Branchen-Report; Chemische Industrie, ifo-Schnelldienst July 14, 1975, 3. In the medium term, however, the real growth effects were significantly lower, as was evident in 1975; on this see below.

support overall for the economy.[412] Since the mid-1960s, the foreign activities of the large chemical companies had increased noticeably.[413] This meant that international perspectives also became more attractive in the chemical trade, although the business still retained local ties.

Figure 34: Members of the board of managers and directors of Brenntag in 1974.

412 Branchen-Report; Chemische Industrie, ifo-Schnelldienst July 14, 1975, 3.
413 Marx, *Wegbereiter*.

Brenntag Turns 100

The economic situation in the chemical industry also gave *Brenntag's* business a tailwind. For 1974, the company expected a sales volume of one billion D-Mark – a magnitude that had never been achieved in the company's history.[414]

For *Brenntag*, 1974 was not only the most successful year in its history to date but also an anniversary year: In October 1974, the company was able to look back on its centenary of business activity. They celebrated this occasion at the end of September with a large ceremony at Hugenpoet Castle in Essen.[415] The *Brenntag* workforce now numbered around 600 employees – working at the headquarters in Mülheim, in twelve sales offices in Germany, and in the eleven foreign subsidiaries.

According to the Stinnes annual report, anyone who wanted to understand the success of *Brenntag* would not encounter "capital power." "The material resources were always limited." Rather, management and employees contributed "with new ideas, daring, and agility." "Success in change" – that was *Brenntag's* company motto, the report boasted.[416]

The industry's economic situation offered favorable conditions for continuing to expand bases for the chemical trade, with the focus at this time still being on Europe and the USA. However, *Brenntag* now also took steps to specifically promote trade with the Soviet Union. Together with *V/O Sojuzchimexport Moscow, Brenntag AG* founded the trading company *Sobren-Chemiehandel GmbH Mülheim an der Ruhr* in 1974. The idea was to use *Brenntag's* sales know-how to sell products from the Soviet chemical industry in the Federal Republic. At the same time, the aim was to support small and medium-sized companies in exporting chemical products to the Soviet Union.[417] This joint venture was an unusual project. As a *Brenntag* chronicler pointed out, apart from *Sobren*, there was only one other German-Soviet joint venture in the Federal Republic at that time – the import company for Russian vodka.[418] "The tried and tested relationships with the state trading countries have now been anchored in

---

414 *Frankfurter Allgemeine Zeitung*, September 23, 1974, 14. In fact, the chemical trading division of Hugo Stinnes AG broke through the one billion sales mark and, based on the extraordinary price developments, increased sales significantly compared to the previous year – by sixty or even over 80 percent, if you add agency sales. See Hugo Stinnes AG, annual report 1974, 9; Hugo Stinnes AG, annual report 1975, 11. Frank & Schulte GmbH was added in 1973, which significantly increased the total sales of the chemical trading department in the short term. From 1978/79, the mineral trade was reported separately.

415 Scheffels, *125 Jahre*, 30.

416 Hugo Stinnes AG, annual report 1974, 5.

417 Ibid., 20.

418 Scheffels, *125 Jahre*, 30.

corporate law," said the Stinnes annual report. The fact that such a joint venture came into being had something to do with the changed political climate, which created new opportunities for German companies to do business in the East.[419]

"The 'politics of strength' gave way more and more to the view of 'change through rapprochement,'" stated the historian Peter Fäßler, with a view to the programs of the chancellors from Adenauer to Kiesinger.[420] Around 1973, the chemical company *Bayer* also concluded an agreement with the Soviet State Committee for Science and Technology to promote cooperation in the field of agrochemicals for the Soviet market. Five years later, *Bayer* opened an office in Moscow.[421]

The changed political climate also affected trade relations between the Federal Republic and the GDR. Since 1966, a whole series of liberalization measures had signaled a more relaxed atmosphere for the exchange of goods in intra-German trade.[422] The guiding principle of "change through trade" became increasingly important for policy toward the East, which Willy Brandt initiated first as foreign minister in the grand coalition and later as federal chancellor. In 1966, the GDR Council of Ministers founded the "Commercial Coordination" department, or Koko for short, in the Ministry for Foreign Trade and Inner-German Trade (MAI), which now functioned as a unified management for the GDR companies *Zentralkommerz, Intrac, Transinter,* and *Intershop,* among others. *Brenntag* had business connections with *Intrac,* especially in the 1980s. *Brenntag* also had business relationships with the Koko company *Berag Import Export GmbH.*

The new structure Koko, which was under Alexander Schalck-Golodkowski's control from December 1966, was intended to help the planners of the GDR economy to meet their need for foreign currency more systematically with specially designed business practices in a phase of forced reform efforts. In some cases, these efforts occurred outside the legal framework. This step represented an important turning point for the development of the GDR's foreign trade transactions.[423]

---

419 For the GDR business of West German companies, see André Steiner, "Ostgeschäfte: westliche Unternehmen in der DDR," in: *ZUG 2018,* 63/2, 221–234. For GDR trade, see also Peter Krewer, *Geschäfte mit dem Klassenfeind, Die DDR im innerdeutschen Handel 1949–1989,* Trier 2008. For a look at the Eastern Bloc states, see Karsten Rudolph, *Wirtschaftsdiplomatie im Kalten Krieg. Die Ostpolitik der westdeutschen Großindustrie 1945–1991,* Frankfurt a. M. 2004.

420 Peter Fäßler, "Zwischen 'Störfreimachung' und Rückkehr zum Tagesgeschäft. Die deutsch-deutschen Wirtschaftsbeziehungen nach dem Mauerbau," in: *Deutschlandarchiv* 3/2012 (March 20, 2012), available online at https://www.bpb.de/themen/deutschlandarchiv/126613/zwischen-stoerfreimachung-und-rueckkehr-zum- tagesgeschaeft/ [last accessed June 10, 2023], here 11.

421 Erik Verg et al., *Milestones. The Bayer Story 1863–1988,* Leverkusen 1988, 516.

422 For the liberalization measures, see Fäßler, *Eiserner Vorhang,* 256 ff.

423 For the history of commercial coordination, see Matthias Judt, *Der Bereich Kommerzielle Koordinierung. Das DDR-Wirtschaftsimperium des Alexander Schalck-Golodkowski – Mythos und Realität,* Berlin 2013, and BT-Drucksache 12/7600, 87 ff.

Church Business from 1966

Since Koko was founded in 1966, the head of the Diakonie Ludwig Geißel, as a trustee of the federal government, made the specific agreements for handling Business B with a Koko official as soon as a state secretary from the Federal Ministry for Pan-German Issues (from 1969: for Intra-German relations) and a representative of the GDR government had drawn up the rough outlines for the next period of business. The procedural steps in Church Business B largely corresponded to those in Business A but with the difference that the raw material deliveries went to the Koko company *Intrac* and the financing came from federal funds.[424] In the 1970s, the goods delivered were only marketable goods such as crude oil, rough diamonds, and precious metals. Geißel mainly used the companies he had already worked with in Business A as his trusted companies. This is where *Brenntag* came into play, supplying crude oil. *Essener Stahl- und Metallhandelsgesellschaft mbH*, which had succeeded *Hugo Stinnes*, was also already involved in Church Business A and supplied silver and copper for Business B transactions. In addition, *Diedrich Kieselhorst/Seefahrt Reederei GmbH*, as a supplier of industrial diamonds, was among the narrow circle of trusted companies in Church Business B. *Intrac* also had business relationships with these companies in other areas of domestic German trade. Although the federal government requested the involvement of other companies, Ludwig Geißel prevailed with his preference to stick with the companies that already had experience in church business.[425]

How did the handling of this business work? The trusted companies such as *Brenntag* received information about framework agreements and then concluded a contract with *Intrac Handels-GmbH* about the products and quantities to be delivered and the delivery period. The transport companies also received a commission of around 0.85 percent of the value of the goods. As soon as the companies had concluded the contracts with Koko, payment to the trusted companies was initiated via the representative of the EKD Council at the seat of the federal government. The church institutions took care of the transit trade permit and the "Supply Note U." Deliveries were only made once the approval of the Federal German authorities was received, as they did not want to deliver up front.[426]

---

424 BT-Drucksache 12/7600, 310.

425 BT-Drucksache 12/7600, 312.

426 After the delivery, the trusted company sent its invoice, the delivery note, and the confirmation of receipt from Intrac to Geißel, BT-Drucksache 12/7600, 310.

In the beginning, the trusted companies apparently did not know that their deliveries were a component of the prisoner release program. They were "initially not aware" that "the federal government's humanitarian efforts were hidden behind the term 'Special Business B,'" the final report of the Bundestag investigative committee, which investigated the activities of the Koko in the early 1990s, stated.[427]

Since the early 1970s, petroleum had also been part of the Business B product range. The first oil deliveries began in 1971, with *Brenntag* involved from the start.[428] For example, representatives of *Intrac* and *Brenntag* met in East Berlin in the spring of 1971 to discuss the ongoing Special Business and possible additional business. The plan was to deliver around 100,000 tons of crude oil from the Middle East, worth around ten million D-Mark, by the end of the first half of the year. For this purpose, the Liechtenstein-based company *Elmsoka*, short for *Establishment Internationale Import-Export Handels-Gesellschaft,* was to be commissioned as a preliminary supplier to *Brenntag* and to transport the crude oil in five shiploads via Rotterdam and Rostock for import into the GDR by the end of June 1971. The managing director of *Elmsoka* also took part in the meeting. *Brenntag* regretted not acting as a supplier itself and, in return, asked to be released from all complaints relating to this business that were not caused by *Brenntag* itself with regard to quality, quantity, and adherence to delivery dates, which *Intrac* accepted.[429] *Brenntag* also requested a corresponding exemption for future orders in this arrangement.[430]

The meeting was also noteworthy in other respects, since those involved explored options for deepening relationships beyond the Special Business through additional dealings with petroleum products. "The Intrac representative reacted with great interest to us pointing out that Brenntag could take delivery of 90% of the USSR's crude oil imports into the Federal Republic of Germany," according to the minutes of the meeting.[431] For the current year, *Intrac* signaled

---

427 BT-Drucksache 12/7600, 312.

428 The responsible head of department in the Ministry for Intra-German Relations reported a delivery worth 16.9 million D-Marks for 1971, of which 2.9 million D-Marks were heating oil and 4.0 million were gas oil, and a sum of ten million Deutsche Mark remained for crude oil; see Armin Volze, "Eine Bananen-Legende und andere Irrtümer," in: *Deutschland-Archiv*, 26th Vol. 1993, H. 1, 65. See also BT-Drucksache 12/7600, appendix volume (Anhangband), 78. The order of magnitude fits the file traces in the Berlin Brenntag archive, which point to the first Brenntag activities in the B business amounting to ten million D-Mark in 1971. Brenntag Berlin archive, Unterlagen Erdöl/Rohöl, Intrac.

429 Brenntag Berlin archive, Unterlagen Erdöl/Rohöl, Intrac, meeting on May 8, 1971.

430 "We are exempt from all possible claims that are related to this transaction and cannot be proven to be due to our fault – in particular those related to quality, quantity, deadlines, etc. You will settle this directly with Intrac, which is the buyer of the crude oil we have purchased with this order." Brenntag Berlin archive, Unterlagen Erdöl/Rohöl, Intrac, passim.

431 Brenntag Berlin archive, Unterlagen Erdöl/Rohöl, Intrac, confidential note for Mr. vom Bruck dated May 8, 1971 (Berlin branch).

an additional requirement of around 500,000 tons. Among other things, they were interested in whether "the goods could be processed into final products in the Federal Republic of Germany" and whether – and how – the goods could also be obtained via Antwerp. There was also the question of whether *Brenntag* could "specifically provide refineries." The *Brenntag* representatives took up the last point directly. "Regarding processing options in our own division," those involved noted that they wanted to "immediately make contact and move in this direction."[432]

Regrettably, it is not possible to reconstruct from the available documents exactly what the result of these preliminary talks was. However, soon afterward, a refinery that temporarily belonged to the *Veba Group* was engaged in the contract processing of crude oil for *Elmsoka*: The *Ölwerke Frisia AG* in Emden processed crude oil into finished products such as heating oil and different grades of gasoline and sold the products to companies in the Federal Republic.[433] According to the Koko, *Elmsoka* had around one million tons of crude oil processed by *Frisia* between 1973 and 1975.[434]

In the meantime, the general conditions for trading in GDR petrochemical products had changed. As early as 1964, the price advantage for GDR petroleum products had rapidly disappeared because the Federal Republic had revised the tax and customs regulations for mineral oil. Closer Western European integration made it necessary to unify the EEC's external tariffs.[435] The Federal Republic dropped import tariffs for mineral oil, in line with the EEC consensus. At the same time, the federal government increased the mineral oil tax in order to keep the domestic market stable and to provide adjustment aid for domestic oil production and for the coal industry.[436] Thus, the previous customs privilege for GDR products disappeared, while a new tax surcharge was added.[437] As a result, sales of GDR products fell significantly. This gave rise to resentment

---

432 Ibid.

433 See, for example, VAT accounting for the processing fees and storage costs calculated in 1973 as part of the contract processing agreement concluded between Frisia and Elmsoka from February 1, 1974, in: BArch, DL 210/6596. Frisia AG joined the Veba Group in 1973 and was sold again in 1976. In the course of this, there were investigations by the Düsseldorf Regional Finance Directorate (Oberfinanzdirektion Düsseldorf) in 1977; see letter from Oberfinanzdirektion Düsseldorf to Bundesministerium der Finanzen, dated June 1, 1977, in: Abschlussbericht des 1. Untersuchungsausschusses des 12. Deutschen Bundestages. Der Bereich Kommerzielle Koordinierung und Alexander Schalck-Golodkowski. *Werkzeuge des SED-Regimes*, Anlagenband 3, Doc. 694, 2769–2772. For information on the investigation, see also below.

434 "Inhalt und Ziel der behördlichen Ermittlungen gegen Elmsoka und Intrac in der BRD," in: BArch, MFS AG BKK 1567, 31 ff., here 33.

435 See Stokes, *Faktor Öl*, 305 ff.

436 See "Gesetz über die Umstellung der Abgaben auf Mineralöl" (i.e., law on the conversion of taxes on mineral oil) from December 31, 1963; for the discussion, see, e.g., the 84th session of the German Bundestag on October 9, 1963, BT-Plenarprotokoll 04/84, 4116 ff.

437 Fäßler, *Eiserner Vorhang*, 283.

Figure 35: Tanker truck at the Brenntag branch in Berlin-Britz, 1970s.

between the trading partners and to demands for compensation from the GDR Politbureau, which the Federal Republic complied with at times. Between 1967 and 1968, the GDR no longer supplied any petroleum products at all to the Federal Republic.[438]

The trade in petroleum and petroleum products between East and West, therefore, depended on a favorable foreign trade policy framework. The drastic changes in the price of oil from fall 1973 also put the usual supply relationships to the test. Under these conditions, the long-term supply agreements that GDR foreign trade companies had made with companies in the Federal Republic were of particular importance. The West Berlin company *Rex Handelsgesellschaft Schulte Frohlinde & Co.* played an important role in the trade in mineral oil products between West and East. It had been active in the mineral oil trade with the GDR since 1950 and was to move closer to *Brenntag* in the course of the 1970s.[439]

---

438 Fäßler, *Störfreimachung.*
439 Judt, *Bereich Kommerzielle Koordinierung,* 62.

Rex delivered crude oil to the GDR and took back the mineral oil products processed there – such as carburetor and diesel fuels as well as heating oil. In 1959, *Rex* and the GDR Chemical Foreign Trade Company had reached an agreement that guaranteed *Rex* extensive rights to sell heating oil, gasoline, and diesel from GDR origins in West Berlin and the Federal Republic, while *Rex* guaranteed the purchase of GDR mineral oil products.[440] The "exclusive contract," which *Rex* was able to rely on for many years, also had a political dimension insofar as it concerned the oil supply in West Berlin. During the customs policy unrest in 1967/68, deliveries were stopped but continued with a new agreement in 1969. From 1969 to 1974, *Rex* purchased the crude oil destined for the GDR from *Deutsche BP*. In addition, *Rex* had a contractual relationship with the Koko company *Intrac* lasting several years, during which they brokered deliveries from *BP* to *Intrac* on a commission basis.[441] At the beginning of the 1970s, *Intrac* covered around a quarter of West Berlin's consumption of oil products, *Der Spiegel* estimated.[442] Purchasing fuel – as well as other goods – from the GDR was also attractive from a tax perspective because of the entitlement to VAT reduction. *Intrac* estimated the volume of business between *Rex* and the GDR trading companies for 1974 at around 1.5 million tons of products worth 401.2 million accounting units.[443] From 1975 onward, under the Berlin Agreement, the *Rex* trading company delivered around one million tons of Libyan crude oil to *Intrac* every year and, in return, took the same amount of refined products.[444]

Brenntag, which itself operated in the petroleum business in Berlin, took note of the activities of its high-profile competitor. *Brenntag* had a vital interest in expanding its own position as a joint source point on the West Berlin market and in the trading operations dominated by *Rex*. In contrast to the past, since the mid-1960s it had a parent company that had the necessary capital strength to further advance this business policy goal with equity investments if the opportunity arose. An episode from the early 1970s may illustrate this: When *Brenntag* celebrated its centenary in Mülheim in 1974, business partners from the GDR were also invited, such as the director of the East Berlin foreign trade company *Berag Import Export GmbH*, which also worked within the Koko organization.

440 Ibid.

441 See documents from the public prosecutor's investigations against *Rex* (due to alleged violations of the MRG [tenancy act]) in the 1970s, traces of which have been preserved in the files of the GDR Ministry for State Security, Intrac file note dated July 10, 1975, in: BArch, MfS, AG, BKK, 1126, 6; see also file note about a conversation with the public prosecutor's office from April 2, 1979, ibid., 12.

442 *Der Spiegel* 33, August 13, 1973 (Article: "Erdöl: Schon ein Fortschritt."), also quoted in Judt, *Bereich*, 63.

443 BArch, MfS, AG, BKK, 1126, 6.

444 "Inhalt und Ziel der behördlichen Ermittlungen gegen *Elmsoka* und *Intrac* in der BRD," in: BArch, MFS AG BKK 1567, 31 ff., here page 34.

Under the code name "Peter Reimann," the *Berag* boss wrote regular reports as an unofficial employee (IMB)[445] for the GDR Ministry of State Security about his business contacts with Western companies, including *Brenntag*. Despite all the caution that is generally required when evaluating these types of sources, given the special circumstances in which they were created, the IMB's report on the *Brenntag* celebration seems quite plausible. According to this report, the CEO of *Stinnes AG*, Günter Winkelmann, asked the East German invited guest about oil and fuel exports to the Federal Republic. He wanted to know about the attitude of the GDR Chemical Foreign Trade Company. For the *Stinnes* chairman of the board, the chosen form for conducting business was "personally incomprehensible" because "the Rex Handel company had earned many millions from the overall fuel business," and the "entire business constellation […] was completely inscrutable" to him. "The company Rex Handel does not have the personal or other qualifications to carry out the entire business process in the required quality, nor to achieve corresponding economic results."[446] This remark shows the interest of the *Stinnes* CEO in bringing the *Stinnes Group* further into this German-German business sector.

In fact, just over a year later, the balance of power around the Berlin hub changed. On January 1, 1976, the *Stinnes Group* acquired a stake in the newly founded *Rex* through *Brenntag*. *Brenntag AG & Co. OHG* initially acquired a 50 percent stake, which was later increased to a majority stake of 51 percent in the newly constituted *Rex Handelsgesellschaft Schulte Frohlinde GmbH & Co KG*.[447] This also gave *Brenntag* access to the advantageous position that *Rex* had at that time as the leading trader in Berlin in two respects: on the one hand, the exemption permit from the Federal Ministry of Economics for the delivery of crude oil to the GDR, and on the other hand, the exclusive contract for the purchase of GDR mineral oil products within the framework of the intra-German agreement.[448]

Rex supplied the mineral oil to the large oil companies such as *Esso* and *Shell* and the heating oil to local traders such as the Berlin-based *Vaubeka*, which was also a *Stinnes* subsidiary. The West Berlin market was considered attractive

---

445 "Unofficial intelligence employee with hostile connections," see the role of Menzel, who also acted as an informant for the German foreign intelligence service BND (Bundesnachrichtendienst), in BT-Drucksache 12/7600, 522 as well as 119 and 129; see also Abweichender Bericht der Berichterstatterin der Gruppe Bündnis 90/Die Grünen, Ingrid Koeppe (MdB) im 1. Untersuchungsausschuss, 17 ff.

446 BArch BStU, MfS HA, VIII, 37490, report "Peter Reimann" from October 5, 1974, 18 f.

447 See *Stinnes AG* 1976 annual report, group diagram; see also Monopolkommission, Hauptgutachten 1976/77: Fortschreitende Konzentration bei Großunternehmen, Baden-Baden 1978.

448 Confidential note, "Geschäfte mit der DDR" from April 25, 1979, and May 14, 1979, as well as a statement from the Federal Ministry of Economics from June 5, 1979, in: BArch B 126/81543.

because fuel prices were higher here than in other major German cities. Industry observers attributed the special situation to the island location and the resulting cost and competition situation, because the large providers had a comparatively greater weight than providers with "aggressive pricing."[449] Even in the 1980s, fuel imports to West Berlin from the GDR were to be carried out via *Rex*.

"As if the Production Facilities Weren't Beyond the Borders"

When *Brenntag* acquired a stake in *Rex*, the chemical trading division of the *Stinnes Group* had grown into the second largest business area after fuel trading. New bases supplemented the international organization, such as a *Brenntag* sales office in Tehran (*Brenntag AG Branch Office*) and subsidiaries in Australia (*Brenntag Australia Pty. Ltd. Melbourne*) and Taiwan (*Brenntag Co. Ltd. Taipei*).[450]

The aim was to simplify distribution for customers, "as if the production facilities were not across the borders or even the Atlantic but right next door."[451]

The buoyant chemical economy shortly after the oil price shock gave a tailwind to the expansion plans for operations abroad. However, the record sales in the chemical industry concealed comparatively low real growth overall. Net production and new orders had been declining since mid-1974, prompting the Chemical Industry Association to warn against optimism. "Despite an increase in sales, no progress," was one press comment, which from the association's point of view aptly described the situation.[452] The sometimes-overheated business climate was followed by disillusionment when the recession hit the chemical industry with force in 1975, and the industry's sales, employment, and profits shrank. However, the industry was still in the black. But now the problems became noticeable in sales in important customer industries such as the automotive and textile sectors.[453]

The fluctuations in the chemical economy were reflected in the chemical trading market. In the *Brenntag* business, the dimmed business climate was reflected in the fact that chemical producers temporarily turned back to areas that they had previously handed off to commercial traders. This meant that in

---

449 See, for example, *Der Spiegel*, 16/1989, "Benzinpreis – Mysterium der Marktwirtschaft." See also Ulli Gericke, "Benzinmarkt in West Berlin," manuscript for the radio broadcast on March 16, 1986, on the Sender Freies Berlin, Brenntag archive headquarters, still unsigned.

450 Stinnes AG, annual report 1976, 18. Since 1976, the company name had been Stinnes AG.

451 According to Hugo Stinnes AG, annual report 1974, 5.

452 "No progress despite increase in sales," in: *Chemische Industrie* Vol. 27, March 1975, 121 f.; see also Branchen-Report: *Chemische Industrie*, ifo-Schnelldienst 14.7.75.

453 Quoted here from Felix Spies, "Nach dreißig fetten Jahren," in: *Die Zeit*, No. 40/1975.

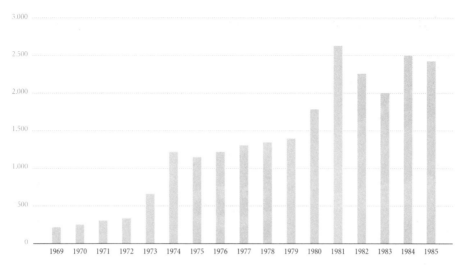

Chart 3: Stinnes AG, sales in the chemicals division* 1969–1985 (in million D-Mark)[454]
*Incl. Plastics, between 1973–1978, including mineral trade.

times of underutilized capacities, *Brenntag* was also in competition with chemical producers. However, due to the wide range of products traded and the firm's presence in different regions, *Brenntag* had a certain amount of leeway to be able to compensate for losses in earnings in one place or another if necessary. From 1975 to 1978, *Brenntag's* business continued to develop in general "in welcome ways," as the annual reports put it.[455] When the chemical industry was in "full swing" in 1979, *Brenntag* continued to expand its organization intensively at home and abroad.[456] In 1979, the *Brenntag* administration in Mülheim moved from Reichspräsidentenstrasse to a new location on Humboldtring, on a former coal mine site of *Stinnes*.[457]

When *Brenntag* sought to develop new markets, it usually started with a sales base. The next step, however, was to consolidate the structures for local distribution and expand the sales network within the new markets. Investments in the second half of the 1970s were made with this strategic goal. By 1979, *Brenntag* had strengthened its structures in Belgium (*Tradia S. A.*), Portugal (*A. F. Gouveia Lda.*), the Netherlands, and Brazil through investments and company takeovers.

---

454 Compiled from the annual reports of [Hugo] Stinnes AG, 1969–1985. From the 1986 financial year onward, the survey system changed, so that different information was available for some financial years (e.g., 1985). There are also minor deviations, e.g. varying figures for the financial year 1974 in the annual reports of 1974 and 1975.

455 [Hugo] Stinnes AG, annual reports 1975–1978, passim.

456 Stinnes AG, annual report 1979, 14.

457 Scheffels, *125 Jahre*, 30.

Abbildung 36: The Hugo Stinnes public limited company surrounded by subsidiaries, 1973.

In the USA, additional distribution centers were added in Houston and Dallas.[458] In Texas, the *Stinnes Oil & Chemical Company*, part of the *Brenntag* business division, founded the *Texas Oil & Chemical Terminals* together with a US refinery in the mid-1970s and began building a large tank farm at the Beaumont site.[459]

During this time, the number of companies belonging to the *Veba Group* also grew rapidly. Over the course of the 1970s, there was an increasing number of voices criticizing the expansion of the *Veba Group*. In a report, the Monopolies Commission[460] accused *Veba* of making "the absorption of small and medium-sized companies" part of its "long-term corporate strategy." The accusation was that the growth was due to the *Stinnes Group's* "eagerness to expand" and was damaging to medium-sized businesses. In contrast, *Stinnes* saw the expansion of structures as a prerequisite for successful trading. It claimed the group was primarily involved in areas in which small companies could no longer keep up

458 See group overview in Stinnes AG, annual report 1979.

459 Hugo Stinnes AG, annual report 1975, 18 f., 36.

460 The Monopolies Commission (Monopolkommission) is a panel of experts that advises the federal government on competition issues.

Figure 37: Brenntag chemicals warehouse, 1970s.

and were approaching the big ones of their own accord. They added that the number of *Stinnes* subsidiaries was declining due to targeted divestments.[461] The conflicting objectives between the interests of the federal government, the *Veba Group,* and its subsidiary, *Stinnes,* could not be resolved. External growth remained a strategic approach to accelerate the development of trading areas within the *Stinnes Group.*[462] *Brenntag's* strategic goal of systematically expanding its organization on the domestic market and abroad was in line with the parent company's mission statement. The funds for the gradual expansion were raised within the group with low interest rate charges.[463]

461 See note from Ministerial Councilor Blättner dated September 8, 1980, in: BArchB126/93025, folder "Veba AG. Expansionsfreudigkeit und Diversifizierung b. d. Stinnes AG" with further documents on the matter (statements from the Monopolies Commission; statement from the Veba board chairman).

462 For the discussion, see the documents in BArch B126/93025, folder "Veba AG. Expansionsfreudigkeit und Diversifizierung b. d. Stinnes AG"

463 This applies especially to acquisitions in the 1980s, while the financing of the early acquisitions had to remain open in some cases; see contemporary witness interview with Rainer Herrmann on August 16, 2023. On corporate financing, see also the guidelines for group financial transactions of Stinnes AG, in: BArch, DL 210/851.

Growing "Eastern Business" and Continuation of Church Business

While expanding its international trading network, *Brenntag* was also interested in opening up markets beyond the "Iron Curtain," as the *Sobren* joint venture had already demonstrated. Over the course of the 1970s, the annual reports repeatedly confirmed the "welcome" development of business "with the state trading countries of the Eastern Bloc."[464] These trading relationships had now reached a "considerable volume."[465] For 1976, *Stinnes* board member Hermann vom Bruck, who was responsible for the *Brenntag* business, estimated the so-called "Eastern business" at around 200 million D-Mark, and the trend was rising. Measured against the chemical division's sales volume in the 1976 financial year, this corresponded to a share of 16.7 percent – thus, the business was definitely important.[466]

However, no further details are known, so it remains unclear at this point which markets this figure refers to.

Meanwhile, activity in the church business also grew noticeably. Over the course of the 1970s, an average of over a thousand people per year were released through federal government transactions with the GDR authorities. Since the middle of the decade, the total annual expenditure for prisoners' release had amounted to a three-digit million amount in D-Mark.[467]

As the number of ransomed prisoners grew, the volume of crude oil deliveries from *Brenntag* also increased. According to a compilation from the Ministry for Intra-German Relations, oil deliveries in 1976 reached a value of 32 million D-Mark.[468] Ten years later, the approved delivery value for crude oil was 122 million D-Mark.[469] The highest volume was reached in 1984 – with seven "special agreements B," *Brenntag's* oil deliveries as part of the church business amounted to a total of 185 million D-Mark.[470] Already included in these figures was a

---

464 Hugo Stinnes AG, annual report 1975, 18.

465 Stinnes AG, annual report 1977, 17.

466 Note about the supervisory board meeting on December 8, 1976, from December 10, 1976, in: BArch B 126/81542. Vom Bruck's statement is noted here: "Eastern business will expand" (1976 sales of 200 million DM). Hermann vom Bruck was appointed deputy board member on January 1, 1975, and appointed full board member in May 1976. See submission for the supervisory board meeting of May 19, 1976, TOP 9, in: BArch B 126/77038.

467 Armin Volze, "Kirchliche Transferleistungen in die DDR," in: *Deutschland-Archiv*, Vol. 24, 1991/1, 59–66, here 63; see also Wölbern, *Häftlingsfreikauf*, 437 f.

468 Armin Volze, "Eine Bananen-Legende und andere Irrtümer," in: *Deutschland-Archiv*, Vol. 26, 1993, H. 1, 65. See also BT-Drucksache 12/7600, appendix volume (Anhangband), 78.

469 It should be noted here that approved delivery values may differ from actual deliveries. Volze, *Transferleistungen*, 63. BT-Drucksache 12/7600, appendix volume (Anhangband), 79.

470 See the contracts of April 18, 1984; May 29, 1984; June 29, 1984; August 22, 1984; September 4, 1984; October 30, 1984. Archive Diakonie, ADW, HgSt 7939 and 7840.

commission of 0.85 percent that *Brenntag* received for its activities. This was a traditionally low friendship price for the Diakonisches Werk. Even at the time of *Hugo Stinnes OHG*, only a friendship margin was charged to support the church. According to the memories of former employees, the Diakonisches Werk was one of *Brenntag's* largest customers in the early days of the church business.

"We are normally not prepared to work for a percentage level of just 0.85," explained contemporary witness Hermann vom Bruck in retrospect. "You can't support a trading company with 0.85 percent."[471] The church business was a "routine business," he claimed, "that was established and running" – always "between one and two percent of sales."[472]

Investigations into Brenntag and Rex

When representatives of the Koko company *Intrac* met with representatives of *Brenntag* in East Berlin at the beginning of the 1970s to discuss oil deliveries as part of the church business, something unusual was already apparent that differentiated the Special Business from other intra-German trade. The negotiating partner on the GDR side, *Intrac*, presented concrete ideas about where the goods should be obtained from. *Intrac* told the trusted companies the exact source that was supposed to supply them with the goods. This included the Vaduz-based company *Elmsoka*. Looking back, it became known that *Intrac* had held a 50 percent stake in *Elmsoka* since 1963 and even 100 percent from 1983 onward.[473]

The inclusion of *Elmsoka* in the delivery network in Special Business B resulted in the strange circumstance that – as the Bundestag committee of inquiry into Koko's activities said – *Intrac* was "simultaneously the supplier and recipient" of the ordered goods.[474] *Intrac* traded the raw materials directly on the stock exchange. The goods did not necessarily have to be physically transported to the GDR, as the warehouse receipts or bills of lading were sufficient for international marketing. Especially in the 1980s, deliveries often involved Soviet crude oil, which had already arrived locally via the Druzhba pipeline and was

---

471 See vom Bruck's statement before the Koko investigative committee, stenographic minutes of the 132nd meeting of the investigative committee on April 28, 1993, in: Parliamentary Archives of the German Bundestag (Parlamentsarchiv des Deutschen Bundestages), 3327, 12te Wahlperiode, Protokoll132 (in the following quoted as PA-DBT 3327 12. WP Prot. 132), 1–78, here 24.

472 Stenographic record of vom Bruck's interrogation, PA-DBT 3327 12. WP Prot. 132, here 73. Measured against the turnover of the chemical trading division of Stinnes AG, however, the crude oil deliveries from 1984 amount to 7.5 percent of the revenues.

473 BT-Drucksache 12/7600, 313.

474 Ibid.

stored in Schwedt.[475] The inclusion of *Elmsoka* in the supply circuit made it easy for the GDR to generate foreign currency. As can be seen from *Elmsoka's* order confirmations, *Brenntag* was supposed to make its payments for oil orders mostly in dollars or pounds to banks in Liechtenstein, London, and New York.[476]

The involvement of the Liechtenstein company *Elmsoka* in the special transactions aroused the interest of Federal German customs investigators in 1977, who suspected violations of the regulations in intra-German trade. However, after discussions with the Federal Ministry of Finance and the Federal Ministry of Economics, it was decided that the church business was "taboo" for the tax authority. "The past will no longer be checked," it said in a file note.[477] However, the investigations into two proprietary transactions that *Brenntag* and *Intrac* concluded in the mid-1970s continued, and the Bochum public prosecutor's office was now in charge. This involved two oil orders from *Elmsoka* for *Intrac*, each worth 20 million D-Mark, from 1975 and 1976. The accusation was that no separate permits for the transactions had been issued, while *Brenntag* argued that they had not needed separate permits because the transactions in this constellation had, in principle, already been approved and they could use the existing license.[478] After statements from the federal ministries, the Bochum public prosecutor's office discontinued the investigation.[479] *Brenntag* paid a fine,[480] and after an interruption of a few weeks, they were able to resume the transactions.

The public prosecutor's office also made similar allegations against the Berlin company *Rex Handelsgesellschaft Schulte Frohlinde*, in which *Brenntag* had held a 50 percent stake since January 1, 1976.[481] After the oil price shock in

---

475 The GDR obtained this in exchange for transfer rubles from the USSR, BT-Drucksache 12/7600, 313.

476 See the landing certificates and the orders from Brenntag to Elmsoka and the confirmations from Intrac to Brenntag.

477 See a file note that the Stinnes board brought to the attention of the Federal Ministry of Finance on May 15, 1979 – note "Geschäfte mit der DDR" from April 25, 1979, and May 14, 1979, as well as a statement from the Federal Ministry of Economics dated June 5, 1979, in: BArch, B 126/ 81543. For further information on the investigations, see Judt, Area, 64 and BT-Drucksache 12/7600, 315 f.

478 Note from the Stinnes board "Geschäfte mit der DDR" from April 25, 1979, and May 14, 1979, as well as a statement from the Federal Ministry of Economics from June 5, 1979, in: BArch B 126/81543. See also the minutes of a meeting between the public prosecutor's office and lawyers from Cologne: File note about a conversation with the public prosecutor's office on April 2, 1979, in the investigation against the Rex company, in: BArch, MFS, BKK, 1126, 15 ff.

479 In the final report of the investigative committee, the termination of the investigation is attributed to the intervention of the SPD parliamentary group leader Herbert Wehner, who was Federal Minister for all-German issues at the beginning of the prisoner release. A fine was issued to Brenntag; see BT 12/7600, 315 f.

480 Hermann vom Bruck explained that the fine was due to a mere formal error that had emerged during the routine check; see PA-DBT, 3327, 12te WP, Prot. 132, 1–78, here 70 ff.

481 File note about a conversation with the public prosecutor on April 2, 1979, in the investigation against the *Rex* company, in: BArch, MFS, BKK, 1126, 15 ff. See also an informant's report about a conversation in the Stinnes high-rise on April 18, 1979, BArch MFS HA XVIII 36325.

the fall of 1973, it was difficult to find suppliers, which is why *Elmsoka* became significantly more important as a supplier, *Brenntag* said in internal notes.[482] Records about the investigations into *Rex* have also been preserved in the Stasi documents, for example about a meeting between the Bochum public prosecutor's office and lawyers in Cologne in April 1979.[483] According to the minutes, the participants discussed how to assess the "material content" of the business and whether *Elmsoka's* involvement was "purely on paper." The public prosecutor's office did not see any economic damage to the Federal Republic, arguing that a lack of permits was an administrative offense, not a criminal one. For comparison, they also looked into *Brenntag,* concluding that *Brenntag* had received "explicit approvals for trading with *Elmsoka*" and was also currently receiving approvals for trading with *Elmsoka*. However, in a *Rex* transaction with the Prague company *Chemapol*, the prosecutors saw the first indications of circumvention transactions by the *Rex* company and suspected support from higher authorities.[484]

The Second Oil Price Shock and the
Energy Agreement with the GDR

During 1979, the price of oil rose rapidly again in the wake of the Iranian revolution.[485] This surge in inflation was one aspect of a whole package of generally difficult macroeconomic conditions that caused the Federal Republic's economy to slide into recession in the early 1980s. For the chemical industry and chemical trade in the Federal Republic, the price surge temporarily caused a noticeable increase in sales.

In the GDR, the effects of the oil price shocks occurred with a delay because long-term supply agreements with the USSR had fixed prices over several years. Toward the end of the 1970s, however, the price increases from the first oil price crisis had a noticeable impact, and the West became more important as an energy supplier.[486] In the fall of 1979, the Federal Republic concluded an

---

482 See note "Geschäfte mit der DDR" from April 25, 1979, and May 14, 1979, as well as a statement from the Federal Ministry of Economics from June 5, 1979, in: BArch B 126/81543.

483 File note about a conversation with the public prosecutor on April 2, 1979, in the investigation against the Rex company, in: BArch, MFS, BKK, 1126, 15 ff.

484 Ibid.

485 While a barrel of crude oil cost $ 12.70 in 1978, the price of oil in 1980 was $ 28. From Prollius, *Wirtschaftsgeschichte*, 183; see Hohensee, Ölpreisschock, 78.

486 See Frank Bösch *Zeitenwende 1979. Als die Welt von heute begann*, München 2019.

energy agreement with the GDR that stipulated mutual deliveries until 1985. What was particularly new was the long term of the agreement, which provided for deliveries of mineral oil to the GDR and the purchase of GDR mineral oil products by West German companies.[487] The most important trading partners in the mineral oil sector were *Brenntag, Rex,* and another company from the *Veba Group, Veba Öl.* About half of West Berlin's needs were covered by this agreement from 1980 onward, the *Frankfurter Allgemeine Zeitung* estimated. The GDR was to supply 370,000 tons of gasoline, 400,000 tons of heavy fuel oil, and 1.15 million tons of diesel and light fuel oil, while it received about one million tons of crude oil.[488]

At this point, the most important oil processing plant in the GDR, the *"Petrochemical Combine" (PCK) Schwedt,* had built a new plant that could split long-chain hydrocarbons using Japanese conversion technology. *Brenntag* became an important sales partner for this plant. In the fall of 1978, the state-owned company *AHB Chemie Export Import* granted *Brenntag* exclusive rights to sell fuels and aromatics from the new Schwedt fission and aromatics complex. With the long-term contract, *Brenntag* received sole distribution rights for GDR benzene and C-8 aromatics in Europe, with the exception of the quantities supplied directly to *Dow Chemical Europe* and *Rhone Poulenc.*[489] For the GDR, petroleum products were considered important sources of foreign currency. The business partners in the East saw the advantages of exclusive cooperation: They emphasized *Brenntag's* storage capacities, its presence at important transshipment points for international business, its own shipping company, and the long-term charter contracts with international shipping companies. Additionally, the cost-effective transport processing and the company's network – the feature of "conducting joint sales and pricing work using import-export coordination for individual groups of companies" – was also a plus on the list. According to one assessment, *Brenntag* had "the most comprehensive sales and purchasing system for chemical products from petroleum processing with sales organizations in Europe and the USA."[490]

---

487 "Energie-Abkommen mit der DDR," *Frankfurter Allgemeine Zeitung,* September 6, 1979, 2.

488 Energie-Abkommen mit der DDR," *Frankfurter Allgemeine Zeitung,* September 6, 1979, 2. See also a conversation in the Stinnes high-rise on April 18, 1979, in: BArch MFS HA XVIII 36325.

489 See the contract with VEB AHB Chemie Export Import and the Brenntag dated September 6, 1978, in: BArch, MfS, FFO, KD Schwedt 350, 127–140. From 1983–1988 the original delivery was of 265,000 tons of benzene and 40,000 tons C8 aromatics intended for sale in Europe and the Federal Republic. Fine-tuning took place in annual additional agreements. Deliveries began as early as 1982, and there were some deviations in terms of quantities – in 1983, 65,000 tons of benzene and 15,000 tons of C8 aromatics were delivered; see ibid.

490 Various information about Brenntag 1980/81, compiled by hand, in: BArch, MfS, FFO, KD Schwedt 350, 20 ff., here 20–21.

"More Thrust Through Reinforcement": Brenntag 1980–1985

Since the 1970s, the conditions for economic development in Western Europe began to change significantly. Historians of this period speak of a time "after the boom," after the decades of a stable post-war order ended and a new era took shape, which was characterized by different guiding ideas, changing economic situations, and changing forms of economic activity.[491]

The complex process of change also included the contemporary view of economic growth, progress, and future development. The crises of the 1970s ended "public confidence in the unstoppability of progress," said historian Konrad Jarausch, assessing one aspect of the change.[492] Ecological issues also moved higher on the political agenda, and environmental associations gained in profile. With the rise of the environmental movement, the public began to look differently at the chemical industry and became more concerned about the externalities of chemical production. At the beginning of the 1980s, the environmental and nature conservation organization BUND e.V. proposed "chemical policy" as a new policy field in a position paper, calling for containing the risks of chemical production as a political task.[493] Since the Seveso disaster, the discussion about the dangers of chemistry and chemical transport had gained media momentum.[494] In 1976, an accident at a chemical factory near Milan resulted in the highly toxic byproduct tetrachlorodibenzodioxin being released during the synthesis of trichlorophenol. As a result, a dioxin cloud contaminated the surrounding area, caused livestock and plants to die, and severely polluted the environment.[495]

During this phase, there were increasing attempts in the German economy to change the existing regulations for the transport of dangerous goods and make it safer. At the beginning of the 1980s, the Federal Minister of Transport called for the list of highly dangerous chemicals subject to special safety regulations

---

491 See Anselm Doering-Manteuffel/Lutz Raphael, *Nach dem Boom. Perspektiven auf die Zeitgeschichte seit 1970*, Göttingen 2010². See also Werner Plumpe/André Steiner (eds.), "Der Mythos von der postindustriellen Welt," in: *Der Mythos von der postindustriellen Welt. Wirtschaftlicher Strukturwandel in Deutschland 1960 bis 1990*, Göttingen 2016, 7–14.

492 Konrad Jarausch, "Verkannter Strukturwandel. Die siebziger Jahre als Vorgeschichte der Probleme der Gegenwart," in: ibid. (ed.), *Das Ende der Zuversicht. Die siebziger Jahre als Geschichte*, Göttingen 2008, 9–26, here 9.

493 Frank Claus, "Neue Wege zur Austragung von Umweltkonflikten im Bereich der Chemiepolitik. Dornenreicher Weg zum Dialog," in: *politische ökologie 31 – Positionen und Perspektiven der Umweltbewegung*, May/June 1993, 74–80.

494 In the context of this company history, the reasons for the rise of the environmental movement cannot be discussed; see Frank Uekötter, *Deutschland in Grün. Eine zwiespältige Erfolgsgeschichte*, Bonn 2015, 137ff. See also Frank Uekötter/Claas Kirchhelle, "Wie Seveso nach Deutschland kam. Umweltskandale und ökologische Debatte von 1976 bis 1986," in: *Archiv für Sozialgeschichte 52*, 2012, 317–334.

495 On the accident, see Matthias Hofmann, *Lernen aus Katastrophen: nach den Unfällen von Harrisburg, Seveso und Sandoz*, Berlin 2008, 201ff.

to be expanded. In addition, the Dangerous Goods Ordinance for road traffic stipulated that from autumn 1981, drivers of tank trucks carrying dangerous goods required a certificate of competency from the Chamber of Commerce and Industry.[496] An EEC directive (Seveso I directive) issued in 1982 required the member states of the European Economic Community to create a set of rules by the mid-1980s that would better limit the risks of producing and transporting chemicals than before.[497] The chemicals trade, organized in the Association of German Chemicals and Foreign Trade, advocated measures to contain risks but criticized contradictory regulations and warned of the costs that could result from new legal regulations for the chemical industry in terms of occupational safety, storage technology, and transport.[498]

At the same time, industry representatives saw the opportunities that could arise from long-term structural changes in the chemical industry. "The producers have realized that retailers can simply fulfill the distribution function more economically," summarized *Brenntag* board member Hendrik Rudhart in the spring of 1981. This trend had already become more pronounced in the USA and was now becoming increasingly established in other regions. This meant that traders could market products that the manufacturers did not bring onto the market themselves – for example, in other trading units or in other combinations. This meant that the task of the "distributor" gained more weight as an independent field of activity in contrast to the classic wholesale trade.[499] In particular, products that were sent to customers in small quantities and not as a full truckload by the chemical producer were often too complex for the manufacturers to distribute and were therefore increasingly outsourced to the chemical trade. Parallel to these ecological developments, *Brenntag* further expanded its network of locations in the Federal Republic of Germany in the early 1980s. Since the early 1970s, *Brenntag* had held a 50 percent stake in the established Frankfurt company *Emesco*, which celebrated its 250th anniversary in 1983. With the acquisition of all remaining shares in *Emesco GmbH & Co. KG, Brenntag* gained additional locations.[500] *Emesco* had eight branches and

---

496 "Chemikalienhandel eher pessimistisch," in: *Chemische Industrie* 33, April 1981, 191 ff.

497 Council Directive 82/501/EEC of 24 June 1982 on the major-accident hazards of certain industrial activities, Amtsblatt der Europäischen Gemeinschaften [Offical Journal of the European Union] No. L 230 of 05/08/1982, 1–18.

498 "Chemikalienhandel eher pessimistisch," in: *Chemische Industrie* 33, April 1981, 191 ff.

499 For the distinction, see Cord Matthies, "Marktentwicklungen und Trends," in: Carsten Suntrop (ed.), *Chemielogistik: Markt, Geschäftsmodelle und Prozesse*, Weinheim 2011, 25–50, here 39 f.

500 Stinnes AG, annual report 1982, 15. The Frankfurt-based Andreae Noris Zahn AG sold its Emesco shares to Brenntag; see *Frankfurter Allgemeine Zeitung*, June 1, 1983, 15.

around 10,000 regular customers, whom it mainly supplied with small batches of chemical products. As a result, *Brenntag* now covered a larger range that it could supply as a full-range supplier.[501]

When some areas within the *Veba* group of companies were strategically repositioned in 1985 in order to further sharpen the profile of the individual business sectors, further bases for *Brenntag's* activities were added. As early as December 1976, the *Stinnes* supervisory board had discussed better coordination of the activities of *Stinnes* and *Raab Karcher*, who were in fierce competition in some market segments.[502] About a decade later, the boards of both companies reached corresponding agreements. They had observed that, in order to expand their advantageous positions in their respective markets,

Figure 38: Inspection work in the chemicals warehouse, mid-1980s.

cutthroat competition had taken place in certain areas. They now concluded that the required growth could only be achieved in the medium term by taking over competitors, not through market growth. Based on this analysis, the management developed the idea of swapping some divisions of both companies and combining synergies so that *Stinnes* and *Raab Karcher* could "improve each other's market position in a cartel-free area."[503]

As part of a division swap on October 1, 1985, *Brenntag* took over the chemical activities of *Raab Karcher*, including the Lehrte chemical factory, while in return, *Stinnes AG* handed over, among other things, the wood trading, heating technology, and heating oil sales to *Raab Karcher*.[504] "More thrust through

---

501 Scheffels, 125 Jahre, 30. See also: "Für 1984 wieder eine Anzag-Dividende?", in: *Frankfurter Allgemeine Zeitung*, June 1, 1983, 15. On Emesco's 250th anniversary, see 250 Jahre Emesco Chemikalien, 1983. Today's Brenntag location in Plochingen is closely linked to Emesco's history.

502 See documents for the supervisory board meeting on December 8, 1976, in: BArch B 126 81542.

503 Documents on the supervisory board from June 27, 1986, Historisches Archiv der Deutsche Bahn AG, quoted hereafter as Deutsche Bahn Archive, HA-50-8.

504 Stinnes AG, annual report 1985, 6; Scheffels, *125 Jahre*, 30.

Figure 39: Bronze plaque to mark the 40th anniversary of Textile Chemical in 1959.

reinforcement," concluded the annual report, because *Brenntag* had, on the one hand, significantly expanded its product range and, on the other hand, significantly enlarged its sales network in both Germany and Western Europe.[505] *Raab Karcher* had locations in Hamburg, Hanover, Lehrte, Kassel, Düsseldorf, Frankfurt, Stuttgart, and Munich, as well as in Antwerp, Paris, Milan, and London. With 312 employees, *Raab Karcher's* chemical division generated sales of 446 million D-Mark in the 1984 financial year with an increasing profit forecast.[506] *Brenntag* also saw the fine chemicals area, which the Lehrte chemical factory contributed, as a welcome addition to its GDR business.[507] However, this reorganization entailed considerable adjustment requirements for the employees involved. This was evident not only in the negotiation process with the works council that preceded the exchange[508] but also in the newly created structure. Both companies had their own corporate culture, which was also expressed in the basic understanding of how operational routines were to be implemented.[509] Contemporary witnesses reported that *Raab Karcher's* stringent, well-structured organizational world initially stood in striking contrast to the familial organizational culture that *Brenntag* had cultivated up to that point. The "psychological significance" of the changes was "noticeable everywhere," stated the new CEO of *Stinnes*, Hans-Jürgen Knauer, a few months after the integration.[510] It was necessary to find a new common denominator, merge duplicate structures, standardize information and communication systems, adapt sales programs, and, if possible, not irritate

---

505 Stinnes AG, annual report 1985, 19.

506 Draft of an agreement dated August 12, 1985, between Raab Karcher AG, Essen and Stinnes AG, Mülheim, attachments "Raab Karcher Chemie," in: *Rheinisch-Westfälisches Wirtschaftsarchiv* (hereafter quoted as RWWA), 200-807_8.4.F.

507 On individual questions regarding the exchange of activities in the chemical sector, see Raab Karcher's board meeting on August 30, 1985 (TOP 11: Interim report on the transfer of the RK Chemiehandel to Brenntag AG, RWWA, 200-100:2.2.1.AH21).

508 Report on the activities of the Stinnes-Raab-Karcher Commission and meeting of the commission on October 14 in Duisburg (most important problem: the union IG Metall's collective agreement), in: RWWA, 200-807_8.4.F, passim.

509 Draft of an agreement dated August 12, 1985, between Raab Karcher AG, Essen and Stinnes AG, Mülheim, in: RWWA, 200-807_8.4.F.

510 Knauer's remarks on TOP 1 of the agenda, supervisory board meeting on April 27, 1987, Deutsche Bahn Archive, HA-50-11-a.

the suppliers who had previously worked exclusively with *Raab Karcher*.[511] About a year later, management already noted progress on this path.

By taking over the chemical activities of *Raab-Karcher, Stinnes AG* had taken an important step toward rounding off its interests and given its own chemical division an integration task that was something new for *Brenntag* on this scale. Overall, *Stinnes AG* intended the *Brenntag* division to play an important role in the restructuring program that the group pushed forward in the mid-1980s, because the withdrawal from self-service retail was countered by the expansion of the chemical trading division.[512] The planned expansion of *Brenntag's* activities was therefore a high priority.

In the USA, too, a targeted expansion of the foreign organization for the chemical division had continued since the early 1980s. The acquisition of *Textile Chemical* in Pennsylvania in 1981 was a significant step.[513] Founded in 1919 and headquartered in Reading in southeastern Pennsylvania, the company primarily

Figure 40: Textile Chemical warehouse, circa 1950s.

511 On individual questions regarding the exchange of activities in the chemical sector, see Raab Karcher's board meeting on August 30, 1985 (TOP 11: Interim report on the transfer of the RK Chemiehandel to Brenntag AG), in: *Rheinisch-Westfälisches Wirtschaftsarchiv* (RWWA), 200-100:2.2.1.AH21.

512 In 1985, Stinnes AG sold its stake in Deutsche SB-Kauf GmbH & Co. OHG (DSBK). See Deutsche Bahn Archive, HA-50-2, supervisory board meeting on August 18, 1985.

513 Scheffels, *125 Jahre*, 30.

supplied chemicals to the textile industry in Pennsylvania, New Jersey, and New York until the 1960s. With the decline of the US textile industry, the company focused on other industrial sectors – and supplied the paint and coatings industry, steel processing, water treatment, and food industries with chemical substances, even though the attribute "Textile" in the company name was still reminiscent of the beginnings of the company's history.

Philipp Mühsam AG also started trading chemicals to the textile industry at the time – after withdrawing from trading in agricultural products at the end of the 19th century. *Textile Chemical* operated in Pennsylvania, New Jersey, Maryland, Delaware, Virginia, and parts of New York and Ohio in the early 1980s. To this day, Reading is a key location for *Brenntag* in North America. Through this takeover, the *Stinnes Oil & Chemical Company*, which was part of the *Brenntag* division and had been known as *SOCO* since 1980, moved into the ranks of the leading chemical distributors in the USA. Like the parent company, *SOCO* relied on a local presence and decentralized procurement and marketing functions.[514] At the same time, the takeover of *Textile Chemical*

Figure 41: Textile Chemical premises in Reading, aerial photograph 1974.

514 Stinnes AG, annual report 1981, 7, 18; see also Overview of Soco, Inc. (1984), in: Brenntag Archive, still unsigned.

by *SOCO/Brenntag* also formed a building block in a longer-term process of change underway in the USA's chemical distribution market. While no company covered the entire US market until the 1970s, with many companies coexisting in their local or regional markets and not contesting their traditional territories, competition intensified in the early 1980s as more and more companies with greater range emerged. Several factors appeared to increasingly favor the approach that large corporations were able to apply to the business. The increasing level of regulation for handling chemicals, which gradually became apparent with the growing awareness of chemical-specific risks, needed to be more cost-neutral and influenced new business standards. At the same time, incentives emerged to exploit rationalization advantages through bundling in a more extensive network, thus absorbing increased market pressure – such as certification, documentation, or insurance costs.[515]

Brenntag came closer to its goal of gaining more weight on the US market in the summer of 1986 when it bought the US company *Delta Distributors*. Their solvent sales organization, with locations in Texas, Louisiana, and Oklahoma, formed a useful complement to the parent company *SOCO*, which mainly traded in inorganic chemicals and specialties.[516] The merger of *SOCO* and *Delta* was considered a milestone.[517] The supervisory board said that *Brenntag* had now implemented a significant step in its long-term strategy and achieved a significant market position in US metropolitan areas.[518] In order to take account of increasing internationalization, *Stinnes AG's* annual report has been published bilingually in English and German since the 1984 financial year.[519] The international trading activities were now combined in *Brenntag Interchem GmbH*, based in Mülheim.[520] Both forms of transaction in the international chemicals trade – warehouse-based distribution and trading as a warehouse-independent drop-ship business – stood side by side and ideally were to work closely together.[521]

---

515 See note from contemporary witness Bob Moser, who started working at Textile Chemical in 1978, dated January 22, 2024. Archive Brenntag headquarters, still unsigned.

516 Stinnes AG, annual report 1986, 20. Since the spring of 1982, SOCO had been an important element in the USA structure of the Brenntag division; see Stinnes AG, annual report 1982.

517 See overview for the supervisory board meeting on April 27, 1987, which compiles major investments with groundbreaking character from the last 1.5 years, in: Deutsche Bahn Archive, HA-50-11a.

518 See files for the supervisory board meeting on June 27, 1986, in: Deutsche Bahn Archive (see also documents for the general meeting in HA 50, 8).

519 Stinnes AG, annual report 1984.

520 Stinnes AG, annual report 1985, 20.

521 Stinnes AG, annual report 1985, 20.

"Then Let's Go to Brenntag": Brenntag's GDR Business as Reflected in the Stasi Files 1980–1985

Apparently *Brenntag's* GDR business also gained noticeable momentum in the 1980s. This picture emerges from documents that came together from various departments of the GDR's State Security Service, such as the Commercial Coordination Working Group, the Main Department XVIII (Securing the National Economy), and the Schwedt District Office. Since *Brenntag's* own materials on this matter are largely missing, the sources only reflect the perspective of the Ministry for State Security (MfS) on *Brenntag*. However, the operational documents are not necessarily unreliable with regard to the facts described, because the MfS was interested in "established facts." Nevertheless, the political classifications and assessments by those reporting should be read critically.[522]

According to these documents, *Brenntag* had relied on an agency agreement with *Berag Import Export GmbH* since the early 1980s. *Berag* advised *Brenntag* on trading in GDR products and on sales to the GDR. For this service, it received a commission that fluctuated between 0.75 and 1.5 percent of the value of the goods.[523]

The focus of business between *Brenntag* and the GDR chemical industry was the petrochemical products from Schwedt, calcined soda and caustic soda from the *Bitterfeld Chemical Combine,* and solvents from the *Buna Chemical Combine.*[524] In the early 1980s, contemporary participants saw *Brenntag's* parent group, the *Veba Group,* as a "crucial pillar of the GDR's chemical exports business."[525] This was particularly true when the long-term purchase agreement for benzene from Schwedt and petroleum aromatics began to be implemented in 1982. Companies such as *BASF, Bayer, Hüls, ICI,* and *Montedison* purchased the products.[526] The *Stinnes Group* was developing "high levels of activity in

---

[522] See, for example, Bettina Altendorf, *Quellenkunde anhand von Stasi-Akten,* www.stasi-unterlagen-archiv.de/assets/bstu/de/ Bildungsmaterialien/Bildung_Quellenkunde.pdf [last accessed September 6, 2023]. See also Klaus-Dietmar Henke/Roger Engelmann, *Die Bedeutung der Unterlagen des Staatssicherheitsdienstes für die Zeitgeschichtsforschung,* Berlin 1995.

[523] According to official approval documents, the commissions were allowed to reach a predetermined level per year – for 1983, according to the service approval, this was 700,000 D-Mark or accounting units. According to a handwritten list by the head of Berag, the commissions actually paid for 1983 were around 916,000 billing units. See also the individual documents and the service authorization, in: BArch, DL 210 618.

[524] Report from IMB Peter Reimann on a conversation with a *Brenntag* board member on August 26, 1981, in: Mülheim, BArch, MfS, AG, BKK, 768, 101.

[525] For example, the head of the PCK AHB Export Import in Berlin; see information about a conversation with Werner Lange on October 11, 1982, in Berlin, in: BArch, MfS, FFO, KD Schwedt 350, 112 ff., here 114.

[526] See the handwritten report by IM "Hecht" from September 21, 1983, in: BArch MfS HA XVIII 17349, 153 ff., here 153.

Figure 42: Veba press conference at the Leipzig Trade Fair with Erich Honecker, probably 1983.

business relations with the GDR," they claimed.[527] With the combination of *Rex's* petroleum businesses and *Brenntag's* chemical businesses, the company carried weight in intra-German trade.[528] At the same time, a certain risk of dependency was also observed in the diverse business relationships. Some managers "make things very easy for themselves and always say: 'Let's go to *Brenntag* then.'"[529]

It fit *Brenntag's* growth strategy to further expand the GDR business and to "carefully" maintain long-term business relationships, as *Brenntag* board member Hendrik Rudhart put it in an interview.[530] According to state security documents, *Stinnes* board member Hermann vom Bruck saw the GDR business as "a safe bet, especially for the future," since it was "not subject to the conditions of the free market in Western Europe."[531]

At the Leipzig fall trade fair in 1983, companies from the *Veba Group* presented themselves together for the first time – with fifty employees for export and import consultancy and a "strong contingent of CEOs and board members."[532] The visit of the GDR State Council Chairman Erich Honecker to the *Veba* stand attracted

527 Annex Veba Aktiengesellschaft, 4.9. 1983, in: BArch MfS HA XVIII 17349, 186 ff., here 186.

528 Ibid.

529 Ibid. Information about a conversation with Werner Lange on October 11, 1982, in Berlin, in: BArch, MfS, FFO, KD Schwedt 350, 112 ff., here 115.

530 "Chemikalienhandel eher pessimistisch," in: *Chemische Industrie 33*, April 1981, 191 ff., here 193.

531 Information about the visit to Stinnes/Brenntag on July 3 and 4, 1984, in: BArch MfS AG BKK 447, 34 ff., here 36.

532 Conversation note from September 4, 1983, Veba-AG trade fair stand, BArch MfS HA XVIII 17349, 197 ff., here 200.

attention within the industry. One reporter summarized that "nothing was left open in terms of business in 1983."[533] The sales between *Veba* and the GDR foreign trade were estimated at 2.3 billion accounting units for GDR exports and 900 million accounting units for GDR imports.[534] This meant that the *Veba Group* had considerable weight in trade with the GDR: In 1983, the federal territory's purchases of goods with the GDR amounted to a value of 6.878 billion D-Mark, and the federal territory's deliveries to the GDR amounted to around 6.947 billion D-Mark.[535] In addition to mineral oil and lignite, *Brenntag's* chemical business also made a significant contribution to *Veba's* sales. Other forms of cooperation were considered. A report explained that *Brenntag* wanted to give *PCK Schwedt* support through its own company, *Pluto,* including with regard to marketing, design, waste, and packaging technology.[536] For the agricultural chemical trade, *Stinnes* board member vom Bruck put forward the proposal to organize the sale of products from the Rostock fertilizer plant via *Stinnes AG* and *Intrac,* based on the model of the oil business transactions with the GDR.[537]

Apparently, it was possible to accompany business with the GDR with sophisticated credit operations. There are references to this in various pieces of unofficial information. For example, *Brenntag* delivered solvents to the GDR, bought them back, and granted the GDR a loan through different terms of payment.[538] In the fall of 1983, the *Berag* director also reported that the *Stinnes* company had decided to grant the GDR a "global loan of 50 million."[539] He said that *Brenntag* had been criticized "because of its so-called credit policy." In the future, *Stinnes* no longer wanted to issue the loans "in small, little-by-little amounts."[540] Looking back, Hermann vom Bruck explained that these were only commercial loans, not financial loans.[541]

533 Information on the Brenntag discussion on September 6, 1983, in: BArch MfS HA XVIII 17349, 177 ff., here 177.
534 This is the estimate of the Stinnes board member from vom Bruck according to the conversation note of the trade policy department dated September 4, 1983, in: BArch, MfS HA XVIII 17349. See also *Statistisches Jahrbuch für die Bundesrepublik Deutschland 1984*, 257.
535 *Statistisches Jahrbuch für die Bundesrepublik Deutschland 1984*, 257.
536 Information on the Brenntag discussion on September 6, 1983, in: BArch MfS HA XVIII 17349, 177 f., here 178.
537 Discussion notes from the trade policy department dated September 4, 1983, in: BArch., MfS HA XVIII 17349, 197 ff., here 199.
538 Note about a conversation on February 23, 1984, at Brenntag/Stinnes in Mülheim, in: BArch, MfS AG BKK768, 59 ff., here 60.
539 Report of the IMB "Reimann" from September 8, 1983, "Einschätzung über künftige Aktivitäten führender Chemiekonzerne," in: BArch MfS AG BKK 768, 69 ff., here 72.
540 If necessary, Stinnes was also prepared, according to another report, to increase the volume of any special transactions – meaning transactions with a long-term payment term of, for example, 540 days and a third partner, for example in the Far East – the currently 50 million convertible D-Mark could be increased twice or one and a half times. For such commercial loans, the interest rate would be 3–4% above normal bank loans; see IMB Reimann's report on a conversation on December 13, 1983, at Stinnes AG in Mülheim, in: BArch, MFS AG BKK 768, 49 ff., here 51. See also "Hinweise zur chemischen Industrie der DDR und BRD vom 19.9.1983," in: BArch, MFS HA XVIII 17349, 157 ff., here 158.
541 See vom Bruck's statement before the Koko investigative committee, stenographic minutes of the 132nd meeting of the investigative committee on April 28, 1993, in: PADBT 3327, 12. WP, Prot. 132, 1–78, here 40 f.

Another piece of information after the Leipzig fall fair in 1983 stated that *Brenntag AG* had recently carried out credit operations on special export-import transactions with benzene on a "significant scale" and that similar operations were also planned for 1984.[542] It stated further that *Brenntag* organized the "transshipment via Hamburg and the onward delivery in ships to Rotterdam and Antwerp in order to reach the end customers in the Federal Republic of Germany by inland waterway vessels and to partly unload them in the Federal Republic of Germany by exchanging the goods for convertible foreign currency."[543] *Brenntag* had also carried out swap transactions in Italy between Prague and *Chemapol*.[544] These transactions were similar to an idea that the *Berag* director reported on after discussions with representatives of the chemical industry, including *Brenntag*. The debate there had been about "importing certain basic chemicals into the GDR and securing long-term payment for this." At the same time, however, the individual companies should agree to "buy the basic chemicals and transport them back into Western Europe in order to trade via a GDR/BRD detour and provide additional convertible foreign currency."[545] Apart from the fact that such a transaction did not correspond to the principles of intra-German trade, from an EEC perspective it could amount to price dumping. The number of EEC anti-dumping proceedings against GDR foreign trading companies increased rapidly in the early 1980s, signaling that competitors and the EEC were reacting to increasing imports into the Common Market.[546] For example, there were allegations against *Brenntag* and its trading activities for *AHB Chemie* from the *Solvay Group* reported in the files, saying the group took action against the import of soda ash from the GDR.[547]

In addition to intra-German trade, the GDR's foreign chemical trade offered a starting point for establishing an even broader international presence, e.g., toward the Far East. *Brenntag* management apparently thought about making greater use of the opportunities in South Korea and Japan and integrating the *Brenntag* subsidiary in Tokyo into the trade in GDR goods.[548]

---

542 See the handwritten report by IM "Hecht" from September 21, 1983, in: BArch MfS HA XVIII 17349, 153 ff., here 154.

543 Ibid.

544 See also BArch, MfS, FFO, KD Schwedt 350, 28 (according to the minutes, Brenntag wanted to look into the idea of doing swap transactions with France).

545 Report from IMB Reimann about a conversation with a Brenntag board member on October 19, 1982, in: BArch MfS HA XVIII 36325, 60 ff., here 60.

546 Maximilian Graf, "Die DDR und die EWG 1957–1990," in: *Revue d'Allemagne et des pays de langue allesmande* [Online], 51-1 | 2019, published online on: July 2, 2020, last accessed June 1, 2023. URL: http://journals.openedition.org/allemagne/1352; DOI: https://doi.org/10.4000/allemagne.1352

547 See BArch MfS AG BKK 768, 87, 92; BArch MfS AG BKK 447, 17 f.; BArch HA XVIII 36325, 9 f., 61 ff.

548 Report on a conversation at Stinnes/Brenntag on August 27, 1984, in: BArch MfS AG BKK 768, 2 ff., here 5.

Meanwhile, work in the German-Soviet joint venture *Sobren* apparently did not turn out as *Brenntag* had originally imagined. In the summer of 1983, *Brenntag* was already considering dissolving the joint company. The Soviet side was not prepared to give *Brenntag* access to important documents, the *Berag* director explained in a report to the MfS. Apparently, there were also conspiratorial activities of individual employees into which *Brenntag* did not want to be drawn "under any circumstances."[549] *Brenntag* had allegedly asked the *Berag* director whether he himself would like to coordinate the *Sobren* collaboration in Düsseldorf for *Brenntag*, but he had declined.[550]

In the medium term, the chemical producers in the GDR also wanted to offer more highly refined products, in accordance with the goals of the GDR government. This approach was not met with universal approval within the ranks of *Brenntag* management because some *Brenntag* executives were skeptical about the future prospects of it, given the high market shares of the German producers. Nevertheless, around 1984, *Brenntag* made an agreement with the GDR chemical combines to market not only basic chemicals, but also products with higher processing levels.[551] For the time being, business in the East continued to progress. In August 1984, Hermann vom Bruck reported to the *Stinnes AG* supervisory board that the department "International Ost" had once again "significantly exceeded" the target figures due to good business developments in the GDR and the USSR.[552]

Brenntag in the Late 1980s, 1986–1989

Around the mid-1980s, the markets once again became agitated because crude oil prices had dropped significantly since the fall of 1985. Within a few months they fell by around 60 percent, which noticeably changed the price structure for other raw materials and chemical products. In the ten months prior, the *Stinnes* CEO explained in November 1986, market structures, prices, supply flows, currency relations, and customer wishes had changed more than in the previous five years.[553] While chemical producers initially tended to benefit from the new

---

549 Report IMB Reimann June 7, 1983, in: BArch MfS AG BKK 768, 80.

550 Tape copy from August 18, 1983, of a report from IMB Reimann on August 1, 1983, in: BArch MfS AG BKK 768, 75 ff., here 77. The joint venture was dissolved in the 1980s.

551 Minutes of the meeting of the supervisory board of Stinnes AG on May 14, 1984, in: BArch B136 22832.

552 Room document for the supervisory board meeting on August 8, 1984: Report on the development of the company's divisions from January 1, 1984, to June 30, 1984, in: BArch B136/22832.

553 Statements by Knauer on TOP 1 supervisory board meeting of Stinnes AG on November 17, 1986, in: Deutsche Bahn Archive, HA 50, 10.

framework conditions, margins in chemical trading fell.[554] The chemical trading division at *Brenntag* usually participated somewhat delayed in an upturn in the chemical economy.[555] However, with the fall in oil prices, there were signs of a positive development in the chemical industry.

For a while, the outcomes in *Brenntag's* business area fell short of the planned targets due to the changed market conditions.[556] Customers were reluctant to order and initially only ordered the smallest sizes, since they expected further price reductions. Nevertheless, it had a stabilizing effect that the range was now broader, after the capacities of *Emesco* and *Raab-Karcher* had been added and given the range more depth with regard to inorganic chemicals, acids, and alkalis.[557]

Shortly before the fall meeting of the *Stinnes* supervisory board in 1986, a chemical accident occurred in Schweizerhalle near Basel, Switzerland, which once again fueled the public discussion about the risks of the chemical industry. A major fire in a *Sandoz* warehouse in November 1986 required extensive extinguishing work so that tons of chemicals flowed from the warehouse into the nearby Rhine with the extinguishing water, including mercury, thiophosporic acid esters, and a dye that colored the Rhine water red.[558] The first consequences for the Rhine ecosystem became visible shortly after the event. The chemical water flowing downstream killed the fish in the river, and drinking water production had to be temporarily stopped.

At *Brenntag*, the *Sandoz* accident was perceived as a turning point for its own business activities. Just a few months later, *Stinnes* board member Hermann vom Bruck, who was responsible for the *Brenntag* businesses, stated on the supervisory board that official requirements for the transport and storage of products had increased since the chemical accident. He had seen this on site during the approval process for some *Brenntag* projects. In Munich, some local politicians now spoke out against the construction of a new *Brenntag* warehouse. The approval for the new central warehouse in Plochingen was subject to the condition that *Brenntag* financed additional equipment for the local fire

---

554 Knauer's remarks on TOP 1 of the agenda, supervisory board meeting on April 27, 1987, in: Deutsche Bahn Archive, HA-50-11-a.

555 Frank Bösch, *Zeitenwende 1979. Als die Welt von heute begann*, Munich 2019, 330. Bösch interprets the fall in oil prices as a "huge economic stimulus program" for the West.

556 Minutes of the supervisory board meeting of April 27, 1987, in: Deutsche Bahn Archive, HA-50-11. Business in Belgium, Portugal, Austria, and Japan was unsatisfactory in 1986. See minutes of the supervisory board meeting of Stinnes AG on November 17, 1986, in: Deutsche Bahn Archive, HA 50, 10.

557 Deutsche Bahn Archive, HA -50-11b, statements from vom Bruck at the supervisory board meeting on April 27, 1987 (April 3, 1987).

558 The accident was referred to in environmental history research as a "chemical Chernobyl." Uekötter/Kirchhelle, 329. Mathias Hofmann, *Lernen aus Katastrophen. Nach den Unfällen von Harrisburg, Seveso und Sandoz*, Berlin 2008, 279 ff.

department. In Dormagen, a *Brenntag* warehouse keeper, a freight forwarding company, was supposed to "fulfill requirements that the neighboring giant EC [= Erdölchemie] had probably not known before" for the storage of a few hundred kilograms of pesticides – according to vom Bruck's assessment.[559]

Meanwhile, another *Brenntag* project now seemed to be becoming more popular: the recycling plant in Goch on the Lower Rhine. A *Brenntag* subsidiary had been processing contaminated solvents here for several years.[560] In 1986, *Brenntag* had still had to buy the goods to be processed and pay for them. "Today, most suppliers pay us a fee for taking over the contaminated material," explained the responsible board member in the spring of 1987.[561] The CEO of *Stinnes* even recognized the disposal option as a strategic competitive advantage.[562]

In the wake of the *Sandoz* disaster, the chemical industry association had agreed on a package of voluntary measures to increase operational safety in the industry. The catalog of measures included, among other things, guidelines for fire protection in chemical storage facilities and for the construction of collection facilities for fire-fighting water.[563] Accordingly, *Brenntag* began converting various warehouses and implementing new safety measures in 1987.[564] The modern *Brenntag* central warehouse near Plochingen with the large underground tank system for solvents was considered internally as a showcase project with regard to soil and water protection; it also influenced the conversion plans for other warehouses.[565] The original warehouse at the parallel port in Duisburg was regularly flooded whenever the Rhine was in flood, which raised safety questions and suggested relocation in the medium term. For the time being, technical improvements were undertaken to increase operational safety. By 1990, *Stinnes AG* wanted to invest 60 million D-Mark in modernizing *Brenntag's* warehouses in order to limit the potential danger posed by dangerous goods.[566]

This investment program formed a building block in an overarching strategy: *Stinnes* management prepared *Brenntag* for developments that it expected

---

559 Statements from vom Bruck at the supervisory board meeting on April 27, 1987 (from April 3, 1987), in: Archives of Deutsche Bahn, HA-50-11b.

560 Annual report of Stinnes AG 1987, 16. See also annual report of Stinnes AG 1981, 16.

561 Statements from vom Bruck at the supervisory board meeting on April 27, 1987 (from April 3, 1987), in: Archives of Deutsche Bahn, HA-50-11b.

562 Statements by Knauer on the 1987 financial year, in: Deutsche Bahn Archive, HA-50-14.

563 Mathias Hofmann, *Lernen aus Katastrophen. Nach den Unfällen von Harrisburg, Seveso und Sandoz*, Berlin 2008, 305 f.

564 Stinnes AG, annual report 1987, 16.

565 Ibid.

566 At the general meeting of Stinnes AG on June 30, 1988, the question of the potential danger from contaminated sites arose; see HA 50-15b, supplementary documents for the supervisory board meeting, and the shareholders' general meeting on June 30, 1988. The modernization of the warehouses was further discussed in the supervisory board; see, e.g., Deutsche Bahn Archive, HA 50/16, documents for the supervisory board meeting of Stinnes AG on November 23, 1988, including explanations of the investments in property, plant, and equipment in 1989.

in the chemicals trade in the coming years. *Brenntag's* internationalization was still progressing too slowly, *Stinnes* board member Hermann vom Bruck diagnosed in a meeting of the supervisory board in the spring of 1987, and, he noted further, it had been costly in the past. However, there was no question for *Brenntag's* management that the targeted expansion of foreign business was the right path for the future. Now it wanted to promote its international presence and combine that with a more clearly defined orientation of the company. With regard to the markets in the Far East, the company was still looking for a new approach. At least in Japan, it became apparent that the attempt to assert oneself against the Japanese trading houses was encountering great difficulties, and that continuing activities in their current form no longer made sense in the medium term. During the second half of the 1980s, *Brenntag* gave up the loss-making distribution business and focused on trading activities.[567]

However, the focus of the growth strategy was still on Europe and the USA in this phase. *Brenntag* wanted to further expand its structures there through acquisitions. *Brenntag* had now become the market leader in the Federal Republic. After a lengthy review, the cartel office agreed in 1987 that *Brenntag* would be allowed to increase its stake in the Bremen company *Tietjen* – a step that the company interpreted as an important stage for expansion on the German market.[568] During this phase, there was a generational change in management. Dr. Erhard Meyer-Galow, who was appointed to the *Brenntag* Board of Directors in the spring of 1988 and took over as CEO at the beginning of 1989, advocated a determined continuation of the internationalization and growth strategy.[569]

During this phase, *Brenntag* management discussed the market changes that they attributed to the *Sandoz* disaster. The relationship between the producers and the large distribution companies had changed "noticeably." "In a number of cases," said the *Stinnes AG* supervisory board in the spring of 1988, "real partnerships" had emerged. Producers increasingly shared their know-how regarding storage, transport, and handling in order to avoid negative reporting. They had apparently realized that one has to offer customers not just products

---

567 The locations in the Far East were at times considered important bases for GDR chemical exports. The supervisory board said that in 1986, 40 percent of GDR chemical exports to this region were processed through Brenntag's Far East offices; see Deutsche Bahn Archive, HA 50, 3 (supervisory board meeting on December 4, 1985). For the perception of Japan as a "problem child," see also the supervisory board meetings 1986–1989, Deutsche Bahn Archive, HA 50, 11 and HA 50, 5a (speech manuscript by vom Bruck from April 25, 1989, for the supervisory board meeting in May 1989).

568 See, for example, an overview of the supervisory board meeting on April 27, 1987, which compiles "major investments that are breaking new ground" from the last 1.5 years, in: Deutsche Bahn Archive, HA-50-11a.

569 Deutsche Bahn Archive, HA 50/14. See also Deutsche Bahn Archive, HA 50/26. See also Brenntag archive headquarters, Brenntag Report, 1993/3.

Figure 43: Brenntag subsidiary Recycling-Chemie Niederrhein GmbH truck, 1988.

but solutions to problems. The recycling plant in Goch was considered a successful example of this. With these new focal points, the requirement profile for personnel gradually changed: *Brenntag* trained its employees and hired new technicians. In addition, the pressure on sales margins eased.[570]

The strong growth of the chemical industry in the late 1980s promised growth opportunities for trade in chemicals of all kinds.[571] At the European level, the full expansion of the Single European Market was within reach. According to the Single European Act, goods, people, services, and capital would be able to move freely within the European Community until the end of 1992, and the respective markets would be subject to uniform standards across the EC. Industry observers predicted growth in trade, intensifying competition, and falling prices.[572] *Stinnes AG* prepared for a possible increase in the exchange of goods with a strategy concept that was intended to bundle the forces available in the group for logistics and forwarding services and optimize them as an "integrated carrier."[573] *Brenntag's* profile was also to be sharpened: The aim

---

570 Deutsche Bahn Archive, HA 50, 14, supervisory board meeting on April 22, 1988, TOP "Brenntag" (from Knauer's speech manuscript; Dr. Malmström's secretariat from April 12, 1988).

571 See, for example, Stinnes AG, annual report 1988, 15.

572 See, for example, the Cecchini report, a study that predicted particular growth and stability for the twelve countries of the European Community if they succeeded in expanding fully into the internal market; Paolo Cecchini, *Europa '92. Der Vorteil des Binnenmarktes*, Baden-Baden 1988; see also Fred Becker, "Managementprobleme für Industrieunternehmen durch den Europäischen Binnenmarkt," in: Jürgen Berthel/Fred Becker (eds.), *Unternehmerische Herausforderung durch den Europäischen Binnenmarkt 1992*, Berlin/Heidelberg 1990, 3 ff.

573 Deutsche Bahn Archive, HA 50/16, minutes of the meeting of the supervisory board of Stinnes AG on November 23, 1988. See also statements by Dr. Knauer on TOP III, 7. For Stinnes' reorganization approaches around Rhenus, see, e.g., Deutsche Bahn Archive, HA 50, 15, minutes of the meeting of the supervisory board of Stinnes AG on June 30, 1988.

was to make it one of the largest chemical trading companies in Europe.[574] The intention was to enable *Brenntag* to supply any customer with any quantity of the desired chemical products at any point within the framework of the Common Market. In addition to trading activities, the focus would now be on distribution and specialized warehousing, especially for solvents and dangerous chemicals, which would be subject to stricter environmental protection regulations in the future.[575]

Here the competitive advantage for larger companies was obvious: In order to limit possible risks to health and the environment when storing and transporting chemicals, extensive investments were necessary that smaller companies often could not afford.[576] In addition, the capital-rich companies were able to take on a pacesetting role as "first movers" in this phase of change, setting standards with regard to the equipment of locations, facilities, and processes, and in this way establishing a standard that enabled a high level of protection against environmental risks – the kinds of risks that smaller companies might not have the wherewithal to deal with. As the strategic direction of the late 1980s shows, *Brenntag* was aware of this advantage and was willing to position itself in the best possible way in the given initial situation. This also included sharpening its profile for new areas of activity and offering itself to producers of chemical products not just as a dealer, but as a partner for specialized services relating to the handling of chemicals. Cost advantages could arise for specialized chemical distributors because, with established business relationships involving several producers, they covered a much broader range and larger batch sizes than the individual producer was able to. In the near future, it was considered likely that traditional wholesale chemicals would become less important than specialized chemical distribution. It had already been observed, especially in the USA, that producers preferred to commission larger distribution companies with the most modern standards and facilities. As in other sectors in the chemical industry, competitive corporate management gained increased significance over traditional production-centered models. This corresponded to an increasing willingness among producers to optimize distribution and logistics issues and to outsource related activities. As US studies showed, the proportion of business activities that chemical producers conducted with distributors grew from

---

574 See statements by Hermann vom Bruck at the supervisory board meeting on May 11, 1989, in: Deutsche Bahn Archive, HA 50/5a.

575 See also the report of an IM, in: BArch, MfS, HA XVIII, 22129.

576 See statements by Hermann vom Bruck at the supervisory board meeting on May 11, 1989, in: Deutsche Bahn Archive, HA 50/5a.

6 percent at the end of the 1970s to 24 percent at the end of the 1980s. A trend toward further increases was expected in the 1990s as well.[577]

The program for the reorganization of *Brenntag* had a twofold thrust. In addition to internationalizing the business area, its domestic activities needed to be reorganized. The workforce had now grown to 1,784 employees: At the end of September 1988, *Brenntag* employed 1,095 people in Germany and 689 abroad.[578]

Since 1988, *Brenntag* management had been working with the management consultancy McKinsey to develop a new structure that differentiated four core areas: the industrial chemicals division for standard products, *Brenntag Eurochem GmbH* for the distribution of specialty chemicals, *Brenntag Interplast GmbH* for the distribution of plastics, and the *Brenntag Interchem GmbH* for global trading. The new divisional organization was intended to replace the previous product-oriented matrix structure, which had still followed a chemical classification scheme in its basic structure. The reorganization promised to define responsibilities more clearly and reduce the coordination effort, since similar business processes were brought together in the new structure. For standard chemicals that are easily replaceable on the market, the added value that *Brenntag* offered to the customer consisted less in the product than in the associated organizational performance, for which the respective teams now worked together in regional profit centers. When it came to specialty chemicals, it was more about application technology advice for customers with whom *Brenntag* often maintained a long-term business relationship. In order to be able to adapt its own know-how (e.g., recipes for certain chemicals) to specific needs, *Eurochem* was divided into divisions that represented customer groups from different areas. When it came to plastics, *Brenntag* now focused on the small distribution business, which offered more attractive margins. While *Brenntag Interchem* – *Brenntag's* trading company – had been more oriented toward the East in the past, it now wanted to focus on global trade, pool procurement, and demand and act as a global trader on the world market with appropriate batch sizes.[579] Implementation of the new structure was planned for 1990.

The declared growth orientation since the late 1980s outlined more clearly what had already been the subject of public discussion in the 1970s: the group's

---

577 Stinnes intern. Information für unsere Führungskräfte, No. 2, June 1990, 8, in: Brenntag headquarters archive, still unsigned. The market to which the shares relate is not specified.

578 Documents for the meeting of the employee representatives on the supervisory board on November 22, 1988, in: Deutsche Bahn Archive, HA 50/16c.

579 Stinnes intern. Information für unsere Führungskräfte, No. 2, June 1990, 9 ff., in: Brenntag headquarters archive, still unsigned.

acquisition of small and medium-sized companies as part of *Brenntag's* business model. In some cases, this certainly had explosive implications. If the group had an interest in buying a firm that was not reciprocated by the owners, their different interests would conflict on the market. Generally speaking, and detached from the specific history of *Brenntag*, it can be stated that in such a conflict of interests, the company had the best structural conditions to assert its position due to its capital strength, especially in this phase. If the premises of a long-established chemical dealer were contaminated with pollutants due to long-term use – and the probability of this was quite high – the company would face potentially significant cleanup costs, which might exceed the financing capacity of the respective company. According to statements from a Stasi informant, the *Stinnes* board of directors certainly considered unscrupulously using its leverage to force takeovers if necessary or – as the tape transcript read – to "bring stubborn sheep to reason."[580] However, it is not clear from the documents whether such cases actually occurred. Between 1985 and 1990, *Brenntag* only made one acquisition in the Federal Republic of Germany.[581]

Admittedly, concentration tendencies became evident in the global chemicals trade in the late 1980s. Looking at the Federal Republic's market, the number of companies trading in chemicals on a certain scale decreased in the second half of the 1980s. While the statistical yearbook for 1985 listed over 600 companies with a turnover of one million D-Mark or more in chemical wholesale,[582] the corresponding number was 539 in 1987 and 513 in 1989.[583] As a result of the competition, dozens of companies either disappeared from the market, lost business volume, or formed part of a larger group. Nevertheless, the market was very fragmented. Many providers – some with strong regional roots – existed side by side. Market leadership was therefore achieved with comparatively small market shares.

---

580 See IMB Reimann's report on a conversation with a Stinnes board member on September 8, 1988, at the Leipzig trade fair, in: BArch, MfS, AG BKK 679, 75.

581 This involved increasing the stake in Tietjen. Further acquisitions only followed in the 1990s. Brenntag archive, headquarters, data collection Dr. Mörath, acquisitions 1985–1995.

582 See product group 404 – "Wholesale trade in technical chemicals, raw drugs, and rubber."

583 *Statistisches Jahrbuch der Bundesrepublik Deutschland 1987*, 235; *Statistisches Jahrbuch der Bundesrepublik Deutschland 1990*, 234; *Statistisches Jahrbuch der Bundesrepublik Deutschland 1991*, 257. In 1984, 620 companies were listed in the wholesale trade in chemicals; see *Statistisches Jahrbuch der Bundesrepublik Deutschland 1986*, 232. The trade and restaurant census lists 1,064 companies in the chemicals trade for March 29, 1985, although this also includes companies with sales of less than one million D-Mark (companies with sales of 20,000 D-Mark or more were recorded), so that the results of this count are only partially comparable with the other survey category; cf. *Statistisches Jahrbuch der Bundesrepublik Deutschland 1987*, 227 f. and 235.

German-German Business 1986–1989/90

The business partners in the GDR also took note of the strategic adjustment processes at *Stinnes AG* and its *Brenntag* division. "You will hear a lot more about *Brenntag* in the future" is how *Stinnes* board member Hermann vom Bruck is said to have commented on the new concept to representatives of the *Schwedt Petrochemical Combine* in the fall of 1987.[584] In the GDR, *PCK Schwedt* was considered to be one of the largest *Brenntag* suppliers in the late 1980s.[585] The fact that the distribution contract for petrochemicals from the GDR was extended by five years in the fall of 1988 was one of the *Brenntag* business transactions mentioned individually by the supervisory board of *Stinnes AG*.[586]

Overall, the petroleum, heating oil, and petroleum aromatics route was considered to be a reference model for good cooperation, something similar to what *Stinnes AG* wanted to see in the fertilizer sector.[587] In order to reduce the focus on commodities, *Stinnes AG* was probably also interested in agreements for products in the area of higher-value chemicals, e.g., for pharmaceutical raw materials.[588]

However, based on the available documents, it is not possible to reconstruct all of *Brenntag's* GDR businesses. The files reveal more about *Brenntag's* distribution of GDR products than about its chemical deliveries into the GDR. For example, *Brenntag* also had the sole distribution rights for dry sorbitol from GDR production, manufactured primarily at *VEB Kosmetik-Kombinat Berlin* (KKB) and at *Deutsches Hydrierwerk* Rodleben.[589] A piece of operational information from the Stasi estimated the *KKB's* market share in the Federal Republic at 30

---

584 Report on consultations with Stinnes AG, in: BArch, MfS, BV, FFo, KD Schwedt 350, 150.

585 "It was assessed by both sides that the business development between PCK and Brenntag AG had developed steadily since 1982 and that PCK had now developed into the largest supplier (more than 10% of Brenntag sales); see report on consultations with Stinnes AG, in: BArch, MfS, BV, FFo, KD Schwedt 350, 150. Nevertheless, the data is too fragmentary to reconstruct details about the supplier structure. According to the documents (BArch, MfS, BV, FFo, KD Schwedt 350, passim), Brenntag must have marketed around 17,000 tons of C8 aromatics and 48,000 tons of benzene from Schwedt and Böhlen in 1987, which corresponded to around 43 million accounting units – that was a significant share of sales in Brenntag Interchem's business (sales of this unit are estimated at around 300 million D-Mark) but only a comparatively small share of Brenntag's total sales, which in 1987 were around three billion D-Mark. A Stinnes board member estimated sales with AHB Chemie – without the Intrac business – at around 110 million D-Mark in 1988; see BArch, MfS, BKK, 679. This fits with a list of the VE Außenhandelsbetrieb Chemie-Import-Export, which estimated exports (mainly benzene, xylene, and soda) via Brenntag for 1987 at 106 million D-Mark; cf. BArch, MfS, HA, XVIII, 22129, 26.

586 See documents for the supervisory board meeting on November 23, 1988, in: Archives of Deutsche Bahn, HA 50/16.

587 BArch, MfS, AG, BKK, 447, 81.

588 BArch, MfS, HA, XVIII, 22129, 28.

589 The exclusive distribution rights for DHW Rodleben go back to the 1970s. BArch, MfS, BV Halle KD Roßlau, 1154, 248. See also BArch, MfS, BV Halle, KD Roßlau, No. 440.

percent. The most important buyer for this sweetener was the *Aldi* company, so the *KKB* was in a position of dependence because *Aldi's* purchasing strategy was consistently aimed at the cheapest price. There were potential competitors in this sector, including the company *Merck* and a French provider. In this constellation, the business partners valued *Brenntag's* networks. In the event of complaints, *Brenntag* took over the negotiations with customers and offered the prospect of selling quantities not purchased by *Aldi* elsewhere. In a similar way, *Brenntag* promised to use its US business connections to help the GDR paint industry with bottlenecks in the procurement of specialty resins.[590]

This account of the company history can only make assumptions about some of the flows of goods. This also applies to a distressing topic in the GDR's industrial history. In several chemical combines in the GDR, prisoners were employed under health-damaging, extremely stressful working conditions, for example in old chlorine chemical plants in Bitterfeld and Schkopau.[591] GDR foreign trade also sold products from the old plants to Western European countries and the Federal Republic.[592] This raises the question of whether and to what extent *Brenntag* sold GDR chemical products manufactured using forced labor and – if this was the case – whether the circumstances under which these products were produced were known within the company. Several West German companies were active in the trade of GDR chemicals. However, it is quite likely that *Brenntag*, as an important partner in the GDR chemical trade, was also involved in the distribution of these products.[593] Nevertheless, assumptions about this issue must remain speculative based on the available documents. According to current research, there is no reliable information on this matter.[594]

---

590 See operational information and appendices to travel directives from 1987, in: BArch, MfS, BV Halle KD Roßlau, 1154. The fact that Brenntag's extensive business connections and its contacts with producers were seen as a plus point in the GDR can be seen again and again over time. The bottleneck in the GDR's paint industry in 1989 was caused by operational disruptions at the Bayer plant (Bayer was sole supplier). Brenntag wanted to solve this bottleneck with US goods. BArch, MfS, AG, BKK, No. 679, 87.

591 See Julius Vesting, *Zwangsarbeit im Chemiedreieck. Strafgefangene und Bausoldaten in der Industrie der DDR*, Berlin 2012, 86 ff.

592 Rainer Karlsch, "Das Milliardengeschäft der Hoechst AG mit der DDR-Chemieindustrie von 1976," in: *ZUG* 2018, 63/2, 235–274, here 274.

593 According to MfS documents, Brenntag traded in chlorine chemical products, e.g., soda and caustic soda, which were produced in Bitterfeld, according to an IMB report from August 1981; cf. BA, MfS, AG, BKK, 768, 101. From which systems these products came from is not discussed. In the mid-1980s, Brenntag is said to have been concerned with expanding its business with CKB: "Brenntag keeps trying to establish greater contact in the Bitterfeld Chemical Combine and obviously […] does not have the necessary sympathy with AHB Chemie and also with the Bitterfeld Chemical Combine," IMB Reimann reported to the MfS in February 1985 after a visit to the Brenntag branch in West Berlin; see BArch, MfS, AG, BKK, 1177, 13.

594 Concerning the old chlorine electrolysis plants, see Karlsch, *Milliardengeschäft*, 260 ff. Open questions cannot be answered in the context of this company history without archival sources from Brenntag's own business operations. To achieve a better understanding of historical developments from the perspective of the producers and trading partners, a reappraisal of the corporate history of the chemical combines and GDR foreign trade companies is required.

In the late 1980s, further opportunities for cooperation between *Brenntag-Stinnes* and GDR business partners came onto the agenda. The electricity agreement agreed upon in March 1988 between the *Veba* subsidiary *PreußenElektra* and the GDR trading organizations *Berag* and *Intrac*, in the negotiation of which *Stinnes* board member Hermann vom Bruck played a key role, apparently served as a pacesetter for further ideas.[595] According to conversation notes in the *VEB Chemie-Import-Export-Außenhandel*, Hermann vom Bruck now had projects in mind that would improve the storage and transport processes in the GDR.[596] As the Single European Market was filling out, stricter regulations were expected for the storage and transport of chemicals classified as dangerous goods. A basic assumption in the *Stinnes Group* was that the explosiveness of logistical questions would become more acute.[597] This raised the question of how logistics problems could be solved when marketing GDR goods.[598] While *Brenntag's* location concept for the Federal German territory took into account that there would be restrictions on the range for the transport of flammable liquids in the medium term, ideas were now being discussed about how to expand the storage capacities for the *Buna* and *Bitterfeld Chemical Combines* and where to build a larger warehouse in Dessau on the Elbe.[599]

Meanwhile, the well-established business relationships of the *Brenntag* subsidiary *Rex* to supply the West Berlin market with mineral oil products continued into the late 1980s. In traditional annual meetings, the GDR company *Intrac* negotiated with *Rex Handelsgesellschaft* and the oil companies *BP, Shell, Aral,* and *Esso* about delivery dates and tender quantities that exceeded the agreement. The existing arrangements between *Intrac* and *Rex* for the GDR delivery of gasoline and diesel fuels attracted increasing criticism.[600] Berlin's Economics Senator Pieroth fought to break up the existing sales structure and allow additional retailers. His aim was to involve medium-sized companies more directly in the supply of the Berlin fuel market. The business partners that had been involved so far rejected this initiative.[601] In contrast, officials in the Federal

---

595 In the late 1980s, Veba CEO Bennigsen-Foerder campaigned to enable electricity deliveries between the Federal Republic and West Berlin via GDR territory; the "electricity agreement" was agreed upon in March 1988; see Leonard Müller, *Handbuch der Elektrizitätswirtschaft. Technische, wirtschaftliche und rechtliche Grundlagen*, Berlin 2001, 49. See also BArch, MfS, HA, XVIII, 22129, 31.

596 For example, it was about the handling options in the PCK Schwedt or for solvents in the Buna Combine, BArch, MfS, HA, XVIII, 22129, 31.

597 BArch, MfS, AG, BKK, 476, 21 f.

598 See also BArch, MfS, AG, BKK, 820, 19.

599 BArch, MfS, AG, BKK, 476, 21; see also BArch, MfS, HA, XVIII, 22129, 44.

600 For early criticism, see, e.g., BArch, MfS, AG, BKK, 1988.

601 BArch, MfS, AG, BKK, 1891, 65 ff.

Ministry of Economics had probably promised a compromise in 1989 of giving smaller parts of the overall business to other companies.[602]

Soon afterward, however, the markets and the general conditions for the mineral oil business in West Berlin changed dramatically. After the peaceful revolution in the GDR in the fall of 1989, the border between the Federal Republic of Germany and the GDR opened. With reunification and the monetary, economic, and social union that took place in the summer of 1990, the chapter of intra-German trade relations came to an end. The ransoming of prisoners as part of church business also ended at this time. The federal government's last reciprocation reached the GDR in January 1990.[603]

New Structures in East Germany in the Early 1990s

But how did *Brenntag's* relationships with its former business partners develop after this turning point? It is not possible to determine from the available documents how this process took place in detail.[604] Looking back, however, the newly established structures can be seen.

As early as March 1990, at a meeting in Mülheim, it was agreed to expand the existing business relationship between *Brenntag* and the *Bitterfeld Chemical Combine* (Chemiekombinat Bitterfeld, CKB). A group of experts was to examine which sales tasks in foreign trade *Brenntag* should take on and how distribution in the GDR area could be organized.[605] The *CKB's* product range included inorganic chemicals, PVC products, potassium chlorine products, manganese compounds, and plant protection products.[606] A few weeks later, the *Brenntag* management also agreed with *VEB Leuna-Werke* to deepen the existing cooperation in the areas of marketing, storage, and distribution of Leuna products – including mineral oil products, fertilizers, resins, gases, and glues – and to build a packaging center. To explore the tasks, experts came together in working groups and developed suggestions as to which tasks *Brenntag* should take on in the future, or whether joint ventures should be founded.[607] In addition, *Brenntag*

---

602 As a note from the conversation states, the Federal Ministry of Economics had temporarily discussed an "optical solution" that would involve awarding around 5 percent of the business volume to other companies. However, it is not clear from the note what the final regulation looked like. BArch, MfS, AG, BKK, No. 679, 90 ff.

603 Wölbern, *Häftlingsfreikauf*, 355.

604 As far as the Intrac and Berag files were already listed, no clues could be found; see BArch, inventory DL 210 in February 2023.

605 Stinnes-intern, 2/1990, 2.

606 Ibid.

607 Ibid.

also wanted to "work in partnership" with *VEB Chemiehandel Chemnitz* and VEB *Chemiehandel Rostock* for chemical distribution in Saxony, Mecklenburg, and Western Pomerania. In addition to logistical support, investment funds were to be mobilized to technically improve systems, adapt them to environmental protection concerns, and train employees.[608]

In the meantime, the Treuhandanstalt [a transitional privatization agency], which was set up in June 1990, had been given the task of unbundling and privatizing the combines. As the economic historians Rainer Karlsch and Raymond Stokes pointed out, serious problems soon emerged with the privatization of the East German chemical plants. In view of the technological backwardness and incalculable contamination and waste issues, a huge need for investment became apparent, and the future of the chemical sites was discussed amid considerable controversy.[609] "The capacities of the West German chemical industry were sufficient," as Karlsch and Stokes explained the prevailing view on the management floors of West German chemical producers, "to supply the market in the new federal states."[610]

From the preliminary considerations carried out by *Brenntag* together with former VEBs, three joint ventures ultimately emerged in which *Brenntag* had a majority stake: *NordChem Brenntag Venoc Chemiehandel* with its headquarters in Berlin and a branch in Rostock, *Erfurt Chemie GmbH,* and *Chemiehandel Chemnitz Brenntag GmbH.* There were 130 employees spread across four of the former seven locations of *VEB Chemie-Handel.*[611] At the *Stinnes AG* general meeting in June 1991, CEO Knauer was "very satisfied" with the progress of the *Brenntag* organization in East Germany. After a base was added in Magdeburg, *Brenntag* was represented region-wide with functional warehouses. In 1992, after reaching an agreement with the Treuhandanstalt, *Brenntag* was able to take over the remaining shares in the new investment companies.[612] Despite high start-up costs, the company was soon in the black.[613] Nevertheless, *Brenntag* complained about losses in sales because some East German sources of supply were no longer available – for example, solvents. In addition, it was necessary to compensate

---

608 Stinnes intern, 2/1990, 3.

609 Rainer Karlsch/Raymond Stokes, *Die Chemie muss stimmen. Bilanz des Wandels 1990–2000*, Leipzig/Berlin 2000.

610 Ibid., 242

611 See documents from the supervisory board of Stinnes AG in 1990 and 1991, in: Deutsche Bahn Archive, HA 50/19; HA 50/20; HA 50/21; HA 50/21a; HA 50/22. See also Scheffels, *125 Jahre*, 33.

612 Documents from the meeting of the supervisory board of Stinnes AG on May 13, 1992, in: Deutsche Bahn Archive, HA 50/24, see also HA 50/21. See also the annual report of Stinnes AG for the 1992 financial year.

613 See Stinnes AG, annual report 1990.

for the expiring aromatics business with the Schwedt refinery, because the new owners – including the *Veba* subsidiary *Veba Öl* – had terminated the contracts for petroleum aromatics that were originally signed to last until the mid-1990s.[614] In order to better exploit new market opportunities in countries of the former Eastern Bloc, *Brenntag* set up offices in Warsaw, Moscow, and Prague.[615]

The circumstances in the Berlin fuel market had also changed. With the unification of the two German states, the Berlin Agreement, which had regulated the status quo for Berlin, ceased to be in force. This eliminated the basis for cooperation between the *Brenntag* holding company *Rex Handelsgesellschaft Schulte Frohlinde* and *Intrac* in the mineral oil business. In order to reduce the double structure in intermediary trading, the legal basis of *Rex Handelsgesellschaft* was changed, and *Intrac* was granted a limited partnership interest in *Rex* of 30 percent. This share was transferred back to *Brenntag* on October 1, 1991.[616] *Brenntag* acquired the remaining shares in *Rex* in 1993 when the former gave up the petroleum business as part of the restructuring of its activities.[617]

Investigation of Koko and the Role of Brenntag

During this time, knowledge about illegal practices in the realm of the GDR organizational unit Koko increased, fueled by media reports about the opaque dealings of its leader, the State Secretary and Central Committee member Alexander Schalck-Golodkowski. Since the summer of 1991, the first investigative committee of the 12th German Bundestag had also been dealing with the questionable activities of the GDR's Commercial Coordination unit. The discussion also revolved around the prisoners' release and the role of the trusted companies in the Federal Republic involved in these transactions, including *Brenntag*.[618] How should *Brenntag's* participation in the prisoners' release be assessed from a historical perspective of the company? A contribution from the NDR research format "Panorama" caused *Brenntag* management to proactively

---

614 See information in the documents of the supervisory board 1991–1993, in: Deutsche Bahn Archive, HA 50/22; HA 50/23; HA 50/24; HA 50/25; HA 50/26.

615 Deutsche Bahn Archive, HA 50/26. See also Stinnes AG, annual report 1993.

616 See BArch, DL 210/3570. Schulte-Frohlinde's limited partnership interest was reduced accordingly to 19 percent. See also the business transactions that were discussed in the supervisory board on November 28, 1991, in: Deutsche Bahn Archive, HA 50/22.

617 See the business transactions requiring approval at the supervisory board meeting on March 19, 1993, in: Deutsche Bahn Archive, HA 50/26.

618 See, e.g., Wolfgang Brinkschulte, Hans-Jürgen Gerlach, Thomas Heise, *Freikaufgewinnler. Die Mitverdiener im Westen*, Frankfurt a. M. 1993; see also Thomas Kleine-Brockhoff/Oliver Schön, "Das Kirchengeschäft B," in: *Die Zeit* 36/1992 from August 28, 1992. For a critical view, see Armin Volze, "Eine Bananen-Legende und andere Irrtümer," in: *Deutschland-Archiv*, Vol. 26, 1993, H. 1, 65. 58–66.

address all employees with information in August 1992. "*Brenntag* carried out these transactions conscientiously and transparently for a small commission and thus contributed to the release of innocent prisoners," the company said in a statement. The question of why they helped obtain foreign currency for the GDR was seen as a legitimate one. However, they argued, this could not have been prevented. In addition, the "central aspect" should not be lost sight of. "The freedom or reunification of hundreds of thousands of people was achieved through the ransoming of prisoners. We are proud to have helped achieve this."[619]

The company's statement thus addressed the ambivalences of barter, which were being debated at the time. From the perspective of the Federal Republic, the ransom operation walked a fine line between the humanitarian objective and "chumminess" in a dubious, extremely morally questionable deal for the benefit of the SED regime.[620] As the historian Philipp Wölbern pointed out, the political leadership in the GDR's motive for the barter was its financial advantage for the SED dictatorship – political prisoners became an "'export hit' of the GDR."[621] Although the proceeds from Church Business B represented firmly planned sources of financing for the GDR state budget, they represented an "ultimately ineffective attempt" to halt the GDR's economic decline.[622] For *Brenntag*, it was a business that emerged from other church business activities, and the firm's involvement was politically desired by the federal government and the EKD. What must be stated, however, is that *Brenntag* did benefit from this at times. Although the margins were actually very low, the proportion of sales that were generated with this "routine business" was at times higher than the one or two percent of sales mentioned by witnesses at the time. What seems more significant in retrospect is that, due to its involvement in the church business, *Brenntag* grew into a network of business relationships and personal contacts early on, which also gave it a tailwind in other transactions in intra-German trade. By its GDR business partners, *Brenntag* was considered a trustworthy and discreet company with excellent contacts to the Koko companies *Berag* and *Intrac*. It also had a long-term business relationship with the latter through its associate company *Rex*.

---

619 Brenntag AG, Information an die Mitarbeiter. Beteiligung der Brenntag am Häftlingsfreikauf der Bundesrepublik Deutschland von der ehemaligen DDR, August 26, 1992, in: Brenntag headquarters archive, still unsigned.

620 See Wölbern, *Häftlingsfreikauf*, 497. See also Emmanuel Droit, review of: Wölbern, Jan Philipp: *Der Häftlingsfreikauf aus der DDR 1962/63–1989. Zwischen Menschenhandel und humanitären Aktionen.* Göttingen, 2014, ISBN 978-3-525-35079-9, In: H-Soz-Kult, May 4, 2015, www.hsozkult.de/publicationreview/id/reb-21381. For the assessment by the Bundestag investigative committee, see BT-Drucksache 12/7600, 501 ff.

621 Wölbern, *Häftlingsfreikauf*, 437.

622 Wölbern, *Häftlingsfreikauf*, 446.

Due to the confusing structure of some Koko transactions, the work of the investigative committee in the early 1990s again raised the question of whether the Koko company *Elmsoka* had fabricated mineral oil transactions and disguised them through triangular business dealings. In this context, *Brenntag* and other trusted companies were investigated on suspicion of involvement in unauthorized foreign exchange transactions – a violation of the Allied Military Government Act No. 53.[623] Observers at the time noted that it was customary in international oil transactions to only trade freight documents. From the fact that some of the crude oil shipments traded were already stored in the GDR, it could not be deduced that these were fictitious transactions.[624] The investigation was ultimately closed, and there are no new findings known about this matter.

"Powerfully Moving Forward"[625] in the Core Business: Brenntag in the 1990s

Since the late 1980s, *Brenntag* had changed its business and structures on various levels. As early as June 1991, management saw the first successes from the reorganization of their activities.[626] Focusing on the core business was the motto with which *Brenntag* now optimized its organization and divested business outside of chemicals trading. This meant that the traditional mineral oil business no longer existed, the recycling plant went to another *Veba* subsidiary, and the distribution of dry materials as part of *Emesco* was also halted.[627] In addition, *Brenntag* largely gave up trading in plastics and only kept technical plastics in its product range.[628] Trading in small units increasingly came to the fore in their activities.[629]

As a result of the reorganization, sales initially fell. The loss of *Rex's* business became noticeable. In addition, the chemical industry collapsed worldwide around 1992,[630] which caused demand to shrink. Despite the decline in sales, *Brenntag* was able to improve its outcomes overall, which was due to increased

---

623 Archives of the Brenntag headquarters, search warrant (Durchsuchungsbeschluss) dated June 6, 1994.

624 Volze, *Bananen-Legende*; see also vom Bruck's statements before the Koko investigative committee (stenographic minutes of the 132nd meeting of the investigative committee on April 28, 1993, in: PADBT, 3327, 12. WP, Prot. 132, 1–78).

625 Brenntag Report, 4/1995, Report from the Board of Directors, 3.

626 This was the attitude of the supervisory board in spring 1991; see Deutsche Bahn Archive, HA 50/20; HA 50/20a; HA 50/21; HA 50/21a.

627 Stinnes AG, annual report 1991.

628 Stinnes AG, annual report 1992.

629 Ibid.

630 Rainer Karlsch/Raymond Stokes, *Die Chemie muss stimmen. Bilanz des Wandels 1990–2000*, Leipzig/Berlin 2000, 98 ff.

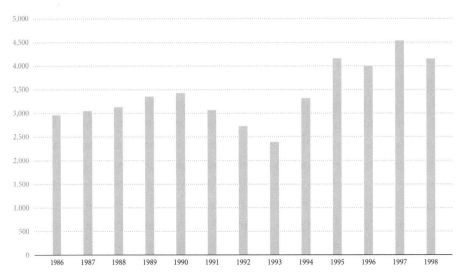

Chart 4: Stinnes AG, External Sales in the Chemicals Division, in Million D-Mark[631]

international activities.[632] *Brenntag* had "no gross profit problem despite the recessionary environment," explained CFO Armin-Peter Bode. Nevertheless, it was important to continue to reduce costs and to streamline regional structures, especially domestically, he said. The aim was not to thin out the network of locations but rather to continue to have their own bases in as wide a range as possible. However, it was a cost driver to have their own handling facilities or filling facilities at many locations. In this context, *Brenntag* was then focusing primarily on joint projects with regional competitors in domestic chemical distribution in order to realize economical solutions through cooperation. A warehouse alliance had already been started with *Biesterfeld* in Berlin-Hoppegarten in 1991, which was later expanded to Hamburg and Nuremberg.[633] Together with the *Rühl* company, a new tank and dry storage facility in Lohfelden in the Kassel district had been planned since fall 1993. In Bavaria, too, where *Brenntag* was in competition with traditional chemical trading companies, the market was approached differently, and in 1994 the Nuremberg and Munich branches were incorporated into the family business *Staub & Co. Chemiehandelsgesellschaft*, in which *Brenntag* and the Frank family each owned 50 percent of the shares. *Staub* had a strong position in inorganic chemicals and solids, which complemented

---

631 Data taken from Stinnes AG, annual reports 1986–1998.

632 Deutsche Bahn Archive, HA 50/26, documents from the supervisory board meeting in March 1993. See also Brenntag archive headquarters, Brenntag Report, 1/1993, 5.

633 Deutsche Bahn Archive, HA 50/22, HA 50/28, HA 50/29.

Brenntag's regional strength in solvents.[634] *Brenntag* also bought the chemical company *Wülfing* in Gevelsberg.[635]

Internationally, *Brenntag* continued to strengthen its position in the relevant markets in Western Europe and the USA.[636] In 1992, *Brenntag* had 20 bases in Europe.[637] With the acquisition of the Belgian market leader *Boucquillon* in 1989, the foreign organization had gained momentum. In the neighboring French market, the aim was still to build a strong local base and then network this with the bases in Belgium. The acquisition of *GDC* and *Orchidis* and the expansion of *Boucquillon* were important steps on this path.[638] In keeping with *Stinnes'* historically grown corporate culture, *Brenntag* largely relied on personal responsibility in the local units. In most cases, the former managing directors or long-term co-owners remained in their positions. The idea behind this was to have as little on-site impact as possible on existing customer relationships due to the change in ownership. The subsidiaries were also to retain their individual character, as this was the foundation of their local market strength. One of the principles of *Brenntag's* growth strategy was that there was no need to constantly reinvent the wheel.[639] It was more about bundling the strengths of smaller companies. This principle took on sharper contours in the course of the 1990s. *Brenntag's* corporate culture was "glocal," said Rients Visser, who took over as CEO from Meyer-Galow in 1994. "We need the local heroes. […] We work globally and locally at the same time."[640] However, this approach reached its limits when the local management culture no longer seemed up to date. "Only the bishop is missing from this accumulation of titles," griped a *Brenntag* manager, for example, about the management structures of an investment company in France. The organizational structure established through a *Brenntag* state holding company acted as a control and management authority for the companies to be integrated into the larger structure.[641]

---

634 Archives of the Brenntag headquarters, Brenntag Report, 2/1994. See also Brenntag Report 1/1996.

635 Archives of the Brenntag headquarters, data collection Dr. Mörath. See also Brenntag Report 2/1994.

636 See documents from the meeting of the supervisory board in November 1991, Deutsche Bahn Archive, HA 50/22.

637 Stinnes AG, annual report 1992.

638 Archives of the Brenntag headquarters, Brenntag Report 3/1994.

639 Archives of the Brenntag headquarters, Brenntag Report 3/1992.

640 See Scheffels, *125 Jahre*, 44 f.

641 See archives of the Brenntag headquarters, Brenntag Report 2/1992 and 1/1993. The decentralized corporate organization, which was cultivated at Stinnes AG until the 1990s, left the subsidiaries room to maneuver that could theoretically be used to the detriment of the parent company. Some cases of this have been known over time, but not from the Brenntag division. In the mid-1990s, Stinnes AG changed some principles of auditing and controlling. See, for example, the Middle East business of the Stinnes subsidiary Vaubeka as well as embezzlement at another Stinnes-subsidiary, and there is also a known case at a Frank & Schulte subsidiary. For the restructuring, see Deutsche Bahn Archive, HA 50/32.

"Grow to be great" was a motto of *Brenntag's* parent company in the 1990s.[642] The fact that *Brenntag* was a focus of growth for *Stinnes AG*, or rather, the *Veba Group*, was evident from the ongoing internationalization. The acquisition of the US companies *Southchem* and *Eaken* for around 14.6 million US dollars closed gaps in the location network of the eastern USA.[643] The internationalization of the group was also reflected in the composition of the Board of Directors. *Brenntag* had "the most international management team in the *Veba Group*," the in-house magazine reported at the end of 1993.[644] At the end of 1994, the *Brenntag* network comprised 49 bases in the USA, one in Mexico, and 87 in Europe.[645] Important domestic acquisitions in the second half of the 1990s included *CVH* (*Chemie-Vertrieb Hannover*) with various locations and *Schuster & Sohn*. In the mid-1990s, CEO Rients Visser expected not only an increase in importance for chemical distribution per se but also growth for *Brenntag* of around 20 percent in 1995 and 10–15 percent in 1996.[646]

Table 2: Brenntag's Foreign Acquisitions 1990–1999[647]

Year	Acquisition/Investment
1990	Nederlandsche Benzol Maatschappij (Netherlands)
1991	Weiss (Italy)
1992	Groupe Distribution Chimie (France); Volkers (Netherlands)
1993	Southchem (USA); R. W. Eaken (USA)
1994	Guzman Iberica (Spain); Groupe Orchidis (France); Sepic (Italy)
1995	Easttec (USA); Neuber-Brenntag Joint Venture (Czech Republic)
1996	Chemproha (joint venture; Netherlands); Brunner (Portugal)
1997	PQS (Spain); Bonnave-Dubar (Belgium); Burris (USA); PQP (Portugal); Christ Chemie (Switzerland)
1998	Milsolv (USA); Whittaker, Clark & Daniels (USA); Teile der Bombardieri-Cambiaghi-Gruppe (Italy); Farleywey Chemicals (UK)
1999	Danby (Netherlands)

642 Deutsche Bahn Archive, HA 50/33.

643 See documents from the supervisory board meeting in November 1993 and spring 1994, in: Deutsche Bahn Archive, HA 50/28 and HA 50/29. On Southchem, see also the archives of the Brenntag headquarters, Brenntag Report 2/1993.

644 Archives of the Brenntag headquarters, Brenntag Report 3/1993.

645 Charles Thurston, "An international affair," *Chemical Market Reporter*, December 19, 1994.

646 *Chemical Market Reporter*, November 27, 1995.

647 Information according to: Scheffels, *125 Jahre*, 35.

In addition to chemical distribution, trading in chemicals remained an important pillar of *Brenntag's* businesses in the 1990s, which were bundled into *Brenntag Interchem*. "Brenntag's second face," said the in-house magazine – "the cream on top," said the responsible board member.[648] On the one hand, *Brenntag* marketed products worldwide on the basis of master agreements with Eastern European producers – similar to what it did in Eastern business in the 1980s. On the other hand, it was active in the international spot business and acted as an intermediary to compensate for short-term mismatches in production and demand on the spot market. In the mid-1990s, *Brenntag* had trading bases in Essen, Berlin, Prague, Warsaw, Moscow, Philadelphia, and Taipei, as well as in Rotterdam and Houston.[649]

In the core business of distribution, *Brenntag* continued its course during the 1990s, intercepting chemical producers' outsourcing interests in sales and logistics and converting them into service offerings. "*Hüls, Bayer,* and *Henkel,* for example, have already transferred corresponding functions and accounts to us on the sales side," the tune went at the supervisory board in the spring of 1996.[650] An example of new services was the *Henkel* Ecolab service concept, in which *Brenntag* supplied *Henkel* Ecolab customers directly with its own mixtures.[651] *Brenntag* saw its role as "an extended arm of the producers."[652] This function had the potential to result in further growth impulses. When a well-known chemical producer wanted sales tasks to be solved for Europe, *Brenntag* sought to take over a specific product or application package for the whole of Europe and align its structures accordingly.[653] In the 1990s, *Brenntag's* regional presence was not yet dense enough to become the exclusive distributor in Europe for a chemical company such as *Dow Chemical*.[654]

In the meantime, the warehouse in Duisburg Ruhrort, central to the large submarket in North Rhine-Westphalia, had reached its limits. *Brenntag* therefore invested around 50 million D-Mark in a modern distribution center in Duisburg-Hüttenheim, which was scheduled to open in 1998.[655] The new standard now included innovative solutions such as the storage of solvents using the so-called

---

648 Archives of the Brenntag headquarters, Brenntag Report 3/1993. See also the Interchem brochure.

649 Stinnes AG, annual reports 1993 and 1995; see also archives of the Brenntag headquarters, Brenntag Report 3/1993. Brenntag withdrew from aromatics trading in Houston and Rotterdam toward the end of the 1990s; see Stinnes AG, annual report 1998.

650 Deutsche Bahn Archive, HA 50/33.

651 Stinnes AG, annual report 1995.

652 Archives of the Brenntag headquarters, Brenntag Report 1/1996.

653 Ibid.

654 *Börsenzeitung* on May 22, 1999, No. 97, 9 (BZ conversation with Wulf Bernotat).

655 Deutsche Bahn Archive, HA 50/33. Stinnes AG, annual report 1998.

Figure 44: Aerial view of the Brenntag site in Duisburg-Hüttenheim, between 1999 and 2004.

gas pendulum process, which could capture and recirculate gases produced during the filling process, as well as an air washer to handle the process exhaust air in inorganic operations.[656]

Brenntag and the IPO of the Parent Company

On December 11, 1997, the supervisory board of *Stinnes AG* came together for a special meeting. The reason was the parent company *Veba's* plans to reorganize its trading, transport, and service areas. *Stinnes AG* was to separate itself from the conventional bulk goods business, concentrate its offering on sophisticated transport chains, and thus reposition itself as a "focused" distribution and logistics company. For this purpose, *Stinnes AG* was scheduled to go public in 1999 in order to allow the capital market to participate in the control of the company with up to 49 percent and to open up future sources of financing. At this point, *Brenntag* was considered the market leader in Europe.[657]

656 Stinnes AG, annual report 1998.
657 Deutsche Bahn Archive, HA 50/39.

With the IPO in mind, preparations were now underway to make the "Stinnes Story" transparent and known to the public. "Nationwide awareness is zero percent," said the head of communications at *Stinnes AG* at the start of the plans.[658] The previously practiced operational management model with various group companies and business areas and *Stinnes AG* as a pure holding company was considered a complex and cumbersome construction that was difficult to convey on the capital market. A reorganization would make the structures clearer. *Brenntag AG* and *Stinnes* founded *Brenntag AG & Co. OHG*, into which they brought the chemical logistics business in return for the granting of corporate rights.[659] As part of the "equity story" of *Stinnes AG*, the dynamic *Brenntag* business was an important driving force. In 1998, the operating output of the *Stinnes* chemical division amounted to 89 million D-Mark, and the return on sales was 2.1 percent.[660] *Brenntag* would continue to strive for a leading global position and, to do so, would continue with its current business model of acquisitions. Nonetheless, on the other hand, it would also systematically develop potential for internal growth – for example, by transferring best practices from the regional subsidiaries.[661] The market presence in the Far East – which had actually been part of the strategic plans from the mid-1990s – was initially put on hold in view of the Asian economic crisis in the second half of the 1990s.

The agenda also included optimizing and standardizing the IT systems. *Brenntag* saw a need to catch up in this area, since in the past the focus had often been more on the acquisitions themselves than on the downstream networking of information technologies.[662] Over the previous decade, *Stinnes AG* had relied on a pragmatic strategy for its data processing. While accounting was managed centrally by the head office, they worked with the companies according to the profit center principle and found special software solutions for operational tasks with SAP. About a thousand workstations were connected to two *IBM* systems.[663] For the future, the management now visualized a global communications and information system that would be based on the *Stinnes* intranet and set new standards across the industry.[664] A chemical logistics concept was developed for

---

658 Quoted from Manfred Helms, "Schwerer Gang," in: *Werben und Verkaufen*, August 20, 1999, Vol. 33, 92.

659 The newly founded divisional companies were operating departments of Stinnes AG that were dependent on income tax and were not tax-independent partnerships. Stinnes AG remained liable to tax, regardless of the civil law reorganization. Supervisory Board meeting on November 11, 1998. Deutsche Bahn Archive, HA 50/42.

660 Information according to *Börsenzeitung*, May 22, 1999, No. 97, 9 (BZ conversation with Wulf Bernotat).

661 Deutsche Bahn Archive, HA 50/39.

662 Deutsche Bahn Archive, HA 50/42.

663 Herbert Schramm on software strategy on November 1, 1988, in: *Blick durch die Wirtschaft*, November 1, 1988.

664 Stinnes AG, annual report 1998.

major customers that could trigger automatic replenishment based on a probe in the chemical container tank that was connected to a modem.[665]

After the IPO of *Stinnes AG* on June 14, 1999, initially met with a rather mixed response from analysts, and attracted interest mainly from institutional investors, the *Stinnes* share price rose sharply by the end of the year.[666] *Brenntag* entered the e-commerce era at approximately the same time as the parent company went public. For the first time, orders could be placed online. [667] It would still take a while for the according practices to work out and for a fully differentiated process to develop in the company.[668] By the end of the 20th century, the *Brenntag Group* had grown to around 4,400 employees worldwide.

---

665 Stinnes AG, annual report 1998.

666 "Die Stinnes-Story spricht sich herum," *Börsenzeitung*, November 3, 1999, No. 212, 9.

667 Stinnes AG, annual report 1999.

668 For more on this, see the next chapter.

12.

Development Under Changing Owners: As a Subsidiary of Stinnes AG, Deutsche Bahn AG, and Under the Ownership of International Financial Investors

When *Stinnes AG* presented the business figures for the previous financial year after the turn of the millennium, the recently slimmed-down logistics group looked back on a record year in its more than 190-year company history: The *Brenntag* parent company's sales were 11.8 billion euros, and the consolidated profit before taxes had grown by over 30 percent to around 165 million euros. The chemicals division – *Brenntag* – made one of the most important contributions to the improved operating figures.[669]

Right at the start of the new millennium, *Brenntag* made a strategically important acquisition: The company acquired the *Neuber Group (Degussa Chemie Handels GmbH)* from *Degussa Hüls* for 33.7 million euros, which gave it new market access in some European countries.[670] With the Vienna-based *Neuber GmbH, Brenntag* was able to significantly strengthen its position in East Central Europe with a view to the upcoming EU accession of Poland, the Czech Republic, Slovakia, and Hungary. The Viennese company was already the market leader in Poland and in the following years would also achieve this position in the other accession countries and in Croatia.[671] In East Central Europe, *Brenntag* had previously only held insignificant market positions. After the acquisition, the company immediately became the market leader and was now the only distribution company able to "offer virtually comprehensive pan-European distribution solutions," a Brenntag executive concluded.[672]

The fact that *Brenntag* was now resolutely pursuing its globalization strategy became even more apparent with another acquisition in 2000. The takeover of the world's fifth largest distributor, *Holland Chemical N. V. (HCI)*, with an

---

669 Information according to Stinnes sees the urge to go to the stock market with mixed feelings, in: *Frankfurter Allgemeine Zeitung*, March 28, 2000, 25. In the chemicals division, sales were up around 10 percent compared to the previous year to 2.3 billion euros; the result was a 56 percent increase to around 71 million euros.

670 See Deutsche Bahn Archive, HA-50-AR-2000-1b, supervisory board meeting on March 22, 2000 (see Baumeister's statements on TOP III).

671 *Prozesstechnik Online*, March 1, 2000, www.prozesstechnik.industrie.de/chemie/degussa-huels-trennt-sich-von-neuber/ [last accessed October 5, 2023].

672 See Gabriele Roolfs-Broihan, "Durch Akquisitionen zum Global Player. Der Weg der Brenntag AG," in: Stefan Odenthal/Gerhard Wissel (eds.), *Strategische Investments in Unternehmen*, Wiesbaden 2004, 118 ff., here 124.

estimated transaction volume of over 550 million euros was one of the largest individual investments in the company history of *Stinnes AG*[673] and was considered the preliminary "highlight of globalization" for *Brenntag*. At the time of acquisition, *HCI* achieved sales of around 1.3 billion euros and brought strong market positions in Northern Europe and South America to the table. Both the portfolio and the regional focus of *HCI's* activities formed valuable additions to the *Brenntag* program and network so that it was described as an "ideal strategic fit."[674] For example, *Brenntag* was now able to reach the Scandinavian market, which had previously been considered one of its weak points. After more than 98 percent of *HCI* shareholders accepted the takeover offer, *Brenntag* became the global market leader in chemical logistics. The company now ranked third in the USA and as the market leader in South America and Europe, where this position continued to be expanded. With the *HCI* acquisition, sales increased by almost 27 percent to around 2.2 billion euros.

A merger of this magnitude promised synergies that were estimated at no less than 132 million euros in advance.[675] The integration of the new structures was to take place as quickly as possible, the supervisory board said, with particular attention on bringing together the different corporate cultures of both companies. *Stinnes AG* also brought with it experience from other business areas in which this had been only partially successful.[676] After the takeover, more than 170 employees worldwide worked for 14 months to merge the structures of *HCI* and *Brenntag*. This approach relied on management team events to strengthen team spirit and the idea of "synergy monitoring" to identify potentially redundant structures.[677] The internal assessment was that the cultural integration went smoothly, with the motto of mutual learning being the main focus.[678] The number of *Brenntag* employees worldwide had now increased from 4,700 to 8,600, including 1,000 in Germany.

---

673 The supervisory board proposed a purchase price of 16.20 euros to 16.79 euros per share, which corresponded to a premium of 54 percent on the current stock market price. In addition, liabilities amounting to 257 million euros would be taken over. See Deutsche Bahn Archive, HA-50-AR-2000-3, supervisory board meeting on September 4, 2000, HA-50, see especially Appendix 1, Bernotat's statements on the HCI acquisition project. In retrospect, HCI's acquisition price was estimated at around 290 million euros; see HA-50-AR-2001-1b, Part 1.

674 Roolfs-Broihan, *Akquisitionen*, 118 ff., here 125. Notes on the acquisition in documents for the supervisory board meeting on September 4, 2000, in: Deutsche Bahn Archive, HA-50-AR-2000-3, see especially Appendix 1, Bernotat's statements on HCI acquisition project.

675 See Deutsche Bahn Archive, HA-50-AR-2000-3, documents at the supervisory board meeting on September 4, 2000.

676 The experiences with the integration of the Swedish logistics group BTL (Schenker) were cited as an example; see ibid., supervisory board meeting on September 4, 2000.

677 Deutsche Bahn Archive, HA-50-AR-2001-2b, supervisory board meeting on June 13, 2001.

678 Roolfs-Broihan, *Akquisitionen*, 118 ff., here 126.

> **Risks of Decentralized Organization**
>
> When, at the beginning of the new millennium, balance sheet manipulation was discovered in a subsidiary of *Stinnes – Schenker do Brasil* – which led to a loss of around 20 million euros, *Stinnes AG* recognized that its risk management still had weak points despite being tightened in recent years. One of the conclusions that the CEO communicated to the supervisory board was that one had to manage one's own operating national companies more closely.[679]

Breaking New Ground in E-Commerce

Stinnes AG also put the expansion of online trading on its agenda as one of the central goals for the new millennium. "The growth opportunities in e-commerce are the leading topic of the year for us," confirmed *Stinnes* CEO Wulf Bernotat in June 2000. After the first start in e-commerce in the late 20th century, the company now wanted to move forward with selected projects. For *Brenntag,* the interesting option was to work with a large chemical marketplace that had been initiated by the chemical companies *Dupont, BASF,* and *Dow*.[680] For chemical logistics companies, the boom in e-commerce presented opportunities and risks. There was a classic logistics task behind every internet transaction, since the goods had to be transported to the customers. Nevertheless, *Brenntag's* management feared declining customer loyalty and increasing pressure on margins as a possible side effect of increased online trading. Against this background, the firm felt it was important to use the new approach to open up new service and business areas, too. In a pilot project, *Brenntag* worked on a sales platform for large suppliers, with functions for order processing and scheduling, which promised cost reductions for customers. In addition, a platform was built to optimize the purchase of non-strategic chemicals, the so-called C chemicals, for customers. The platform was designed as a single sourcing partner, meaning it offered the customer the entire product range from a single source and was intended to include chemicals from *Brenntag* and – depending on the customer's wishes –

---

679 See Deutsche Bahn Archive, HA-50-ASR-2000-1b, Part 2, Bernotat's statements to the supervisory board on March 23, 2000. See also the auditor's statements on the presentation of the 1999 annual financial statements, in: ibid., part 1, as well as minutes of the supervisory board meeting of December 14, 1999, in: ibid., part 2.

680 Deutsche Bahn Archive, HA-50-AR-2000-2A, supervisory board meeting on June 7, 2000.

also other suppliers and distributors. *Solvay*, along with other firms, also was to be involved with this platform.[681] For the technical solutions in online trading, some of the same software components that were already in use at other Stinnes companies were also used here in order to exploit synergy effects. One of the new platforms for chemical goods was rolled out at the end of 2000, initially for large customers in the USA.[682] The chemical platform Elemica followed soon thereafter, but *Brenntag* only had a one percent stake in it.[683]

In 2001, Dr. Klaus Engel took over as CEO of *Brenntag* from his predecessor, Rients Visser, who retired after eight years in this position.[684] Shortly before, far-reaching changes had taken place at *Veba*, which still held the majority of *Stinnes AG* after *Stinnes* went public.[685]

Since the middle of 2000, *Veba* had merged with the *VIAG* conglomerate to form *E.on* and, having grown into one of the largest German corporations with around 200,000 employees, was now focusing on its core business of energy. The stake in *Stinnes AG* no longer fit with the future direction of the new energy giant. It therefore became apparent that *E.on* would sell its majority stake in *Stinnes AG* in the medium term, either en bloc or by issuing the shares on the stock exchange. Meanwhile, *Stinnes AG* continued to grow. The focus on logistics activities with higher margins supported this development.[686] Inspired by the *Brenntag* acquisition of *HCI*, *Stinnes AG* exceeded its own target figures in the 2001 financial year and generated a record performance of 317 million euros – which represented an increase of 26 percent compared to the previous year.[687] In addition, *Brenntag's* field of activity would soon be expanded with a targeted attempt to gain access to the Asian markets. The reasoning was that none of its major competitors were currently active in Asia, so in the near future it would initially plan to have 50 percent stakes in Thailand, Malaysia, and Singapore.[688]

681 Ibid.

682 See Deutsche Bahn Archive, HA-50-AR-2001-1b Part 1, table templates for the supervisory board meeting on March 21, 2001.

683 HA-50-AR-2001-1b Part 1.

684 Press release from Brenntag AG, March 19, 2001. Engel had been a board member of Brenntag since 1999.

685 Instead of the planned 49 percent, due to the rather weak public interest in the first tranche, only 34.5 percent of the shares were sold, so Veba and E.on still held 65.5 percent of the shares in Stinnes AG in 2001; the plans for the next stock market step were delayed. See *Börsen-Zeitung*, November 27, 2001, 10; see also "Stinnes plant zweiten Börsenschritt für Jahr 2000," in: *Die Welt*, November 24, 1999.

686 See also Deutsche Bahn Archive, HA-50-AR-2001, 1b, Part 1, supervisory board meeting on March 21, 2001.

687 See "Stinnes übertrifft 2001 eigene Planungen," in: *Die Welt*, March 21, 2002, 14.

688 "Stinnes will auf Einkaufstour gehen," in: *Deutsche Verkehrszeitung*, April 3, 2002.

Deutsche Bahn AG and Stinnes

Soon afterward, *Deutsche Bahn AG (DB)* signaled its interest in taking over *Stinnes AG*. The main focus of *Bahn* boss Hartmut Mehdorn was on the *Stinnes* subsidiary *Schenker*, a freight forwarding company that strategically complemented *Deutsche Bahn's* logistics activities. In July 2002, the basic decision was made that *DB* would acquire the 65.4 percent stake in *Stinnes AG* from *E.on* and make a public takeover offer to the other shareholders of *Stinnes AG*.[689] With a price of 2.5 billion euros for 65 percent of the shares, the purchase of the *Stinnes* share package was *DB's* largest acquisition. In February 2003, *Stinnes AG* and, with it, *Brenntag* were transferred to the *Deutsche Bahn AG* group.[690] This step had significant consequences for both *Stinnes AG* and its subsidiary *Brenntag*. While the *Stinnes* CEO had developed very different goals for 2008 – the 200th anniversary[691] of the AG – at the beginning of the millennium,[692] the long-standing company now found itself in a constellation in which the functionality of its structures had become outdated from the perspective of the decision-makers involved. The *DB* had only wanted to temporarily acquire those parts of the company that did not appear useful for the railway's logistics chain and then sell them again soon. Unlike *Schenker*, *Brenntag's* service profile did not fit into a rail transport and logistics group. The company tied up *DB* capital that was urgently needed for investments in rail transport and improving capital resources.

For *Stinnes AG*, the sale to *Deutsche Bahn AG* marked the beginning of a division of the company, including the dissolution of the company umbrella that previously spanned the business divisions. "Today's *Stinnes AG* will no longer exist in its current form in the long term," explained the new CEO Malmström at a special meeting of the supervisory board in October 2002.[693] However, *DB*

---

689 For the takeover offer, see the special supervisory board meeting on August 20, 2002, in: Deutsche Bahn Archive, HA-50-AR-2002-3b-parts 1 and 2. See also *Börsen-Zeitung*, June 28, 2002, 9.

690 At the special general meeting of Stinnes AG on February 17, 2003, the squeeze-out was approved with 99.97 percent of the votes; see *Deutsche Bahn* Archive, HA-50-AR-2003-1b, Part 2.

691 This year went back to the part of the company that was founded by Mathias Stinnes in 1808, a company that was active in shipping and coal mining. See Domberg/Rathje, *Stinnes*, 9 ff.; Stinnes AG, *175 Jahre Stinnes – Die Kaufleute aus Mülheim*, Düsseldorf 1983; Mathias Stinnes GmbH, *150 Jahre Mathias Stinnes*, Darmstadt 1958.

692 By 2008, Stinnes AG was to become one of the "most profitable logistics companies in the world." See Wolfgang Pott, "Kronprinzen gesucht!", in: *Welt am Sonntag*, August 12, 2001. As expressed to the press on various occasions, Bernotat had preferred the idea of another IPO to a sale to a major investor.

693 Deutsche Bahn Archive, HA-50-AR-2002-4b.

announced that the current headquarters of *Stinnes AG* would continue to exist until at least the end of 2003.

The Separation of Brenntag from the Group of Deutsche Bahn Companies

This marked the beginning of a phase of change for *Brenntag*. Discussions with potential investors began in the course of 2003. In addition, *Brenntag* management prepared for the forthcoming separation from the group by expanding the headquarters and installing functions that had previously been carried out by *Stinnes*.[694] At the same time, *Brenntag* continued its previous business policy of sharpening its profile in distribution, trading, and logistics services in the chemical industry. On the German market, *Brenntag* was in the process of improving its position and profitability through a joint venture with the Hamburg chemical distributor *Biesterfeld,* founded in the summer of 2002.[695] In the US, however, *Brenntag* was confronted with asbestos lawsuits. These were partly due to legacy issues from companies that had been taken over, and they presented themselves differently in individual cases.[696]

At this point, *DB* started preparing for its IPO, which was only called off in 2007 with the start of the financial crisis. In order to maximize the *Brenntag* sales price, it initiated a bidding competition to which financial investors were also invited. By spring 2003, the business press suspected that *Deutsche Bahn* had received various bids and expressions of interest for *Brenntag*, including from private equity firms such as *Kohlberg-Kravis-Roberts, Carlyle Partners, Blackstone, Advent, BC Partners,* and *Bain Capital.* The *Metzler Bank* was supposed to handle the sale for *Deutsche Bahn AG.* The offers submitted at the beginning of 2003 ranged between 1.2 and 1.5 billion euros.[697] By July 2003, the group of interested parties had narrowed down to *Bain Capital* (Boston), *Blackstone Group* (New York), and the two London companies *Cinven* and *CVC Capital Partners.*[698] Ultimately, the favorite among the bidders was the US company *Bain Capital,*

---

694 See Deutsche Bahn Archive, HA-50-AR-2003-1b-Part 2, supervisory board meeting of Stinnes AG on March 17, 2003.

695 For the Biesterfeld project, cf. Deutsche Bahn Archive, HA-50-AR-2002-3b-Part 1. See also Deutsche Bahn Archive, HA-50-AR-2003-1b-Part 2, supervisory board meeting of Stinnes AG on March 17, 2003.

696 Deutsche Bahn Archive, HA-50-AR-2002-3b-Part 1; HA-50-AR-2002-3b-Part 2; HA-50-AR-2003-1b-Part 2.

697 Juliana Ratner/Lina Saigol, "Deutsche Bahn gets eight bids for chemicals arm Brenntag," in: *Financial Times*, April 16, 2003, 15; see also *Chemical Week*, April 30, 2003, 8, and *Chemical Week*, April 23, 2003, 6; see also dpa/afx european focus, January 30, 2003; "Erste Gebote für Stinnes-Tochter Brenntag," in: *Financial Times Deutschland*, January 30, 2003.

698 *Chemical Week*, July 16, 2003, 4.

which was supposed to jointly take over the *Stinnes* subsidiaries *Brenntag* and *Interfer* from *Deutsche Bahn*. "We want to get this done this year," confirmed the railway company spokesman at the end of November 2003.[699]

Brenntag's expected resilience and financing strength were a crucial prerequisite for the success of the transaction. The auditors involved in the due diligence analysis highlighted the growth in sales, EBIT margin, and number of employees that had characterized *Brenntag* over the last decade.

The purchase by the financial investor meant a major effort for *Brenntag*, as it had to raise the funds for the transaction itself. *Bain Capital* only brought in around 20 percent of the necessary funds, a contemporary recalled looking back.[700] In the

Figure 45: Former company headquarters in Mülheim an der Ruhr in 2011.

leveraged buyout process taken by the investor, the burden of financing, which mainly relied on debt capital, was transferred to the company to be purchased.[701] The sale was completed in March 2004 at a price of 1.25 billion euros[702] – which at the time was considered the largest company purchase to date by a private

699 "Bahn steht kurz vor dem Verkauf von Brenntag und Interfer," in: *dpa/afx*, November 28, 2003.

700 See conversation with Mr. Paul Hahn, former Vice President of Finance and Accounting Brenntag AG until summer 2003, on March 16, 2023.

701 Investment funds managed by Bain took over the Brenntag Group via acquisition companies, including share and asset deals through Brenntag Beteiligungs GmbH, an important role; see archives of the Brenntag headquarters, annual report of Brenntag Investor Holding GmbH 2004.

702 Ann-Christin Achleitner et al., *Brenntag. Primary Buyout and Exit Decision of Bain Capital*, Munich 2012, www.thecasecentre.org/products/view?id=110183 [last accessed October 5, 2023].

equity company in Germany.[703] A few years later, a new superlative was to be achieved with the next change of ownership.[704]

From Bain Capital to BC Partners

As a result of the separation from the *DB/Stinnes* group, *Brenntag's* liabilities increased significantly. In spring 2004, total debt amounted to around one billion euros, of which around 800 million euros were bank loans.[705] In two rounds of refinancing, the private equity company *Brenntag* withdrew equity capital in order to benefit from the improved market conditions for debt capital and to increase returns through leverage effects. Given the low-interest rates and high liquidity on the debt capital markets, increasing the debt burden was more profitable from the investors' perspective than using equity capital.[706] During the first "recapitalization" at the beginning of 2005, *Bain* took out around 200 million euros, which were transferred to *Brenntag* as new debt. After the second so-called recap amounting to around 1.9 billion euros – "record volume for 2005," according to the business press – *Bain* probably withdrew around 450 million euros of equity.[707] Due to the higher liabilities, *Brenntag's* rating temporarily fell from BB- to B+.[708] However, given its solid business development, this worsened rating did not mask any real credit risk – *Brenntag* was able to cope with the debt burden and pay it off from its stable cash flow.[709] The Americans had shown "how things work when it comes to buyouts," commented the *Börsen-Zeitung*. The US investor had multiplied its own stake in a comparatively short period of time.[710] In the summer of 2006, *Bain Capital* sold its stake in *Brenntag* for around three billion euros to the London investment company *BC Partners*, in a transaction

---

703 Ann-Christin Achleitner et al., "Value creation drivers in a secondary buyout – the acquisition of Brenntag by BC Partners," in: *Quantitative research in Financial Markets 6* (2014), 278–301.

704 At the time, this transfer was considered one of the largest deals by a financial investor in Germany, see, e.g., *Chemical Week*, July 26, 2006, 7; "Brenntag wird größtes deutsches Buy-out—Preis 3,5 Mrd. Euro," in: *Börsen-Zeitung*, July 26, 2006, 1.

705 Klaus Oster, "Stolperfallen am High Yield Market," in: *Börsen-Zeitung*, May 13, 2004, 17.

706 Walter Becker, "Schlummernde Werte," in: *Börsen-Zeitung*, July 26, 2006, 1; see also https://www.presseportal.de/pm/30377/852676 [last accessed February 5, 2024].

707 Ibid. (In June 2006, around 390 million debts were added; see *Euroweek*, June 2, 2006, 41.) At the beginning of 2006, the parent company's retained earnings were distributed as an advance dividend; Brenntag Investor Holding GmbH, Konzern-Anhang für den Zeitraum vom 1.1.–31.12.2005, 11.

708 The approximately 1.9 billion euros contained, among others, senior secured loans worth € 1.269 billion, a nine-and-a-half year second lien worth € 275 million, and a mezzanine loan worth € 345 million; see Lisa Bushrod, "Refinancings," in: *European Venture Capital Journal*, February 1, 2006; see also Walter Becker, "Schulden-Multiples auf dem Höhepunkt," in: *Börsen-Zeitung* from December 2, 2005, 12th issue, "Marktbedingungen für Rekapitalisierung günstig" in: *Börsen-Zeitung*, January 25, 2006, 2.

709 Walter Becker, "Schlummernde Werte," in: *Börsen-Zeitung*, July 26, 2006, 1.

710 Ibid.

financed primarily by debt.[711] In July 2006, *Brenntag's* debts amounted to 2.15 billion euros.[712] At the time of the closing in September 2006, the *Brenntag* rating slipped deeper into the "junk status" of B-,[713] due to the high liabilities, but the prospects of the chemical distributor, which had now grown to over 9,000 employees worldwide, were still considered promising.[714]

Brenntag was an interesting investment primarily because of its steadily increasing business volume and its strong market position. The return on sales of 5 percent played a minor role. But the return on equity of 24 percent, which had risen to 37 percent by 2006, was impressive.[715] Due to the high investments in technical assets, the advisory investment bankers got the impression that *Brenntag's* systems were "gold-plated."[716]

Since becoming a standalone in 2004, *Brenntag* had remained on course to further expand its market leadership in some core regions. For example, the company had set up new bases in the Czech Republic, Romania, and Poland through the subsidiary *Brenntag CEE* (formerly *Neuber*), which managed business in Eastern Europe, and planned to set up a subsidiary in Russia by the end of 2005.[717] At the beginning of 2005, the *Brenntag Kimya Tic. Ltd. Sti* was founded as a sales company in Istanbul to further strengthen its presence in Turkey, which had existed since 2003.[718] And with the acquisition of *Albion Chemicals*, it was able to gain a stronger presence in the UK market, which it had long sought. In addition, the chemical division of *Schweizerhall* was acquired. Both were considered to round off the European network, as Daniel Pithois, the CEO of *Brenntag Management GmbH* responsible for European business, explained.[719] According to contemporary industry observers, *Brenntag* also

711 Siegfried Grass, "Inside Brenntag. Wette auf die Zukunft," in: *Handelsblatt*, July 31, 2006, www.handelsblatt.com/unternehmen/industrie/inside-brenntag-wette-auf-die-zukunft/2686922.html [last accessed January 18, 2024]. See also "Kirkland führt Bain Capital beim Brenntag-Verkauf," in: *JUVE*, July 27, 2006, www.juve.de/deals/milliardenschwerer-investorenwechsel-kirkland-fuehrung-bain-capital-beim-brenntag-verkauf/ [last accessed October 5th. 2023]; "Bain Capital sells Brenntag to BC Partners," Brenntag press release, July 25, 2006; Achleitner et al., "Value creation drivers."

712 Information according to ibid.

713 "BC Partners zurrt Brenntag-Kauf fest," in: *Börsen-Zeitung*, October 5, 2006, 10.

714 The rating agency Standard & Poors also saw the potential for an investment grade rating, but this was currently not suitable due to the financial strain. "Bain Capital reicht Brenntag für 3.5 Milliarden Euro weiter," in: *Börsen-Zeitung*, August 26, 2006, 9.

715 Return on sales and return on equity after interest expenses, taxes, depreciation, and amortization (EBITDA); information according to Achleitner et al., "Value creation drivers."

716 This is the impression of Dr. Steffen Kastner, Director at Goldman Sachs, as quoted in ibid.

717 "Austrian Brenntag CEE plans Russian Subsidiary 2005," in: *APA (Austrian Press Agency)*, May 10, 2005.

718 *Logistik Inside*, February 2, 2005; *Verkehrs-Rundschau*, February 2, 2005.

719 *Chemical Week*, May 31, 2006, 21. See also "Brenntag makes UK move with Albion," in: *ICIS Chemical Business*, June 5, 2006; "Schweizerhall verkauft Chemiebereich für 93 Mio. CHF an Brenntag (AF)," in: *AWP Premium Swiss News*, May 31, 2006.

continued a brisk growth strategy in the US market.[720] The strategy was intended to remain constant even after the transition from *Bain* to *BC*, although the change in ownership was preceded by a change in personnel at the top. The previous CEO Engel took on the same role at *Degussa* and was replaced by Stephen R. Clark, who had previously headed *Brenntag North America Inc.*[721] Clark had worked for *Brenntag* since 1981 and had been a board member since 1993. He reiterated the "significant role" that acquisitions would continue to play in the company's growth.[722]

In a press release published by *Bain Capital*, management highlighted the "expansion of *Brenntag's* leadership position" due to "profitable organic growth and the integration of key acquisitions."[723] From the perspective of the previous owner, *Brenntag* was in a good position to continue its proven growth strategy with the support of *BC Partners*. The new owner praised the "broad diversification of Brenntag's business," the "very stable business portfolio," and the "significant development potential" and announced his intention to prepare *Brenntag* for a possible IPO. With a global market share of 7 percent, its growth potential appeared to be far from exhausted. By the summer of 2006, the number of employees had increased to around 9,200.[724] The company now wanted to make further acquisitions, especially in Asia.

The takeover of the Asian chemical distribution activities of the French chemical group *Rhodia* in 2008 was an important step toward this goal.[725] This gave *Brenntag* better access to the dynamic markets in the Asia-Pacific region. At the same time, they were now able to distinguish themselves as the exclusive distribution partner for *Rhodia*. Nevertheless, the extent of *Brenntag's* Asian presence was still limited at this time: Around 160 to 200 employees were employed throughout Asia around 2008/09. Since the company's IT was still very closely linked to *Rhodia*, appropriate specialists were initially hired.[726] In other regions, however, the implementation of the expansion strategy continued to progress – in 2006 alone, *Brenntag* bought ten chemical distribution companies

---

720 Chemical Week speaks of an "aggressive growth strategy"; see *Chemical Week*, November 22, 2006, 20.

721 *Frankfurter Allgemeine Zeitung*, May 11, 2006; Achleitner et al., "Value creation drivers."

722 "We are not bound by any constraints with regard to size, geography, or product lines when evaluating acquisitions," explained the new CEO, quoted from: "Distribution: private equity changes face of chemical landscape," in: *Chemical Week*, November 22, 2006, 20.

723 Brenntag press release, July 25, 2006; Brenntag in Übernahmegesprächen," in: *Frankfurter Allgemeine Zeitung*, July 27, 2006.

724 Ibid., 15.

725 *ICIS Chemical News and Intelligence*, September 30, 2008; *Financial Deals Tracker, MarketLine*, September 30, 2008.

726 See archives of the Brenntag headquarters, still unsigned, documentation of discussions between Schmitt-Köpke and former Brenntag employees from January 22, 2024. For the number of employees, see *Magazin Together*, 2009.

with a total sales volume of 700 million euros. A further four company takeovers followed in 2007, nine in 2008, three in 2009, and four in 2010.[727]

From the Financial Crisis to the IPO

Since the transfer from *Brenntag* to *BC Partners*, global economic conditions had changed noticeably. Around 2007, the US market for subprime mortgages was in crisis, which worried international financial markets. When the US investment bank *Lehman Brothers* finally collapsed in September 2008, the turmoil came to a head, and the global economy slipped into a crisis.[728] Thus far, *Brenntag* had usually been able to cushion economic downturns or crises well. The broad international spread of its business and the lack of dependence on one or a few industries strengthened its resilience to crises and compensated for economic fluctuations more quickly. But now the global economy stalled, so *Brenntag* felt the consequences of the crisis despite its level of diversification and its global presence. For the first time, *Brenntag* was not able to avoid redundancy lay-offs.[729]

With the global financial crisis, the scope of action for private equity companies temporarily became narrower: The capital markets relevant for secondary buyouts were in decline – and the banks no longer financed company acquisitions with a high debt-to-earnings value ratio, so it became more difficult to acquire investments to sell from the portfolio to another financial investor. Nevertheless, the new owner, *BC Partners,* had already signaled during the acquisition that it did not intend to keep *Brenntag* in its investment portfolio permanently.[730]

When the price level for shares stabilized again after the crisis-related slump in 2009, *BC Partners* decided to partially sell the company through an IPO. After an ice age on the German IPO market, *Brenntag's* stock debut was seen in the business press as one of the "icebreakers" on this market. *Brenntag's* business model also proved its worth during the financial crisis, provided stable margins, and offered a long-term, transparent cash flow, according to the involved US investment bank *J. P. Morgan*.[731] In fact, the key figures indicated sustainable development. In the 2009 financial year – a year of crisis – *Brenntag* generated

---

727 Information according to Achleitner et al., "Value creation drivers."

728 For details, see *Deutsche Bundesbank,* Konjunktur in Deutschland, Monatsbericht November 2008.

729 See conversation with Dr. Gabriele Roolfs-Broihan on September 7, 2023.

730 *Börsen-Zeitung,* July 26, 2006, 9; see also *Chemical News & Intelligence (ICIS News),* July 25, 2006.

731 See, e.g., B. W. Ehrensberger/K. Schachinger, "IPO- Eisbrecher KDG und Brenntag," in: *Euro am Sonntag,* February 27, 2010, 6. See also *Börsen-Zeitung,* January 8, 2010.

Figure 46: First Brenntag share price at the stock market debut in Frankfurt on March 29, 2010.

Figure 47: "Deutsche Börse welcomes Brenntag."

sales of 6.4 billion euros and was able to reduce the level of debt through its cash flow in recent years.[732]

The plan was to go public in the first quarter of 2010, combined with a capital increase of 500 million euros.[733] "It is not an easy market for new issues at the moment, but we are really confident," explained *Brenntag* CEO Clark in advance of the IPO.[734]

A banking consortium consisting of *Deutsche Bank*, *Goldman Sachs*, *J. P. Morgan,* and *Merrill Lynch* was supposed to take the stock public. The date for the initial listing was set for March 29, 2010. The stock market debut was considered a success: While the first price of 51.50 euros was above the issue price of 50 euros, the first day of trading closed with a price of 54.11 euros, which corresponded to a subscription profit of around 8 percent. The issue volume amounted to 747.5 million euros.[735] A new chapter in the company's 135-year history had begun, said the company's management, who now aimed for inclusion in the MDAX exchange as the next step.[736]

With the capital increase, *Brenntag* was able to further consolidate its financial status and, in particular, reduce the high-interest mezzanine financing, which significantly improved its rating.[737] On June 21, 2010, *Brenntag AG* was included in the MDAX.[738]

Into the Far East: The Acquisition of EAC

After the successful IPO, the conditions were good for a continuation of the expansion course with fresh capital. At the time of its IPO, Brenntag served approximately 150,000 customers and maintained approximately 400 distribution centers in 60 countries.

The takeover of the Asian distributor *EAC Industrial Ingredients (EAC)* formed an important basis for the long-held plan to expand its market position in Asia.[739]

---

732 See Walter Becker, "Brenntag kurz vor Börsengang," in: *Börsen-Zeitung,* March 13, 2010, 9. (At the end of 2009, net debt amounted to 1.8 billion euros. The net debt ratio, i.e., the ratio of net financial debt to operating result, fell between 2006 to 2009 from 6.4 to 3.8.)

733 Karsten Seibel, "Brenntag gibt Startschuss für den Börsengang," in: *Die Welt,* February 26, 2010, 22.

734 Quoted from "Börsenkandidat Brenntag will Marktführerschaft ausbauen," in: *Die Welt,* March 5, 2010, 17.

735 Karsten Seibel, "Brenntag beschert Aktionären hohe Zeichnungsgewinne," in: *Die Welt,* March 30, 2010, 15. See also Stephan Balling, "Erfolgreiches Börsen-Debüt für Brenntag," in: *Börsen-Zeitung,* March 30, 2010, 17.

736 According to CEO Clark and CFO Buchsteiner after the stock market launch; see *Die Welt,* March 30, 2010, 15.

737 *ICIS Chemical News (Chemical News & Intelligence),* March 31, 2010.

738 "Brenntag joins MDAX," in: *ENP Newswire,* June 9, 2010; *Tagesvorschau* June 21, 2010, in: AWP *Premium Swiss News,* June 18, 2010.

739 "Brenntag significantly expands its market presence in Asia Pacific," in: *ENP Newswire,* July 6, 2010; "Brenntag erwirbt asiatischen Distributeur," in *Börsen-Zeitung,* July 6, 2010, 10; "Thailand: East Asiatic Company's industrial ingredients business acquired by Germany-based Brenntag Holding," in: *Thai News Service – Business News,* August 2, 2010.

In the summer of 2010, *Brenntag* acquired the sales company from the Danish *East Asia Company Ltd. A/S* for a price of 160 million euros. With *EAC's* business, *Brenntag* gained approximately 8,000 customers and a network of 27 bases in nine countries – Thailand, Vietnam, Indonesia, Philippines, Malaysia, Singapore, Cambodia, India, and Bangladesh. *Brenntag* CEO Clark explained that they would now be able to develop their own market position "from a mainstay in Asia" to an "established operational network." Exceptional growth opportunities were expected in Asia, especially in the cosmetics, pharmaceuticals, food, and coatings segments. After the takeover, the plan was to integrate the existing structures and introduce the brand name "Brenntag" within a short period of time. The long-established name "EAC," which had been closely linked to the Danish East Asiatic trade in Thailand since the late 19th century, thus faded into the background.[740] At the time of the takeover, *EAC* had around 800 employees, significantly more than *Brenntag* previously employed in Asia. Now the smaller existing *Brenntag* structure had to be implemented into the larger organizational context of *EAC* without majorizing it. Hence, many organizational structures and processes from *EAC* business practice remained in place. The corporate cultures of *Brenntag* and *EAC* fit together well due to similarities, recalled a *Brenntag* manager who helped set up the business on-site.[741] The basic idea was to continue what was already there instead of forcefully imposing a "Brenntag culture."

This consideration corresponded to an approach that the company had already cultivated during Stinnes' time and which – as was ideally hoped – would combine the best of the different corporate worlds. Nevertheless, in practice this approach had repeatedly reached its limits as the company expanded. However, comparatively little is known about the specific course of integrating company functions at the micro level.[742] At the aggregate level, the process can usually only be understood abstractly: *Brenntag* CFO Jürgen Buchsteiner estimated the synergy potential from the *EAC* takeover at over five million euros, which was to be tapped by 2015.[743]

---

740 See the comment of a departing EAC manager, in: "East Asiatic company's industrial ingredients business," in: *Thai News Service*, August 2, 2010.

741 See archives of the Brenntag headquarters, still unsigned, documentation of a contemporary witness conversation by Carola Schmitt-Köpke, January 22, 2024.

742 Due to the lack of availability of sources, it is not possible to reconstruct the integration processes in detail within the scope of this book. Case studies from the perspective of the acquired companies may need to be included here.

743 *Börsen-Zeitung*, July 6, 2010, 10.

After this acquisition, *Brenntag* management's strategy was still aimed at continued growth, both in Asia and in other regions. The CFO explained that the "powder is still dry" and that they wanted to continue to invest around 150 million euros in company acquisitions every year.[744] "We always have five to ten acquisition candidates on our radar."[745]

Meanwhile, the share price developed positively. At the end of September 2010, a *Brenntag* share already cost 61.40 euros. *BC Partners* still held a large proportion of the company's shares. The *Brenntag* shares of *BC Partners* and *Bain Capital*, which still held shares, were pooled in the holding company *Brachem Acquisition S. C. A.*, which had acted as an "acquisition vehicle" during the transition from *Bain* to *BC Partners* and now held 71 percent of the share capital. Internally, however, the low free float of the shares was seen as an obstacle to price development.[746] When it went public, the company had subjected itself to a six-month sales restriction and thus limited the sale of shares. This holding period expired on September 29, 2010, so that a further 20 percent of the capital became available to the Frankfurt Stock Exchange at the beginning of October 2010.[747] The favorable development of the DAX stock index and the high demand for *Brenntag* shares allowed *BC Partners* to increase the issue price from tranche to tranche. Although financial analysts sometimes warned private investors to be cautious when it came to making such investments, the *Brenntag* share should, they claimed, develop into a stable and profitable security in the future.[748]

---

744 Ibid.

745 Annette Becker, "Das CFO Interview – Interview mit Jürgen Buchsteiner," in: *Börsen-Zeitung*, January 15, 2011, 11.

746 Annette Becker, "Brenntag verschreibt sich der Diversifikation," in: *Börsen-Zeitung*, September 21, 2010, 10.

747 "Brenntag mit gelungenem Börsenstart," in: *Manager Magazin*, March 29, 2010, www.manager-magazin.de/finanzen/artikel/a-686126.html [last accessed October 5, 2023]; "Brenntag setzt auf Schuldenabbau und Zukäufe," in: *Frankfurter Allgemeine Zeitung*, March 18, 2010, www.faz.net/aktuell/finanzen/aktien/boersengang-brenntag-setzt-auf-schuldenabbau-und-zukaeufe-1358279.html [last accessed October 5, 2023]; Brenntag AG, annual report 2011. At the beginning of October, BC Partners sold eleven million Brenntag shares at 60.75 euros each; see *Börse online*, October 7, 2010, 53.

748 See, e.g., B. Jörg Lang/Richard Pfadenhauer, "Der große Aktiencheck," in: *Euro*, July 1, 2010, 26; Kathrin Sandmair, "Die Gewinner aus der 2. Reihe," in: *Focus-Money*, June 30, 2010, 8 ("Investors, however, are better off keeping their hands off of papers like Brenntag").

13

Independent Again:
Brenntag from 2010 to the Present

In its first financial year as a listed stock corporation, *Brenntag's* sales rose to 7.6 billion euros, and its net income (EBITDA) to 598 million euros. This meant the company was able to offset and even overcompensate for the 14 percent decline in sales that occurred in 2009, at the height of the financial crisis.[749] In January 2011, the existing shareholders sold a further seven million shares at a price of 71.50 euros each. After this third placement on the stock exchange, almost two thirds of the *Brenntag* shares were now in free float, and the former majority shareholder *Brachem Acquisitions* – the financial vehicle dominated by *BC Partners* – had reduced its stake to 36 percent. *Brenntag's* market capitalization during this time amounted to around four billion euros – a volume in view of which *Brenntag* management classified the risk of a hostile takeover by a financial investor as low.[750]

Drivers of Growth in a Fragmented Market

The global chemical distribution market remained, however, highly fragmented. With local and regional reach, thousands of companies were active worldwide.[751] As the *Boston Consulting Group* assumed in a study, the five largest companies in the industry together had a market share of less than 20 percent.[752] Nevertheless, industry observers saw greater development opportunities in the market for chemical distribution than in the chemical industry in general, since the transfer of tasks from chemical producers to distributors stimulated growth in specific areas. Unlike logistics companies, distribution companies took ownership of the goods to be processed – to transport or store them, repackage them, mix them, and deliver them to customers in smaller quantities.[753] Reducing complexity for

---

749 "Brenntag will 500 Millionen Euro aus Börsengang," in: *Frankfurter Allgemeine Zeitung*, February 26, 2010.

750 *Börsen-Zeitung*, January 20, 2011, 11. See interview with Jürgen Buchsteiner, in: *Börsen-Zeitung*, January 15, 2011, 11.

751 Guido Hartmann, "Auf großer Einkaufstour," in: *Welt am Sonntag*, October 3, 2010. In Brenntag's 2015 annual report, 29, the number is estimated at more than 10,000 distributors worldwide.

752 Quoted from Klaus Schachinger, "Krisenfester Champion," in: *Euro am Sonntag*, October 15, 2011, 24.

753 For the distribution tasks, see Walter Becker, "Brenntag kurz vor Börsengang," in: *Börsen-Zeitung*, March 13, 2010, 9.

producers was considered a key factor in the distribution business – and the distributor's global network was a beneficial factor.[754]

Brenntag's executives therefore constantly emphasized the further expansion of the company as a central strategic goal. As a leitmotif in public statements, two drivers of growth stood side by side: on the one hand, organic growth, which was based on demand for chemicals and benefited from outsourcing trends, and on the other hand, acquisitive growth through company acquisitions, which formed an integral part of the business model.[755]

The focus of medium-term planning initially continued to be on the Asian market, into which around 40 percent of the acquisition funds were to flow.[756] China still represented a "blank spot" on the map of *Brenntag's* activities. Entering the fast-growing, highly regulated market in the People's Republic was considered difficult and could initially only be achieved through joint ventures with Chinese companies.[757] In June 2011, *Brenntag* reached agreements to acquire a 51 percent stake in solvent specialist *Zhong Yung (International) Chemical Ltd.* for 43 million euros, while the second tranche of 49 percent was planned for 2016.[758] A milestone, the management thought. An executive involved explained that five years of market research had been carried out to find the right partner. *Zhong Yung* operated from regional bases in Shanghai, Tjianjin, and Ghuangzhou.[759]

A few months later, with the acquisition of the *British Multisol Group (Multisol Group Ltd.)* for around 127 million euros, a new segment was added to *Brenntag's* activities – the market for lubricant additives. In addition to the home market in Great Britain, *Multisol* was represented in several European countries and in South Africa.[760]

In the meantime, there had been a change at *Brenntag's* top management: Since the general meeting on June 22, 2011, Steven Holland, formerly Chief Operating Officer who had come to the company as part of the *Albion* takeover, was now at the helm of the Mülheim-based firm. Stephen Clark, the outgoing CEO, moved to the supervisory board.[761] "Brenntag should be in the DAX in five years," said the new CEO, defining his next major stock market goal in spring 2012.

---

754 See, for example, graphic representation in the Brenntag 2012 annual report, 12 f.
755 See Buchsteiner Interview; see also *Börsenzeitung*, September 3, 2011, 9.
756 See Buchsteiner Interview.
757 Conversation with Dr. Gabriele Roolfs-Broihan on September 7, 2023.
758 See also *Brenntag Together* 02/11, 4, and *Börsen-Zeitung*, November 11, 2011, 13.
759 *Brenntag Together* 02/11, 5.
760 "Brenntag schlägt bei Schmierstoffen zu," in: *Börsen-Zeitung*, September 3, 2011, 9.
761 For the personal details, see *Börsen-Zeitung*, March 22, 2011, 7.

"We Want to Be the Safest Chemical Distributor"

As a listed company, *Brenntag's* regulatory obligations changed, requiring more centralized control of tasks arising from chemical-specific risks. At the same time, social awareness regarding the use of chemicals had become more differentiated over the past few decades.

At the European level, the chemicals regulation authority REACH ("Registration, Evaluation, Authorization, and Restriction of Chemicals") had overseen the handling of chemicals since 2007. It replaced a large number of existing regulations at the European level and regulated the use of around 100,000 chemical substances: If they were manufactured in the EU or imported into the EU, they had to be registered, while the use of unregistered substances was banned.[762] There were concerns and criticism in advance about the EU's chemical policy initiative from the ranks of the chemical industry and chemical trade, especially medium-sized companies. There were fears about the associated adaptation requirements – for example, the additional costs, the increased administrative effort, and reduced chemical availability. The concern was that these aspects could ultimately affect innovation and competitiveness.[763] Larger companies, on the other hand, found it comparatively easy to implement the new regulations. A new team was formed at *Brenntag* to introduce and control the processes and procedures now required both centrally and locally.[764] *Brenntag* could also support customers and suppliers in meeting the requirements and registering the products in accordance with the REACH regulations.

In line with the tightening of regulations, public understanding of the quality of products and services also developed. Within the group, quality management systems ensured uniform standards at the regional level.[765]

Nevertheless, a few years after its IPO, the company involuntarily gained greater public attention due to an incident that was only indirectly related to its business policy: A French *Brenntag* company had supplied silicone oils to the French health technology manufacturer *Poly Implant Prothèse (PIP)*, which then

---

762 See European Commission, REACH Regulation, www.environment.ec.europa.eu/topics/chemicals/reach-regulation_en [last accessed February 26, 2024]; see also European Chemicals Agency (ECHA), Understanding Reach, www.echa.europa.eu/de/regulations/reach/understanding-reach [last accessed February 26, 2024].

763 See Klaus Löbbe, *Die europäische Chemieindustrie. Bedeutung, Struktur und Entwicklungsperspektiven*, Bonn 2004, 11, 110; see also "Recht Reach. Zwei Experten, zwei Meinungen," in: *Gefahrgut*, August 31, 2007, 13. See as well "Der Streit geht weiter," in: *Logistik Inside*, October 26, 2007, 59.

764 Brenntag AG, annual report 2010, 17.

765 The quality management systems were certified according to ISO 9001. Brenntag AG, annual report 2013, 97.

fraudulently used these industrial silicones for the production of breast implants. The scandal, which was revealed around 2012, fueled a discussion about possible shared responsibility on the part of the supplier and raised the question of whether a closer examination by the French *Brenntag* company would have been necessary with regard to the actual use of the materials ordered.[766] However, *Brenntag* rejected this accusation: The customer had deliberately deceived the distributor about the intended use, while they themselves had correctly informed them about how the supplied preliminary products should be properly used.[767]

In the medium term, the public debates about responsibility in dealing with chemicals may have contributed to the gradual and more detailed and pointed presentation of the company's long-standing principles with regard to existing risks.[768] Shortly after the IPO, *Brenntag* had also postulated challenging ideas with regard to security issues along with its ambitious growth targets for the future. "We want to be the safest chemical distributor" was the explicitly envisioned goal.[769] Continuously working to improve environmental protection, occupational safety, and health protection was not only a high priority but also a basic business principle, the company explained.[770]

As the group-wide accident statistics – now recorded and evaluated centrally – demonstrated, the number of industrial accidents fell by around a third between 2010 and 2015. Global health protection, occupational safety, and environmental protection strategies relied on accident-avoidance and risk-minimization concepts. In the 2010s, examining the group's structures, the topic of sustainability was added to the roster. In 2013, the group published a sustainability report for the first time, which took into account energy consumption, CO_2 emissions, and other ecological indicators. This made *Brenntag* the first company in the chemical distribution industry with a certified sustainability report and also one of the first companies in the industry to join the UN Global Compact.[771]

Safety in dealing with chemical risks also includes dealing with the problem of contaminated sites that can arise from long-term activity in the chemical trade. As the company grew, *Brenntag* also acquired properties that were contaminated with

---

766 In this context, claims were raised against Brenntag. See Brenntag AG, annual report 2013, 119.

767 See *Frankfurter Allgemeine Zeitung*, March 20, 2012, 12.

768 Brenntag AG, annual report 2014, 76. The company's new "2020 vision" includes "preventing all accidents."

769 See Brenntag AG, annual report 2010, 24.

770 Ibid., 17.

771 Brenntag AG, annual report 2017. In 2016, Brenntag publicly announced its medium-term sustainability goals: from 2020 to 2030, greenhouse gas emissions should be reduced by 40 percent and by 2025, 100 percent of consumed electricity should be from renewable sources. Brenntag SE, Non-Financial Report 2022.

chemicals. Suitable procedures for the reclamation of affected properties were usually developed in close coordination with the responsible cities and districts.

Expansion in a Volatile Economy

When *Brenntag* announced in January 2013 that it would take over the Texas-based *Altivia Corporation* for $ 125 million, the *Börsen-Zeitung* commented that *Brenntag* was the "German M&A pioneer of the new year" [M & A = mergers and acquisitions].[772] *Altivia* specialized in the mixing, packaging, and distribution of water treatment chemicals, including aluminum sulfate, chlorine, bleach, specialty polymers, caustic soda, and sulfuric acid. With this purchase, *Brenntag* completed its 39th acquisition since 2007. Over the next two years, 18 additional purchases were made – on average, an additional purchase was made every month and a half until the mid-2010s.[773]

Given this intensive acquisition activity, the M&A process within the company had gradually become more differentiated. If a possible merger generally seemed appropriate, the next step was to check the minimum return requirements against the operational metrics. "The secret of our success lies in due diligence," explained *Brenntag* CEO Holland.[774] Due to the pronounced fragmentation of the market, the acquisition projects often involved small or medium-sized companies with a purchase price in the double-digit million range. Nevertheless, capacities were limited because it was not possible to examine too many companies in parallel at the same time and then acquire, merge, and integrate them.[775] *Brenntag* did not exhaust the budget reserved for acquisitions in the 2013 and 2014 financial years but, for example, with the acquisition of the Australian distributor *Blue Sky* in the early summer of 2013, it made further inroads into the *Ad Blue* market field, and traded with the urea-based solution used for exhaust gas aftertreatment in diesel engines.[776]

Brenntag's expansive business policy also occasionally raised competition issues. In May 2013, the French competition authority imposed an antitrust fine of 48 million euros on the French *Brenntag* subsidiary because it was said to have made market and price agreements with other chemical traders between 1998

---

772 "Brenntag startet mit Zukauf in Amerika ins Jahr," in: *Börsen-Zeitung*, January 3, 2013, 9.

773 In April 2015, Holland spoke of the 57th acquisition since 2007; see Annette Becker, Interview: Steven Holland, in: *Börsen-Zeitung*, April 28, 2015, 11.

774 Ibid.

775 In 2017, Holland talked about auditing an average of five companies in parallel. See Andy Bounds, "A straight talker who brings the right chemistry," in: *Financial Times*, September 18, 2017, 22.

776 "Germany's Brenntag acquires Australian AdBlue distributor," in: *ICIS Chemical News*, May 16, 2013.

and 2005.[777] In addition, allegations of abuse of a dominant market position were examined. However, *Brenntag* appealed against the French authorities' decision because the company had been a key witness in the investigation since 2006 and had disclosed all information.[778] In fact, the decision was overturned in 2017 due to a formal error, but at the same time the proceedings were reopened.[779] While *Brenntag* had been reimbursed for the fine paid and had made provisions for the pending proceedings, the final decision of the appeal court was not yet available by the end of the 2022 financial year.[780]

In 2014, *Brenntag's* sales exceeded the ten-billion-euro threshold for the first time. In terms of sales and earnings development, *Brenntag* was mostly above the industry average. Since the major financial crisis of 2009 had been overcome, sales in the chemical industry initially grew until 2013, then fell until 2016, and amounted to around 136.499 billion euros in that year, slightly more than in 2010.[781] Production in the chemical industry – with the exception of 2013 – declined in the first half of the 2010s, especially for basic chemicals and petrochemicals.[782] The economic environment in the chemical industry was "moderate to difficult," stated the *Brenntag* annual report.[783]

Table 3: Data on the Corporate Development of Brenntag AG 2012–2016[784]

Year	2012	2013	2014	2015	2016
Key figure/criterion					
Sales (in million euros)	9,689.9	9,769.5	10,015.6	10,346.1	10,498.4
Gross profit (in million euros)	1,925.7	1,945.5	2,027.5	2,266.0	2,428.7
Operating EBITDA (in million euros)	706.6	698.3	726.7	807.4	810.0
Employees	12,988	13,185	13,622	14,459	14,826
Distribution centers/ locations worldwide	ca. 450	ca. 480	ca. 490	ca. 530	ca. 550

777 See "Brenntag erwägt Beschwerde," *Frankfurter Allgemeine Zeitung*, May 31, 2013, 18.

778 Brenntag AG, annual report 2014, 132; Brenntag AG, annual report 2015, 130.

779 Brenntag AG, annual report 2016, 139.

780 See the statements on the legal risks in the annual reports of Brenntag AG from 2017–2022.

781 Verband der chemischen Industrie, Chemiewirtschaft in Zahlen, 34. See also Birgit Gehrke/Insa Weilage, *Branchenanalyse Chemieindustrie. Der Chemiestandort Deutschland im Spannungsfeld globaler Verschiebungen von Nachfragestrukturen und Wertschöpfungsketten*, Düsseldorf 2018, 26 f.

782 Verband der chemischen Industrie, Chemiewirtschaft in Zahlen 2023, 8 f.

783 According to Brenntag AG in its 2014 annual report.

784 Compiled according to Brenntag AG, annual reports 2012–2016.

Overall, however, *Brenntag's* key figures remained stable. In 2013, the falling value of the dollar was reflected in sales figures. Although sales increased in real terms, they remained almost constant in euros.[785] In the 2015 financial year, the company recorded "historic highs" in gross profit and operating EBITDA.[786] The high stability of its business development was primarily due to the great diversity of its customer portfolio. Around 2015, the 50 largest of *Brenntag's* 185,000 customers were responsible for less than 10 percent of its sales, and the ten largest customers were responsible for less than 5 percent of its sales. Since the ten products with the highest sales – among more than 10,000 different products – accounted for less than 20 percent of the gross profit, declines in sales in individual production sectors, industries, and customer groups had little impact. Price increases from individual large suppliers had a comparatively small impact on purchasing costs due to the high level of variation. The ten largest suppliers were responsible for less than 30 percent of the purchasing volume, which is why the dependence on the pricing of individual large suppliers was low.[787] The *Brenntag* stock share did not show any spectacular price increases but was attractive for long-term investors due to its stable price development.[788]

Since 2010, *Brenntag* had been taking advantage of the unusually long period of low interest rates to provide itself with cheap borrowed capital through a seven-year bond worth 400 million euros. The second important external source of financing was a large loan from a consortium of international banks, the interest rate of which was based on the current market interest rate on the euro market (EURIBOR).[789] The term and maturity profile was to be optimized in several steps over the next few years. This was followed in 2015 by a low-interest warrant bond for $ 500 million and a term until 2022, and in 2017, a corporate bond for € 600 million with an interest rate of less than 1.2 percent and a term until 2025.[790]

From Essen out into the World

Five years after going public, *Brenntag* made the decision to move its headquarters from Mülheim to Essen. The old administration building was "bursting at the seams," and would have required extensive renovation in order

---

785 At a global company like Brenntag, more than 50 percent of sales are invoiced in currencies other than the euro.

786 Brenntag AG, annual report 2015.

787 Ibid.

788 Due to the later stock split (3:1), the stock prices at that time cannot be compared 1:1 with the current prices.

789 Brenntag AG, annual report 2013.

790 Brenntag AG, annual reports 2015 and 2017.

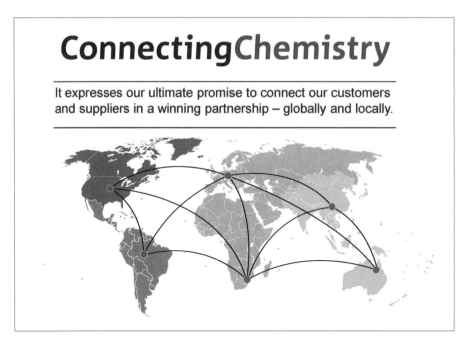

Figure 48: In 2014, Brenntag introduced its global branding "ConnectingChemistry" to express the role of the distribution company in the value chain in the chemical industry.

to tailor it to future requirements. In the winter of 2015, the construction of a new office complex began in Essen's Gruga-Carree, which was intended to offer 650 employees a modern workplace.[791] From the perspective of some long-time employees, it was a change that took some getting used to, leaving the company's traditional headquarters next to the Rhein-Ruhr-Center, which had already been occupied during the *Hugo Stinnes AG* era.[792] Although the decision for a new domicile was based on functional considerations, the move to Essen in 2017 also symbolized how far *Brenntag* had developed as an independent group since it was separated from the group with *DB* and the former *Stinnes Holding*.

Although *Brenntag* continued to have its headquarters in Germany, it could no longer be characterized as a German company at this point. In 2017, it had locations or distribution centers in over 74 countries and employed almost 90 percent of its over 15,000 employees outside of Germany.[793] In addition, around 60 percent of the shareholders were British or US investors.[794] The internationality

791 See also "Brenntag zieht nach Essen um," in: *Börsen-Zeitung*, May 1, 2015, 11.

792 On this change process, see the contemporary witness conversation with Dr. Roolfs-Broihan on September 7, 2023.

793 Brenntag AG, annual report 2017, 84.

794 Bounds, *Straighttalker*.

of *Brenntag* and the geographical focus of its activities were also reflected in the composition of the Board of Directors. In 2017, its five members included three Germans, one Briton, and one Frenchman.[795]

> **Female Managers at Brenntag**
>
> In contrast to the great national diversity of employees and managers, gender diversity at *Brenntag* was less pronounced for a long time. Until 2021, none of the four or five board members were women, although two of the six supervisory board members had been female since 2015. This meant that the target that *Brenntag* had set out to achieve in accordance with the Stock Corporation Act – to have at least a third of the supervisory board appointments go to women by 2017 – was achieved ahead of schedule. From 2020 to 2023, Doreen Nowotne was *Brenntag's* first female supervisory board chairwoman.[796] In addition, with effect from April 1, 2022, the economist Dr. Kristin Neumann was appointed to the Board of Directors as Chief Financial Officer.[797] In the same year, the proportion of women in upper management levels was around a third.[798]

In the year of its move to Essen, *Brenntag* already recorded its 77th acquisition within a decade. Among the companies added to the division in 2017 was a majority stake in specialty chemicals distributor *Wellstar Enterprises Company Limited* in Hong Kong, with three Chinese subsidiaries.[799] In addition, *Brenntag* acquired, among other firms, two British suppliers of food ingredients – *Kluman and Balter Limited* and *A1 Cake Mixes Limited* – thereby strengthening the activities in the food segment, which had already gained momentum in 2014 with the acquisition of the Italian *Chimab*.[800] From 2017 onward, *Brenntag* reorganized its "Food & Nutrition" business segment to emphasize its role as a distributor of ingredients for the food industry.[801]

---

795 Brenntag AG, annual report 2017, 28 f.

796 Brenntag SE, annual report 2020.

797 Ibid.

798 Brenntag SE, non-financial report 2022.

799 The purchase of the remaining 49 percent of the shares was planned for 2021. Natasha Spencer, "Brenntag acquires Chinese Wellstar-group," in: *CosmeticsDesign Asia.com*, July 4, 2017, https://www.cosmeticsdesign-asia.com/Article/2017/07/03/Brenntag-acquires-Chinese-Wellstar-Group [last accessed February 27, 2024].

800 "Brenntag schlägt bei Backzutaten zu," in: *Welt online*, December 18, 2017, https://www.welt.de/regionales/nrw/article171706067/Brenntag-schlaegt-bei-Backzutaten-zu.html [last accessed April 18, 2024].

801 Brenntag AG, annual report 2019, 10.

Over the previous decade, *Brenntag's* market presence in Asia had also gained considerable profile. Looking back in the summer of 2018, *Brenntag* board member Henri Nejade, responsible for the Asian business sector, explained: "Ten years ago we had zero business, and today we are number three in the Asia Pacific region."[802] After various acquisitions in Singapore, Australia, India, and South Korea, the company acquired 65 percent of *Raj Petro Specialties*, which traded more than 700 self-blended petroleum products throughout Asia and achieved sales of 190 million euros in 2017.[803] The *Brenntag* network had also expanded significantly in the Middle East and Africa (MEA) region since 2007. As of 2019, *Brenntag* Africa had around 560 employees and served around 9,960 customers.[804]

Table 4: Activities in Africa

1990	Brenntag Exports
2001	South Africa – Crest Chemicals 50% JV AECI
2006	Morocco / Tunisia / Algeria – Group Alliance Maghreb
2007	Egypt – Tardy
2011	Mauritius – Multisol
2011	South Africa – Multisol
2014	Nigeria / Ghana
2015	South Africa – Lionheart Chemicals
2016	South Africa – Plastichem
2016	Mauritius – Thread Management
2016	South Africa – Warren Chem
2016	South Africa – Multilube
2017	South Africa – Brenntag South Africa
2019	East Africa – Desbro Chemicals
2019	South Africa – Crest Chemicals

Given the accelerated pace of growth, *Brenntag* continued to find itself between the opposing poles of global networking and the local roots of its activities. "At the end of the day, everything is local," commented one executive, referring to

---

802 See *Brenntag Together* 06/18, 17.

803 See Ibid., 16 ff.; Brenntag AG, annual report 2018.

804 See *Brenntag Together* 12/19, 12.

the integration activities.[805] Combining both control perspectives sensibly, and keeping the friction losses in the growing organization with its decentralized components as low as possible, was one of the constant central challenges for management. CEO Holland knew how to protect the organization from becoming "mindlessly global or hopelessly local," summed up a former colleague.[806] When Holland retired at the end of 2019, the baton at the top of the company changed hands: On January 1, 2020, Dr. Christian Kohlpaintner, who had previously served as a member of the Executive Committee at the Swiss chemical company *Clariant*, and had been responsible for the Asia region, among others, took over the position of CEO of *Brenntag AG*.

Corporate Structures Under Pressure

At this time, the global economy was weakening, and the macroeconomic market environment was considered difficult.[807] The visible increase in business output in the double-digit percentage range[808] was essentially the result of the application of a new accounting standard, explained the *Brenntag* annual report. If this effect were subtracted out, there would be no sign of growth.[809] "Overall, we are not satisfied with this earnings development," commented the Board of Directors.[810]

As a result, there were increasing signals that one of the two growth factors, organic growth, was stagnating, and that an important building block in the long-term group strategy was therefore not being realized. "If we take acquisitions out of the equation, *Brenntag* growth has been flat in recent years," explained the new CEO Kohlpaintner. "We urgently need to find possible ways to return to long-term organic growth."[811] With a view to the desired relatively simple business model, the functions and processes in the group were too complicated in some places – now it was important to find an organizational form better suited to this business model, Kohlpaintner commented further.[812] This meant

---

805 See conversation with Dr. Gabriele Roolfs-Broihan on September 7, 2023.

806 According to former Brenntag manager William Fidler, quoted in Bounds, *Straighttalker*.

807 Verband der Chemischen Industrie, *Schwache Chemiekonjunktur in schwierigem Umfeld. Jahresbilanz 2019 der chemisch-pharmazeutischen Industrie*, press release, December 3, 2019.

808 Adjusted for this effect, the consolidated result is slightly below the strong previous year; Brenntag AG, annual report 2019, 40.

809 Operating EBITDA increased by 14.4 percent in 2019 compared to the previous year, and by 11.3 percent on a constant exchange rate basis; ibid.

810 Ibid.

811 *Brenntag Together* 1/20, 10.

812 Ibid., 11.

that the restructuring of the company was identified as a new, necessary plan of action. The "Project Brenntag," which management initiated at the beginning of 2020, was aimed at transforming the company. A key aspect was the transition from regional control to a divisional structure with two global business areas: "Brenntag Essentials" for process chemicals and "Brenntag Specialties" for specialty chemicals. In addition, the transition was to be about reviewing processes throughout the entire group and tapping into the possible potential for increasing efficiency.[813]

After *Brenntag* started the new financial year with an ambitious internal change program, unexpected changes in external conditions and disruptions to economic life soon occurred. Just a few weeks after Kohlpaintner took office, the COVID-19 virus temporarily paralyzed normal business practices and imposed extensive restrictions on business trips and small meetings. *Brenntag* had to adapt its work processes to the infection protection regulations. If work processes permitted it, employees worked remotely from their home offices during this phase. An effort by the IT department to convert the systems quickly created the conditions for meetings of all kinds, including the annual general meeting, to take place in virtual space. The adaptation of business processes to the demands of the pandemic coincided with the overarching efforts to reposition and transform the group.

In September 2019, the Executive Board and Supervisory Board had already decided to change the legal form of the company and converted *Brenntag* from a stock corporation under German law (AG) into a stock corporation under European stock corporation law (SE, Societas Europaea). This change became effective in February 2021 and enabled functional advantages that national corporate law did not provide.[814] The supranational legal form fit better with the current corporate structure, said the CEO's statement. The capital market perceived the SE positively, he rejoiced.[815]

Despite the special challenges of the first year of the pandemic, *Brenntag* prepared the restructuring of its own organizational structure in a far-reaching

813 Brenntag SE, annual report 2020, 5 ff.

814 "Chemikalienhändler Brenntag will Rechtsform ändern," in: *Reuters Unternehmensnachrichten*, September 5, 2019, www.reuters.com/article/deutschland-brenntag-idDEKCN1VQ1Y5 [last accessed October 10, 2023]; see also "Aktuelle Entwicklungen bei der SE," in: *Mitbestimmungsportal der Hans-Böckler-Stiftung*, November 4, 2021, www.mitbestimmung.de/html/datenblatt-aktuelle-entwicklungen-bei-19579.html [last accessed October 10th, 2023]; Brenntag press release, February 1, 2021. Beyond that, no further justification was given for the move. Brenntag AG/Brenntag SE, annual reports 2019 and 2020. As part of the conversion, the establishment of the so-called European Employee Forum was agreed with the employee representatives.

815 https://corporate.brenntag.com/de/media/news/neue-rechtsform-brenntag-ag-in-eine-se-umgewandelt.html.

way in 2020: From January 2021, it relied on functional and divisional control principles that replaced the previously relevant regional criteria. In addition to central departments (Corporate Functions) and service departments (Business Services), the two operational business areas mentioned above took shape, *Brenntag* Essentials and *Brenntag* Specialties.[816] Both divisions were very important: While specialties contributed around 40 percent of gross profit in 2020, industrial chemicals contributed 60 percent. At the same time, *Brenntag* began evaluating mass data in order to optimize the network of 700 locations worldwide by 2022, close around 100 locations in the medium term, and save 1,300 jobs through socially acceptable rationalization.[817] By April 2022, *Brenntag* had already cut 70 locations and saved 925 jobs.[818] Further optimization potential was to be tapped in the medium term by improving internal processes and installing a new digital architecture, with which Brenntag would intensify communication with its customers.[819]

Table 5: Brenntag from 2017–2022. Development of Selected Key Figures[820]

Facts and Figures	2017	2018	2019	2020	2021	2022
Sales Volume (million euros)	11,743.3	12,550.0	12,821.8	11,794.8	14,382.5	19,429.3
Gross Profit (million euros)	2,554.1	2,660.9	2,821.7	2,869.4	3,379.0	4,319.0
Operating EBITA (million euros)	717.1	753.5	757.9	805.3	1.081.9	1.511.7
Employees	> 15,000	> 16,600	≈ 17,500	> 17,000	> 17,000	> 17,500
Worldwide Distribution Centers/ Headquarters	> 530 in 74 countries	> 580 in 73 countries	> 640 in 77 countries	> 670 in 77 countries	≈ 700 in 78 countries	≈ 600 in 72 countries

The severe recession caused by the pandemic did not spare *Brenntag*. And so sales declined in 2020. However, thanks to the higher gross profit per sales volume, total income remained constant. Despite widespread industry supply bottlenecks, global disruptions in transport logistics, and highly strained global supply chains, *Brenntag* even increased its profit after taxes (474 million euros compared to 469 million euros).

816 Brenntag SE, annual report 2020.
817 Conversation with Dr. Gabriele Roolfs-Broihan on September 7, 2023.
818 Brenntag SE, annual report 2021.
819 Conversation with Dr. Gabriele Roolfs-Broihan on September 7, 2023.
820 Brenntag SE, annual reports 2017–2022.

As in the financial crisis, the internationality, the global positioning, the broad product portfolio, and the fragmentation of *Brenntag's* business holdings, as well as the large number of suppliers, continued to prove advantageous. At the same time, it was often a struggle for the teams to make products available in the right places for their customers.

In contrast, the second pandemic year of 2021 was characterized by successful efforts to catch up: The mass vaccinations against COVID-19 that began in the spring enabled the gradual normalization of everyday life and facilitated the return to normality in industry and in the service economy. As a result of the normalization and catch-up effect, *Brenntag* sales rose by 22 percent to 14,383 million euros.[821] While operating profit before taxes, interest expenses, and depreciation (EBITDA) rose by 27 percent and reached a record level of 1,345 million euros, earnings after taxes remained almost constant. Part of this growth was due to acquisitions: *Brenntag* acquired larger capital shares in two Chinese distributors in the specialty chemicals sector and an American distributor of food ingredients.[822]

In addition, during this phase *Brenntag* accomplished the inclusion in the leading stock index DAX. In September 2021, *Brenntag's* market capitalization (the stock market value) exceeded the ten billion euro threshold at around 13 billion euros. As part of the expansion of the German leading index from 30 to 40 companies, entry into the DAX represented a significant milestone in terms of public visibility of the company; it was now one of the 40 largest companies on the German stock market. It was a gratifying recognition, explained CEO Kohlpaintner. Nevertheless, he highlighted another challenge that was mastered at the same time as the greatest achievement of the year: supplying customers with what they needed despite extremely fragile supply chains due to the pandemic.[823]

In the following year, *Brenntag* was able to repeat the extraordinary growth jump of 2021 and increase both sales revenue and operating profit (EBITDA) by 35 percent, although the year was characterized by particular macroeconomic

---

821 Brenntag SE, annual report 2021.

822 Worth mentioning here is the acquisition of a 67 percent stake in Zhongbai Xingye Food Technology (Beijing) Co., Ltd., based in Beijing, as well as a subsidiary. Brenntag also acquired Storm Chaser Holding Corporation, based in Wilmington, Delaware, USA, and its subsidiaries; see Brenntag SE, annual report 2021, 159.

823 "Christian Kohlpaintner im Interview: Chef des weltgrößten Chemiehändlers Brenntag warnt: 'Zügige Preissenkungen eine Illusion',' in: *Handelsblatt*, December 28, 2021, www.handelsblatt.com/unternehmen/industrie/christian-kohlpaintner-im-interview-chef-des-weltgroessten- chemiehaendlers-brenntag-warnt-zuegige-preiswechseln-eine-illusion/27910530.html [last accessed on February 20, 2024].

Figure 49: Parts of the Supervisory Board and Board of Management at the General Shareholders' Meeting 2023, June 15, 2023.

problems with the start of the war in Ukraine and its consequences.[824] Even after adjusting for the price increases, a dynamic development could be seen. The operating results were excellent, according to the *Brenntag* annual report for 2022. Nevertheless, in its 148th year of existence, the company faced a political challenge that seemed unthinkable in the age of military disarmament and political détente. After the start of the Russian war of aggression against Ukraine, the Executive Board of *Brenntag SE* decided at the beginning of March 2022 to suspend all imports to and exports from Russia and Belarus. The business of all *Brenntag* companies in Russia and Belarus would now also be discontinued.

"New Brenntag": Brand Relaunch and New Strategy

During the 2022 financial year, *Brenntag* made many changes and launched various new initiatives. "Let's dive into the new Brenntag" was the title of a special edition of the employee magazine, which presented the company's new brand identity and future growth strategy in the fall of 2022.[825] While the previous logo

---

824 Brenntag SE, annual report 2022.

825 *Brenntag Together,* Special Issue, Fall/Winter 2022.

dated back to the Stinnes era, as the flag based on the "Stinnes-S" in the logo clearly showed, the new "B" for "Brenntag" was intended to signal the break from the old framework and to be a symbol of the modern company.

However, the signals that were soon heard from the German chemical industry were not very optimistic with regard to the development of the chemical sector. In addition to the decline in sales and production and profit warnings from the major chemical producers, there were general concerns about structural problems and high production costs in Germany.[826] The market environment was "adverse," stated CEO Kohlpaintner.

Brenntag also had to specify its earnings targets over the 2023 financial year in a way that was perceived in the press as an adjustment to the forecast and described as a "verbal balancing act" on the company's part.[827]

Against this background, some investors expressed massive criticism of the existing group organization and the current acquisition strategy, agitating against *Brenntag's* business policy course in the run-up to the general meeting of shareholders in 2023. For some time previously, shareholder *Primestone Capital* had spoken out against the idea of taking over US competitor *Univar Solutions*.[828] An activist group among the investors now believed that the company's repositioning in recent years had not been far-reaching enough and called for the two divisions, Essentials and Specialties, to be made quickly independent in order to tap into profitability potential, especially in the Specialties.[829] The activist investors also nominated two of their own candidates for election to the supervisory board. Although voting rights consultants had supported the activists, *Brenntag* successfully fended off the initiative on all points.

In line with the corporate transformation initiated by "Project Brenntag" in 2020 and the growth strategy presented in November 2022, CEO Kohlpaintner announced the next significant step in the company's restructuring at Capital Markets Day in December 2023. Two independent divisions "Specialties" and "Essentials" were planned for both sectors, overlayed by a slim corporate headquarters. According to the CEO, this would fit the market environment,

---

826 See, for example, the criticism of the Chemical Industry Association (Verband der chemischen Industrie), quoted here from Carsten Dierig, in: *Die Welt*, August 10, 2023, 12.

827 "Brenntag schraubt an Prognose," in: *Börsenzeitung*, November 10, 2023, 11.

828 The exploratory talks were broken off; see also "Chemikalienhändler: Brenntag bläst Übernahme von US-Rivalen Univar ab," in: *manager magazin*, January 3, 2023, www.manager-magazin.de/unternehmen/industrie/brenntag-chemikalienhaendler-blaest-uebernahme-von-us-rivalen-univar-ab-a-1471f8e7-c14e-4bab-b487-ac55b7047e3f [last accessed February 26, 2024].

829 "Brenntag wehrt Angriffe der Investoren ab," in: *Süddeutsche Zeitung*, June 15, 2023, www.sueddeutsche.de/wirtschaft/brenntag-haupttreffen-primestone-ridinger-chandrasekaran-1.5934901 [last accessed October 12, 2023].

which had already "sorted itself into the world of specialties on the one hand and industrial chemicals on the other."[830] This would prepare the two divisions for further strategic opportunities by 2026. While 2023 was challenging overall, the business forecast for the 2024 financial year, the 150th financial year in the company's history, was cautious. Brenntag expected a gradual, "sequential" improvement in sales volumes for the rest of the year.[831]

Figure 50: Brenntag's new headquarters, the House of Elements in Essen.

---

830 According to Kohlpaintner at the Capital Markets Day on December 6, 2023, quoted from "Brenntag stößt Entflechtung an," in: *Börsen-Zeitung*, December 6th, 2023, 9.

831 "Ausblick: Brenntag dürfte im Schlussquartal mehr verdienen," in: *dpa/afx* pro feed, March 7, 2024. See also "Brenntag – 2024 wird Erholungsjahr," in: Platow Börse, March 12, 2024.

14.

Conclusion

When the Berlin merchant Philipp Mühsam founded an egg and farm products store 150 years ago, in the fall of 1874, he probably could never have imagined the future success of this step, even in his wildest dreams: 126 years later, the company that evolved into *Brenntag* became a year 2000 world market leader in the distribution of chemicals and ingredients.

Brenntag's history is not a linear success story that was predetermined or predictable. Nevertheless, the predecessor company, *Philipp Mühsam oHG*, developed some characteristics in the first decades of its existence that were to promote its rise. A few years after founding the company, Philipp Mühsam identified a business area with enormous growth potential by entering the chemicals business and then completely changed his business model due to the strong competition in the agricultural products trade. By trading chemicals, he focused on a market segment that offered significant opportunities: The increasing spread of chemical products in commercial production and in people's everyday lives was a strong growth stimulus from which his company benefited. At the same time, the business policy decisions that Mühsam made reflected an interest in technical innovations and the entrepreneurial courage to invest early on in modern means of communication and a sustainable infrastructure. He was one of the first entrepreneurs in his industry to consistently introduce technological innovations and, around 1882, was one of the first Berlin entrepreneurs to have a telephone connection installed on the business premises of his still small company. The purchase of a large office and warehouse building on Alexandrinenstrasse in Kreuzberg in 1886 was a far-sighted investment in the future, as was the development of a commercial property on the not-yet-completed Teltow Canal 20 years later, which provided optimal transport connections and extensive expansion options for future use. In addition, Mühsam and his employees recognized the great opportunities associated with motorization and built what was then the most modern tank farm in the metropolis of Berlin. All this together meant that the founding generation created important foundations for the development of the trading business in the following decades.

When Mühsam died shortly before the start of the First World War, the transition to the next generation went smoothly because the senior head of the company had given his son Kurt an academic education and then groomed him to be his successor. In the critical supply situation starting in 1917 and in the inflationary period after the end of the war, *Philipp Mühsam oHG's* business model showed its resilience. The high investments in storage buildings and tank farms proved to be inflation-proof investments that did not lose their value even in the hyperinflation of 1923. In addition, high inflation caused loan debts to shrink and favored companies that had invested for the long term. Although the company no longer generated the high profits of the last pre-war years and the first years of the war, it was still able to look to the future with optimism as part of a growth industry. As Philipp Mühsam had predicted, the motorization of transport and the chemicalization of the economy gained pace in the 1920s, favoring business prospects in the trade of chemicals and mineral oil.

The change in legal form at this time from an oHG to a stock corporation had no impact on management. Since 1915, Kurt Mühsam had run the company together with his partner and later part-owner Julius Herz. His integration into the management and the circle of shareholders proved to be a salvation for the Mühsam family in terms of the continuity of the company after an unexpected severe stroke of fate: When Kurt Mühsam died suddenly in 1928 at the age of just 40, Herz took up the reins of running *Philipp Mühsam AG* seamlessly. Thanks to very solid financing and a successful sales strategy, the firm survived the severe depression of the global economic crisis without major losses of its equity.

In the first years of National Socialist rule, *Philipp Mühsam AG* benefited from the rapid economic recovery and government support for motorization. Nevertheless, the increasing discrimination against Jewish Germans in economic life and the loss of their civil rights due to the "Nuremberg Laws" forced Herz and the Mühsams to sell the company and emigrate. Like the vast majority of the family members, Kurt Mühsam's widow Ellen emigrated from Germany with her second husband and their daughters, while Herz began looking for buyers in the same year, 1936. He won over the prominent Mülheim entrepreneurial family Stinnes as an interested party, who then took over *Philipp Mühsam AG* in February 1937 at a price that was very advantageous for them. In this precarious situation, the brothers Otto and Hugo Stinnes gave Herz no other choice than to sell the "rock-solid company" (according to Hugo Stinnes) to them for well below the real earnings value.

Just a few months after the acquisition, the Stinnes brothers changed the company name to *Brenntag AG*, erasing the memory of the previous owners. They significantly increased their equity capital and invested in ocean-going and inland vessels in order to take advantage of the increasing transport needs of the National Socialist war economy. *Brenntag AG* was now part of a family-owned conglomerate of transport companies, mines, and coal trading firms and served the *Stinnes Group* to expand their business area geographically and in terms of sector coverage.

In 1943, *Brenntag* moved the company management from Berlin to Mülheim an der Ruhr because of the difficulties in communication caused by the war. While the warehouses and tank facilities at the main location were only damaged, the long-established administrative headquarters in the center of the imperial capital were completely destroyed. And when *Brenntag* had to hand over its two ocean-going ships to the Allies as war reparations in 1945/46, it also lost a significant portion of its assets.

After the end of the war, *Brenntag's* first priority was to get its business back on track. In view of the difficult conditions in the post-war period, the initial company management approach was "driving on sight." Quite inventively, very different business opportunities that presented themselves during the improvised new beginning were seized. The business connections of the Stinnes brothers and their group of companies had a positive effect. *Brenntag* traded in scrap, recycled rubble, produced brick chippings for the construction industry, made bricks from crushed sand, produced large-format building elements in a newly built concrete factory, offered shipping services, and undertook its first business with heating oil when coal was still used everywhere for heating. The company sold fuels and chemicals, invested in inland and ocean-going vessels, and thereby repositioned itself for the booming shipping business.

In addition to the existing *Brenntag AG*, which was under Allied asset supervision from 1949 to 1950, the partners founded *Brenntag GmbH* in 1948, with which the company management promoted business around the traditional Stinnes locations in the Ruhr area. Until the mid-1950s, the focus of activities was on chemicals and mineral oil trading as well as shipping. Favored by tax regulations, shipping represented the "cash cow" at times because generous depreciation principles made corporate financing easier. In the longer term, however, the focus on shipping turned out to be a dead end and a loss-maker for *Brenntag*, as its ships were unable to keep up in the long term in the highly competitive freight market.

However, *Brenntag* had its other mainstay in a growth segment of the economy. Due to the high demand for products from the chemical industry, the opportunities for activity in the chemical trade expanded. In addition, the mineral oil business increased noticeably as motorization expanded dramatically. *Brenntag* recognized the gas station business as a lucrative, future-oriented business area early on and gradually built up a network of gas stations, which at its peak in the early 1960s included around 130 stations. This division helped *Brenntag* solve problems that had their origins elsewhere. During the boom of the 1950s, business had grown well overall, but the undercapitalized company was struggling with liquidity problems on the one hand and earnings problems in some divisions and unfavorable structures on the other. Conflicts within the Stinnes family that owned the company also made it difficult and time-consuming to make changes. Only after a settlement between the Stinnes brothers in 1959 could both parts of the company, *Brenntag AG* and *Brenntag GmbH*, finally be merged. The most important shareholders were now Otto Stinnes and his company, *Hugo Stinnes OHG*. At the end of 1962, *Brenntag* leased a large part of its West German gas station network to *Deutsche Total GmbH*.

Until the early 1960s, *Brenntag's* corporate history reflected the typical strengths and weaknesses of a family business. The connection to *Hugo Stinnes OHG* ensured stability and planning security and gave *Brenntag* scope to explore various business areas and expand its network. At the same time, characteristic problems became apparent – such as the brotherly feud between Hugo and Otto Stinnes and the resulting organizational inefficiencies and weaknesses in corporate financing. *Brenntag's* parent company, *Hugo Stinnes OHG*, also had an open flank structurally, as its capital resources did not match the volume of its trading and banking business. Their business structure stood on feet of clay. When it ran into a crisis of trust and customers withdrew their deposits, the previously stable company ran into sudden liquidity problems and had to file for settlement proceedings.

With the parent company's stumble, *Brenntag's* future suddenly became quite uncertain. For the first and only time in the company's 150-year history, there was a constellation that potentially jeopardized its continued existence. In this phase, *Brenntag's* path could possibly have been interrupted. Nevertheless, Otto Stinnes and his advisors and lenders quickly came to the consensus that the healthy company should be sold and thus separated from the ailing parent company. The mineral oil warehouse in West Berlin helped to get the urgently needed bridging loans from the bank, because *Brenntag* was seen on the market as a company with growth prospects and valuable substance. It is therefore not surprising that various companies had a serious interest in buying the property; the contract was awarded to a subsidiary of the *Bank für Gemeinwirtschaft* at the end of 1963. The new owner, in turn, sold *Brenntag* around a year later to *Hugo Stinnes AG* – that is, to that part of the former Stinnes company conglomerate that had emerged from the US corporation. *Brenntag* came to *Hugo Stinnes AG* at a time when the last step in the "repatriation" of the company, which had recently been bought back from the USA – mainly with federal funds – was still pending: the privatization. *Veba*, as the new owner of *Hugo Stinnes AG*, took this step by issuing *Veba* public shares in the appropriate amount.[832] With the transition to *Hugo Stinnes AG*, *Brenntag* became a "grandchild" of the previously federally owned, now partially privatized *Veba Group*.

As a subsidiary of *Hugo Stinnes AG*, *Brenntag* now had a close connection to a group that wanted to systematically expand the trading divisions of the new acquisitions, go beyond the domestic market orientation, and grow internationally, too. This strategic orientation set the tone for the coming decades. At the same time, it was part of the corporate culture of *Hugo Stinnes AG* to give its subsidiaries and operating companies a great deal of scope for action. This also applied to *Brenntag's* business area. Since its resources had grown over the long term, it brought with it considerable know-how, an extensive network of locations, and business connections in the chemical and petroleum trade.

Since the late 1950s and early 1960s, *Brenntag* had business relationships with the EKD, the national Protestant Church, which was one of its major customers. *Brenntag* had become one of the few "trusted companies" in the so-called church business and was regularly commissioned by the Diakonisches Werk of the EKD to deliver goods to the GDR, the value of which was intended to benefit the Protestant churches in East Germany. In addition, from the 1960s until the end of the GDR, *Brenntag* was active in "special transactions," with which the federal government ransomed political prisoners out of the GDR, using procedural channels that had already been established in the church-initiated goods transfers.

When information about the top secret transactions gradually came to light after the fall of the Wall, public interest revolved around the tightrope which the federal government had walked with the prisoner release – the balancing act between the humanitarian objective and participation in a problematic, ethically highly questionable human trafficking operation through which the GDR earned foreign currency.[833] Looking back, *Brenntag* also reflected on these ambivalences.

---

832 BArch B 126/77037.
833 Wölbern, *Häftlingsfreikauf*, 497.

The historical perspective shows that the "church business" was associated with low earnings margins for the company. Nevertheless, it seems plausible that the role as a trusted company brought advantages for *Brenntag* and supported its business policy interests. What seemed particularly relevant was the personal network that *Brenntag* grew into through its role as a trusted company, which may have helped the firm expand its business connections in the GDR. In the 1980s, it had developed into an important sales partner for the GDR's foreign trade in chemicals; for some products, for example those of the GDR petroleum chemistry, it had long-term exclusive distribution rights. Overall, business with the GDR and other state trading countries was an important area of activity for *Brenntag*, just as the *Veba Group* also played a central role in German-German trade. With its historically evolved location in Berlin, *Brenntag* was in an insular location until the borders between the Federal Republic of Germany and the GDR were opened, which was reflected in the company's business relations. Through the investment company *Rex Handelsgesellschaft Schulte-Frohlinde*, *Brenntag* had occupied a central point in the West Berlin fuel and heating oil trade since the second half of the 1970s.

Gradually, *Brenntag* also gained influence at central hubs in the international chemical trade. *Hugo Stinnes AG*, later *Stinnes AG*, saw itself as a "market intermediary," and saw the expansion of its own network as a prerequisite for being successful as a trading company. It upheld the principle of decentralized leadership, and this guiding principle helped shape *Brenntag's* business model for a long time; pooling the strengths of small companies was also a guideline for the firm's later development. With *Stinnes AG*, *Brenntag* had a group of companies behind it that had the capital strength to support the necessary investments in the long term. In this way, *Brenntag* was increasingly able to combine different approaches to the markets, which were often spread across several distinct firms: local networking and international outreach.

In the 1980s, the building blocks of a business model that would have a long-term impact on *Brenntag* began to take shape. Changes in guidelines for environmental protection contributed to making the requirements for the transport and storage of chemicals more complex and the necessary know-how more intensive. And all this required high investments. In this context, chemical producers became increasingly interested in outsourcing distribution and logistics functions to the chemical trade, tending to prefer larger companies that had a competitive advantage over smaller trading companies in view of the investment requirements. *Brenntag* had already noticed these tendencies in the

US market and strove to distinguish itself more clearly as a distributor while the European internal market was still expanding, which is why it reorganized its activities. While the previous corporate organization had followed a chemical classification system and bundled together very different tasks, the organization that was in effect from 1990 onward differentiated between the business areas of industrial chemicals and specialty chemicals as well as the trading and marketing of plastics.

In the early 1990s, *Brenntag* divested itself of businesses beyond the chemicals trade and gradually concentrated on smaller volume businesses in chemicals. In addition, the company continued on the path of internationalization until the end of the decade and combined this effort with the approach of meeting chemical producers' outsourcing interests with service offerings. The business model that had emerged by the time *Stinnes AG* went public represented a response to the structural changes in the market – such as the outsourcing of parts of the value chain by producers and the concentration tendencies in the fragmented chemical trading market. At the same time, *Brenntag* helped drive some of these changes itself – for example, through its acquisition strategy and expansion of the range of its services.

The turn of the millennium began with the gradual separation of *Stinnes AG* from the *Veba Group*, which merged with *VIAG* in the middle of 2000 to form the conglomerate *E.on* and now focused on the energy industry. While still under the umbrella of the now listed *Stinnes AG*, *Brenntag* achieved a breakthrough into a new dimension with two acquisitions – *Neuber* and *Holland Chemical*: With the purchase of *Holland Chemical*, it became the world's largest company in its industry.

When *Deutsche Bahn AG* bought *Stinnes AG* in 2002 for its logistics division, the spin-off of *Brenntag* from the *Stinnes Group* was only a matter of time. With the transfer of *Stinnes AG* to *Deutsche Bahn AG*, the end of the traditional *Stinnes Group* also loomed large. This development took place a few years before its 200th anniversary, which might have provided an opportunity to review its company history – which has now been told here, at least selectively, from the *Brenntag* perspective.

For *Brenntag*, the 66-year period under the Stinnes umbrella ended in 2003, when the US financial company *Bain Capital* – or funds associated with *Bain Capital* – invested in the company and led it to independence. A phase now began in which *Brenntag's* ownership structure changed in shorter periods of time.

However, the transition to *Bain Capital* initially meant a major effort for the company, as it had to shoulder the majority of the purchase price itself – in accordance with common practices in private equity buyout procedures. The firm's liabilities temporarily increased significantly. From the outset, the merger with *Bain Capital* was not conceived as a long-term project but rather as support for an independent, self-reliant market presence. "You are the experts" was the financial investor's principle to support *Brenntag* in identifying new future business areas in chemical distribution (e.g., "Food," "Life Science," or "Ad Blue") that it should develop in the medium term. While *Brenntag* had previously operated comparatively inconspicuously as a business unit under a corporate umbrella, it was now moving in the direction of record-setting private equity deals. Investors believed the company would be capable of high performance. This was supported by the continued rapid increase in liabilities, which the market environment with low interest rates and liquid debt capital markets had stimulated and which *Brenntag* was expected to pay off from its stable cash flow.

In addition, a significant increase in value was realized during the transfer from *Bain Capital* to the British investment company *BC Partners*, such that the business press spoke of the fact that the private equity company had brought "dormant values" to life and that the previous state owner had missed out on profit opportunities.[834] In fact, *Brenntag* proved to be robust enough to withstand this period of financial stress. Nevertheless, the investor's path also carried risks, as a sudden collapse in operating profit could have thrown the calculation into question. However, the favorable conditions around 2006 gave a tailwind to the private equity firms' buy-and-build strategy. The successor investors from *BC Partners* had no intention of recalibrating *Brenntag* but rather continued the strategic path that was based on organic and acquisition-based growth. *BC Partners* took *Brenntag* public in 2010 and sold all its *Brenntag* shares on the capital market by 2012. With the IPO, *Brenntag* was able to strengthen its equity capital, further reduce its level of debt, and achieve greater visibility.

In doing so, it purposefully further developed its proven business model of global expansion through the purchase of companies. The logistics chains and distribution networks were continuously optimized and extended to markets in Europe, America, Asia, Africa, and Australia. In this context, *Brenntag's* global presence, the pronounced diversification of suppliers, customers, and sales sectors, as well as the broad diversification in industrial and specialty chemicals

---

834 Walter Becker, "Schlummernde Werte," in: *Börsen-Zeitung*, July 26, 2006, 1 (see also https://www.presseportal.de/pm/30377/852676 [last accessed February 5, 2024]); see as well Joachim Müller-Soares/Wolfgang Zdral, "Casino Fatal," in: *Capital*, August 2, 2007, 20.

had a stabilizing effect and added to crisis resilience. The financial crisis of 2008/09 and the global disruptions in logistics chains caused by the spread of the COVID-19 virus interrupted the positive development of company growth and earnings only briefly.

A major corporate structural transformation occurred again in 2020, when *Brenntag* replaced regional organizational principles with a divisional structure based on the industrial and specialty chemicals business areas. This basic idea was to feed more pointedly into a new goal that *Brenntag* aims to implement from 2024 to 2026: the division into two independent corporate units.

Over time, very different phases of *Brenntag's* history can be identified. After starting out in the egg trade, the innovative company founder, Philipp Mühsam, turned to the promising segment of chemicals and mineral oil trading, thereby laying the foundation for a flourishing trading company. Under the ownership of the Stinnes family, *Brenntag* developed into a domestic market-oriented trading company, which later expanded internationally under the umbrella of *Hugo Stinnes AG* and developed a business model that relied on taking on distribution tasks. Overall, *Brenntag* has shown itself to be a versatile company throughout its history, one that embarked on a long-term growth path, at the latest when it joined the *Stinnes AG* group.

At the same time, the history of *Brenntag* reflects essential development phases in the history of chemical distribution. While the path of *Philipp Mühsam AG* and *Brenntag AG* in the first nearly 100 years primarily demonstrated the typical regional networking of such firms at their outset, over the last 50 years, Brenntag has been developing economies of scope through its expansion strategy and the scale it has achieved, thereby setting the course in a fragmented market.

The example of the *Brenntag* story shows how the service concept complemented the trading function and how the field of chemical distribution gained in contour and complexity. Chemical distributors like *Brenntag* not only delivered but also increasingly influenced the marketing of goods through specific filling or mixing operations. In addition, consulting services with regard to regulatory, safety, or quality-related requirements increasingly became part of the business model. Over time, chemical distributors took on tasks that had traditionally been carried out directly by the producers or customers themselves. This change in the division of labor along the chemical industry value chain pointed to structural change tendencies and outsourcing processes, some of which could also be seen in other industries. Over time, distributors like *Brenntag* had moved into an interface position that required flexibility.

Characterizing its history of gradual change, existential crises remained the exception for *Brenntag*, even though its 150-year history also includes periods with difficult, sometimes crisis-like conditions. "Powerfully moving forward" was the formula the company used early on to describe its path. At the time of its 150th anniversary, *Brenntag* has taken further strategic steps along this path to secure and even expand its position for the future as the world market leader in the distribution of chemicals and ingredients.

Appendix

Glossary

German – English

AG – Aktiengesellschaft	joint stock company or public limited liability corporation (Inc.)
Amt für den Vierjahresplan	Office of the Four-Year Plan
Arbeitsgruppe „Bereich Kommerzielle Koordinierung"	Commercial Coordination Working Group
Außenhandelsbetrieb Chemie	Chemical Foreign Trade Company
Brandenburgisches Hauptstadtarchiv	Brandenburg Main State Archives Potsdam
Bundesamt für gewerbliche Wirtschaft	Federal Office for Commercial Business
Bundesanstalt für Gesamtdeutsche Aufgaben	Federal Agency for Pan-German Tasks
Bundesministerium für gesamtdeutsche Fragen (bzw. innerdeutsche Beziehungen)	Federal Ministry for Pan-German Issues (from 1969: for Intra-German Relations)
Bundesaufsichtsamt für das Kreditwesen	Federal Banking Supervisory Office
Bundesministerium für Wirtschaft	Federal Ministry of Economics and the Federal Office for Commercial Business
Bundesnachrichtendienst (BND)	Foreign Intelligence Service
Bundesschatzministerium (1949–1953)	Federal Ministry of the Treasury (1949–1953)
Bundesverkehrsminister	Federal Minister of Transport
Gauleitung	district leadership
Gauwirtschaftsberater	district economic advisor
GmbH – Gesellschaft mit beschränkter Haftung	private limited liability corporation (Ltd.)
Hauptabteilung XVIII (Sicherung der Volkswirtschaft)	Main Department XVIII (Securing the National Economy)
Industrie- und Handelskammer	Chamber of Industry and Commerce
Inoffizieller Mitarbeiter (IMB)	unofficial employee
Kreisdienststelle Schwedt	Schwedt District Office
Kriegsschädenamt für die Seewirtschaft	War Damages Office for Maritime Shipping
Landesarchiv Nordrhein-Westfalen	State Archives of North Rhine-Westphalia
Landeszentralbank	state central bank
Landgericht	Regional Court
Leitsätzegesetz	Guidelines Act
Ministerium für Außenhandel und innerdeutschen Handel (MAI)	Ministry for Pan-German Trade and Inner-German Trade

Ministerium für Wirtschaft und Verkehr des Landes Nordrhein-Westfalen	Ministry of Economics and Transport of North Rhine-Westphalia
Nürnberger Gesetze	Nuremberg Laws
OHG – offene Handelsgesellschaft	open trading company or general partnership
Papiermark	paper mark
Rat für gegenseitige Wirtschaftshilfe	Council for Mutual Economic Assistance
Ratsherr	city councilman
Regierungspräsident	district president
Reichsarbeitsministerium	Reich Ministry of Labor
Reichsfluchtsteuer	Reich Flight Tax
Staatsarchiv Hamburg	Hamburg State Archives
Verband des deutschen Chemikalien- und Außenhandels	Association of German Chemicals and Foreign Trade
Verordnung zum Reichsbürgergesetz	Ordinance on the Reich Citizenship Act
Wehrwirtschaftsführer	Leader of the War Economy
Wiedergutmachungsamt Berlin	Berlin Restitution Office

English – German

Association of German Chemicals and Foreign Trade	Verband des deutschen Chemikalien- und Außenhandels
Berlin Restitution Office	Wiedergutmachungsamt Berlin
Brandenburg Main State Archives Potsdam	Brandenburgisches Hauptstadtarchiv
Chamber of Industry and Commerce	Industrie- und Handelskammer
Chemical Foreign Trade Company	Außenhandelsbetrieb Chemie
city councilman	Ratsherr
Commercial Coordination Working Group	Arbeitsgruppe „Bereich Kommerzielle Koordinierung"
Council for Mutual Economic Assistance	Rat für gegenseitige Wirtschaftshilfe
district economic advisor	Gauwirtschaftsberater
district leadership	Gauleitung
district president	Regierungspräsident
Federal Agency for Pan-German Tasks	Bundesanstalt für Gesamtdeutsche Aufgaben
Federal Banking Supervisory Office	Bundesaufsichtsamt für das Kreditwesen
Federal Minister of Transport	Bundesverkehrsminister

Federal Ministry for Pan-German Issues (from 1969: for Intra-German Relations)	Bundesministerium für gesamtdeutsche Fragen (ab 1969: innerdeutsche Beziehungen)
Federal Ministry of Economics and the Federal Office for Commercial Business	Bundesministerium für Wirtschaft
Federal Ministry of the Treasury (1949–1953)	Bundesschatzministerium (1949–1953)
Federal Office for Commercial Business	Bundesamt für gewerbliche Wirtschaft
Foreign Intelligence Service	Bundesnachrichtendienst (BND)
Guidelines Act	Leitsätzegesetz
Hamburg State Archives	Staatsarchiv Hamburg
joint stock company or public limited liability corporation (Inc.)	AG – Aktiengesellschaft
Leader of the War Economy	Wehrwirtschaftsführer
Main Department XVIII (Securing the National Economy)	Hauptabteilung XVIII (Sicherung der Volkswirtschaft)
Ministry for Pan-German Trade and Inner-German Trade	Ministerium für Außenhandel und innerdeutschen Handel (MAI)
Ministry of Economics and Transport of North Rhine-Westphalia	Ministerium für Wirtschaft und Verkehr des Landes Nordrhein-Westfalen
Nuremberg Laws	Nürnberger Gesetze
Office of the Four-Year Plan	Amt für den Vierjahresplan
open trading company or general partnership	OHG – offene Handelsgesellschaft
Ordinance on the Reich Citizenship Act	Verordnung zum Reichsbürgergesetz
paper mark	Papiermark
private limited liability corporation (Ltd.)	GmbH – Gesellschaft mit beschränkter Haftung
Regional Court	Landgericht
Reich Flight Tax	Reichsfluchtsteuer
Reich Ministry of Labor	Reichsarbeitsministerium
Schwedt District Office	Kreisdienststelle Schwedt
State Archives of North Rhine-Westphalia	Landesarchiv Nordrhein-Westfalen
state central bank	Landeszentralbank
unofficial employee	Inoffizieller Mitarbeiter (IMB)
War Damages Office for Maritime Shipping	Kriegsschädenamt für die Seewirtschaft

List of References

Source materials in print and other forms:

Archiv der Brenntag SE, Hauptverwaltung
  Essen:
  - Bilanzbuch der Philipp Mühsam AG
    1876–1936
  - diverse Akten und gedruckte Berichte
    der Hauptverwaltung der Brenntag
Brenntag AG, Niederlassung Berlin:
  - diverse Akten der Philipp Mühsam
    AG und der Brenntag
Archiv für Christlich-Demokratische Politik
  St. Augustin:
  - Bestand Stinnes (01–220)
Archiv der Deutsche Bahn AG, Berlin:
  - Bestand HA-50 (Akten des
    Aufsichtsrats der Deutsche Bahn AG,
    der Deutschen Bundesbahn und der
    Stinnes AG)
Archiv der Diakonie, Berlin:
  - Bestand Hauptgeschäftsführung

Brandenburgisches Landeshauptarchiv,
  Potsdam:
  - Bestand Rep. 36 A
    (Oberfinanzpräsident Berlin-
    Brandenburg), Steuerakten Familie
    Mühsam
Bundesarchiv Berlin (ehemals Stasi-Unter-
  lagenarchiv):
  - Bestand MfS AG BKK
  - Bestand MfS HA VIII
  - Bestand MfS HA XVIII
  - Bestand MfS Bezirksverwaltung
    Frankfurt/Oder, Kreisdienststelle
    Schwedt
  - Bestand MfS Bezirksverwaltung Halle,
    Kreisdienstelle Roßlau

Bundesarchiv Berlin-Lichterfelde:
  - Bestand DL 210 (Kommerzielle
    Koordinierung)
Bundesarchiv Koblenz:
  - Bestand B 102 (Bundesministerium
    für Wirtschaft)
  - Bestand B 126 (Bundesministerium
    der Finanzen)
  - Bestand B 136 (Bundeskanzleramt)

Deutscher Bundestag, Berlin:
  - Parlamentsarchiv, Akten des Koko-
    Untersuchungsausschusses

Historisches Archiv der Commerzbank AG,
  Frankfurt/Main:
  - Bestand HAC 500

Landesarchiv Nordrhein-Westfalen,
  Duisburg:
  - Abt. Rheinland, Bestand BR 336 m
  - Abt. Rheinland, Bestand NW 1000
  - Abt. Rheinland, Bestand BR 336
  - Bestand Rep. 176
  - Gerichte, Rep. 283
  - Gerichte, Rep. 439

Rheinisch-Westfälisches Wirtschaftsarchiv
  Köln:
  - Bestand Raab Karcher

Staatsarchiv Hamburg:
  - Entnazifizierungsakten
  - Handelsregisterakten
  - Kriegsschädenamt für die
    Seeschifffahrt

Periodicals:

Allgemeiner Wohnungs-Anzeiger für Berlin, various volumes

Amtsblatt der Europäischen Wirtschaftsgemeinschaft

Berliner Fernsprechbuch, 1882

Berliner Börsen-Zeitung, various volumes

Berliner Tageblatt, 1927

Blick durch die Wirtschaft, various volumes

Börsenzeitung, various volumes

Börse Online, various volumes

Brenntag Report, various volumes

Brenntag Together, various volumes

Chemical Market Reporter, various volumes

Chemical News & Intelligence, various volumes

Chemical Week, various volumes

Chemische Industrie, various volumes

Der Schild, 1935

Der Spiegel, various volumes

Deutsche Bundesbank, Monatsberichte, various volumes

Deutscher Bundestag, Drucksachen, various legislative periods

Sitzungsprotokolle, verschiedene Legislaturperioden

Die Welt, various volumes

Die Zeit, various volumes

ENP Newswire, various volumes

Euro am Sonntag, various volumes

Euroweek, various volumes

Financial Times, various volumes

Focus-Money, various volumes

Gefahrgut, various volumes

Frankfurter Allgemeine Zeitung, various volumes

Handelsblatt, various volumes

Ifo-Schnelldienst, various volumes

Logistik Inside, various volumes

Manager Magazin, various volumes

Office of Alien Property, Department of Justice, Annual Reports for the Fiscal Year, Washington D. C. 1947 und 1948

Süddeutsche Zeitung, various volumes

Statistisches Jahrbuch der Bundesrepublik Deutschland, various volumes

Statistisches Jahrbuch für Berlin, 1960

Thai News Service, various volumes

Verkehrs-Rundschau, various volumes

Vossische Zeitung, various volumes

Die Welt, various volumes

Welt online, various volumes

Werben und Verkaufen, various volumes

Wirtschaftsdienst, various volumes

Literature:

Werner Abelshauser, Die BASF. Eine Unternehmensgeschichte, München 2002.

Werner Abelshauser (ed.), Deutsche Wirtschaftsgeschichte seit 1945, München 2004.

Ann-Christin Achleitner, Value creation drivers in a secondary buyout – the acquisition of Brenntag by BC Partners, in: Quantitative research in Financial Markets 6 (2014), pp. 278–301.

Ann-Christin Achleitner et al., Brenntag. Primary Buyout and Exit Decision of Bain Capital, München 2012.

Gerold Ambrosius, Wirtschaftsraum Europa. Vom Ende der Nationalökonomien, Frankfurt/Main 1998.

Peter Auer, Die Verhältnisse zwangen zur Bewirtschaftung …: Streng geheim: Die zweite Blockade, die es nie gab, Berlin 1993.

Johannes Bähr, Industrie im geteilten Berlin. Die elektrotechnische Industrie und der Maschinenbau im Ost-West-Vergleich. Branchenentwicklung, Technologien und Handlungsstrukturen, München 2001.

Frank Bajohr, „Arisierung" in Hamburg, Hamburg 1997.

Nils Beckmann, Käfer, Goggos, Heckflossen. Eine retrospektive Studie über die westdeutsche Automobilmärkte in den Jahren der beginnenden Massenmotorisierung, Vaihingen 2006.

Bericht des 1. Untersuchungsausschusses des 12. Deutschen Bundestages. Der Bereich Kommerzielle Koordinierung und Alexander Schalck-Golodkowski, Bundestags-Drucksache 12/7600.

Jürgen Bethel/Fred Becker (eds.), Unternehmerische Herausforderung durch den Europäischen Binnenmarkt 1992, Berlin/Heidelberg 1990.

Willi A. Boelcke, Die Kosten von Hitlers Krieg. Kriegsfinanzierung und finanzielles Kriegserbe in Deutschland 1933–1945, Paderborn 1985.

Frank Bösch, Zeitenwende 1979. Als die Welt von heute begann, München 2019.

Marcel Boldorf, Ordnungspolitik und kriegswirtschaftliche Lenkung, in: Marcel Boldorf (ed.), Deutsche Wirtschaft im Ersten Weltkrieg, Berlin 2020, pp. 23–66.

Wolfgang Brinkschulte et al., Freikaufgewinnler. Die Mitverdiener im Westen, Frankfurt/Main 1993.

Heinz Brunotte, Die Evangelische Kirche in Deutschland. Geschichte, Organisation und Gestalt der EKD, Gütersloh 1964.

Christoph Buchheim, Die Errichtung der Bank deutscher Länder und die Währungsreform in Westdeutschland, in: Deutsche Bundesbank (ed.), Fünfzig Jahre Deutsche Mark. Notenbank und Währung in Deutschland seit 1948, München 1998, pp. 91–138.

Christoph Buchheim, Die Währungsreform 1948 in Westdeutschland, in: Vierteljahreshefte für Zeitgeschichte 36 (1988), pp. 189–231.

Günter Buchstab, Der Stinnes-Konzern 1933–1945, Rheinbach 1999.

Deutscher Bundestag (ed.), Bericht des 1. Untersuchungsausschusses des 12. Deutschen Bundestages. Der Bereich Kommerzielle Koordinierung und Alexander Schalck-Golodkowski, Werkzeuge des SED-Regimes. Zur Sache 2/94, 5 vols., Bonn 1994.

Paolo Cecchini, Europa '92. Der Vorteil des Binnenmarktes, Baden-Baden 1988.

Frank Claus, Neue Wege zur Austragung von Umweltkonflikten im Bereich der Chemiepolitik. Dornenreicher Weg zum Dialog, in: politische ökologie 31 – Wohin – aber wie? Positionen und Perspektiven der Umweltbewegung, May/June 1993.

Anselm Doering-Manteuffel/Lutz Raphael, Nach dem Boom. Perspektiven auf die Zeitgeschichte seit 1970, Göttingen 2010.

Bernhard-Michael Domberg/Klaus Rathje, Die Stinnes, Wien 2009.

Barry Eichengreen/Albrecht Ritschl, Understanding West German Economic Growth in the 1950s, in: Cliometrica 3 (2009), pp. 191–219.

Barry Eichengreen, The European Economy since 1945, Princeton 2007.

Barry Eichengreen, Vom Goldstandard zum Euro. Die Geschichte des internationalen Währungssystems, Berlin 1996.

Peter Fäßler, Zwischen „Störfreimachung" und Rückkehr zum Tagesgeschäft. Die deutsch-deutschen Wirtschaftsbeziehungen nach dem Mauerbau, in: Deutschland-Archiv 3/2012.

Peter Fäßler, Innerdeutscher Handel als Wegbereiter der Entspannungspolitik, in: Aus Politik und Zeitgeschichte 1/2007.

Peter Fäßler, Durch den „Eisernen Vorhang". Die deutsch-deutschen Wirtschaftsbeziehungen 1949–1969, Köln 2006.

Rainer Fattmann, Bildungsbürger in der Defensive. Die akademische Beamtenschaft und der „Reichsbund der höheren Beamten" in der Weimarer Republik, Göttingen 2001.

Gerald D. Feldman, Hugo Stinnes, München 1997.

Fren Förster, Geschichte der Deutschen BP 1904–1979, Hamburg 1979.

Saul Friedländer, Das Dritte Reich und die Juden, vol. 1 (1933–1939), München 1998.

Christiane Fritsche, Schaufenster des „Wirtschaftswunders" und Brückenschlag nach Osten. Westdeutsche Industriemessen und Messebeteiligungen im Kalten Krieg (1946–1973), München 2008.

Birgit Gehrke/Insa Weilage, Branchenanalyse Chemieindustrie. Der Chemiestandort Deutschland im Spannungsfeld globaler Verschiebungen von Nachfragestrukturen und Wertschöpfungsketten, Düsseldorf 2018.

Ludwig Geißel, Unterhändler der Menschlichkeit. Erinnerungen, Stuttgart 1991.

Herbert Giersch et al., The Fading Miracle. Four Decades of Market Economy in Germany, Cambridge 1992.

Manfred Grieger/Markus Lupa, Vom Käfer zum Weltkonzern. Die Volkswagen-Chronik, Wolfsburg 2015.

Christoph Hamann, Die Mühsams. Geschichte einer Familie, Berlin 2005.

Karl-Heinrich Hansmeyer/Rolf Cäsar, Kriegswirtschaft und Inflation, in: Deutsche Bundesbank (ed.), Währung und Wirtschaft in Deutschland 1876–1975, Frankfurt/Main 1975, pp. 367–429.

Alfred Hartmann, Die Privatisierung bundeseigener Unternehmen in der Bundesrepublik Deutschland, in: Jörn Axel Kämmerer (ed.), Privatisierung. Typologie, Determinanten, Rechtspraxis, Folgen, Tübingen 2001, pp. 209–228.

Klaus-Dietmar Henke/Roger Engelmann, Die Bedeutung der Unterlagen des Staatssicherheitsdienstes für die Zeitgeschichtsforschung, Berlin 1995.

Matthias Hofmann, Lernen aus Katastrophen: Nach den Unfällen von Harrisburg, Seveso und Sandoz, Berlin 2008.

Jens Hohensee, Der erste Ölpreisschock 1973/74. Die politischen und gesellschaftlichen Auswirkungen der arabischen Erdölpolitik auf die Bundesrepublik Deutschland und Westeuropa, Stuttgart 1996.

Carl-Ludwig Holtfrerich, Die Deutsche Bank vom Zweiten Weltkrieg über die Besatzungsherrschaft zur Rekonstruktion 1945–1957, in: Lothar Gall et al., Die Deutsche Bank 1870–1995, München 1995.

Konrad Jarausch (ed.), Das Ende der Zuversicht. Die siebziger Jahre als Geschichte, Göttingen 2008.

Matthias Judt, Der Bereich Kommerzielle Koordinierung. Das DDR-Wirtschaftsimperium des Alexander Schalck-Golodkowski – Mythos und Realität, Berlin 2013.

Rainer Karlsch, Das Milliardengeschäft der Hoechst AG mit der DDR-Chemieindustrie von 1976, in: Zeitschrift für Unternehmensgeschichte 63 (2018), issue 2, pp. 235–274.

Rainer Karlsch, Energie- und Rohstoffpolitik, in: Dierk Hoffmann (ed.), Die zentrale Wirtschaftsverwaltung in der SBZ/DDR. Akteure, Strukturen, Verwaltungspraxis, Berlin/Boston 2016, pp. 249–362.

Rainer Karlsch/Raymond G. Stokes, Faktor Öl. Die Mineralölwirtschaft in Deutschland 1859–1974, München 2003.

Rainer Karlsch/Raymond Stokes, Die Chemie muss stimmen. Bilanz des Wandels 1990–2000, Leipzig/Berlin 2000.

Rainer Karlsch, „Wie Phönix aus der Asche?" Rekonstruktionen und Strukturwandel in der chemischen Industrie in beiden deutschen Staaten bis Mitte der sechziger Jahre, in: Lothar Baar/Dietmar Petzina (eds.), Deutsch-deutsche Wirtschaft 1945 bis 1990. Strukturveränderungen, Innovationen und regionaler Wandel, St. Katharinen 1999, pp. 262–303.

Alexander Koch, Der Häftlingsfreikauf. Eine deutsch-deutsche Beziehungsgeschichte, München 2014.

Christopher Kopper, Der Durchbruch des PKW zum Massenkonsumgut 1950–1964, in: Stephanie Tilly/Dieter Ziegler (eds.), Automobilwirtschaft nach 1945. Vom Verkäufer- zum Käufermarkt?, Jahrbuch für Wirtschaftsgeschichte 1/2010, pp. 19–36.

Christopher Kopper, Handel und Verkehr im 20. Jahrhundert, München 2002.

Patrick Kresse, Finanzierungsstrukturen in der deutschen Automobilindustrie: Bayerische Motorenwerke, Daimler-Benz und Volkswagenwerk 1948–1965, Berlin 2018.

Peter Krewer, Geschäfte mit dem Klassenfeind. Die DDR im innerdeutschen Handel 1949 bis 1989, Trier 2008.

Simone Lässig, Jüdische Wege ins Bürgertum. Kulturelles Kapital und sozialer Aufstieg im 19. Jahrhundert, Göttingen 2004.

Landesarchiv Berlin, Abteilung Zeitgeschichte (ed.), Berlin: Ringen um Einheit und Wiederaufbau 1948–1961, Berlin 1962.

Raimund Le Viseur, Die Kaufleute aus Mülheim. 175 Jahre Stinnes. Eine deutsche Familienchronik, Düsseldorf 1983.

Dieter Lindenlaub, Die Errichtung der Bank deutscher Länder und die Währungsreform von 1948, in: idem et al., Schlüsselereignisse der deutschen Bankengeschichte, Stuttgart 2013, pp. 297–319.

Ludger Lindlar, Das mißverstandene Wirtschaftswunder. Westdeutschland und die westeuropäische Nachkriegsprosperität, Tübingen 1997.

Klaus Löbbe, Die europäische Chemie-industrie. Bedeutung, Struktur und Entwicklungsperspektiven, Bonn 2004.

Christian Marx, Wegbereiter der Globalisierung. Multinationale Unternehmen der westeuropäischen Chemieindustrie in der Zeit nach dem Boom (1960er-2000er Jahre), Göttingen 2023.

Hans-Jürgen Mende/Kurt Wernicke (eds.), Berliner Bezirkslexikon, Mitte, Berlin 2003.

Wolfgang Mertsching, Die Entwicklung der Mineralölindustrie in Mitteldeutschland nach 1945, in: Merseburger Beiträge zur Geschichte der chemischen Industrie Mitteldeutschlands 3/1998, pp. 5–50.

Hans Möller, Die westdeutsche Währungsreform von 1948, in: Deutsche Bundesbank (ed.), Währung und Wirtschaft in Deutschland 1876–1975, Frankfurt/Main 1975, pp. 433–483.

Monopolkommission, Hauptgutachten 1976/77. Fortschreitende Konzentration bei Großunternehmen, Baden-Baden 1978.

Kurt Mühsam, Der gewerbliche Lohnkampf im heutigen Strafrecht, Diss. jur. Heidelberg 1910.

Leonard Müller, Handbuch der Elektrizitätswirtschaft. Technische, wirtschaftliche und rechtliche Grundlagen, Berlin 2001.

Alexander Nützenadel, Die Stunde der Ökonomen. Wissenschaft, Politik und Expertenkultur in der Bundesrepublik 1949–1974, Göttingen 2005.

Werner Plumpe, Chemische Industrie, in: Marcel Boldorf (Hg.), Deutsche Wirtschaft im Ersten Weltkrieg, Berlin 2020, pp. 193–226.

Werner Plumpe/André Steiner (Hg.), Der Mythos von der postindustriellen Welt. Wirtschaftlicher Strukturwandel in Deutschland 1960 bis 1990, Göttingen 2016.

Kurt Pritzkoleit, Männer, Mächte, Monopole. Hinter den Türen der westdeutschen Wirtschaft, Düsseldorf 1963.

Michael von Prollius, Deutsche Wirtschaftsgeschichte nach 1945, Göttingen 2006.

Heiner Radzio, Unternehmen mit Energie. Aus der Geschichte der Veba, Düsseldorf/ Wien/New York 1990.

Thomas Rahlf (Hg.), Deutschland in Zahlen. Zeitreihen zur historischen Statistik, Bonn 2023.

Gabriele Roolfs-Broihan, Durch Akquisitionen zum Global Player. Der Weg der Brenntag AG, in: Stefan Odenthal/Gerhard Wissel (Hg.), Strategische Investments in Unternehmen, Wiesbaden 2004

Karsten Rudolph, Wirtschaftsdiplomatie im Kalten Krieg. Die Ostpolitik der westdeutschen Großindustrie 1949–1991, Frankfurt/Main 2004.

Karsten Rudolph/Jana Wüstenhagen, Große Politik. Kleine Begegnungen. Die Leipziger Messe im Ost-West-Konflikt, Berlin 2006.

Tim Schanetzky, Wirtschaft und Konsum im Dritten Reich, München 2015.

Gerald Scheffels, 125 Jahre Brenntag Stinnes Logistics, hg. von der Brenntag AG, Essen 1999.

Mark Spoerer/Jochen Streb, Neue deutsche Wirtschaftsgeschichte des 20. Jahrhunderts, München 2013.

André Steiner, Ostgeschäfte: Westliche Unternehmen in der DDR, in: Zeitschrift für Unternehmensgeschichte 62 (2018), pp. 221–234.

André Steiner, Von Plan zu Plan. Eine Wirtschaftsgeschichte der DDR, München 2004.

Mathias Stinnes GmbH, 150 Jahre Mathias Stinnes, Darmstadt 1958.

Gerd Sudholt (Hg.), Wanted. Die Fahndungsliste der US-Amerikaner 1945, Stegen 2002.

Carsten Suntrop (Hg.), Chemielogistik: Markt, Geschäftsmodelle und Prozesse, Weinheim 2011.

Sebastian Teupe, Zeit des Geldes. Die deutsche Inflation zwischen 1914 und 1923, Frankfurt a. M. 2023.

Richard Tilly, Willy H. Schlieker. Aufstieg und Fall eines Unternehmers (1914–1980), Berlin 2008.

Richard Tilly, Geld und Kredit in der Wirtschaftsgeschichte, Stuttgart 2003.

Stephanie Tilly/Florian Triebel, Automobilindustrie 1945–2000, München 2013.

Helmut Trotnow/Bernd von Kostka (Hg.), Die Berliner Luftbrücke. Ereignis und Erinnerung, Berlin 2010.

Frank Uekötter, Deutschland in Grün. Eine zwiespältige Erfolgsgeschichte, Bonn 2015.

Frank Uekötter/Claus Kirchhelle, Wie Seveso nach Deutschland kam. Umweltskandale und ökologische Debatte von 1976 bis 1986, in: Archiv für Sozialgeschichte 52 (2012), pp. 317–334.

Erik Verg u. a., Milestones. The Bayer-Story 1863–1988, Leverkusen 1988.

Julius Vesting, Die Zwangsarbeit im Chemiedreieck. Strafgefangene und Bausoldaten in der Industrie der DDR, Berlin 2012.

Armin Volze, Eine Bananen-Legende und andere Irrtümer, in: Deutschland-Archiv 1/1993, pp. 58–66.

Armin Volze, Kirchliche Transferleistungen in die DDR, in: Deutschland-Archiv 1/1991, pp. 59–66.

Tamás Vonyó, War Reconstruction and the Golden Ages of Economic Growth, in: European Review of Economic History 12 (2008).

Rolf Wiegand, Henry Nathan, in: Neue Deutsche Biographie (NDB), vol. 18 (1997), p. 745 f.

Heinrich August Winkler, Der lange Weg nach Westen. Deutsche Geschichte 1933–1990, Bonn 2004.

Barthold Witte, Bericht über kirchliche Transferleistungen im evangelischen Bereich der DDR von 1957 bis 1990, Bonn 1993.

Harald Wixforth, Bielefeld und seine Sparkassen, Bielefeld 2003.

Jan Philipp Wölbern, Der Häftlingsfreikauf aus der DDR 1962/3-1989. Zwischen Menschenhandel und humanitären Aktionen, Göttingen 2014.

Irmgard Zündorf, Der Preis der Marktwirtschaft. Staatliche Preispolitik und Lebensstandard in Westdeutschland 1948 bis 1963, Stuttgart 2006.

List of Charts, Tables, and Figures

Charts

Tables

Figures

Picture Credits

Figure 1, page 14: Christoph Hamann, Die Mühsams. Geschichte einer Familie, Berlin 2005, fig. p. 57

Figure 2, page 16: Berliner Börsen-Zeitung, II. Beilage der Berliner Börsen-Zeitung, Nr. 472, 10.10.1874, p. 5

Figure 3, page 17: Brenntag, photo: Mayk Azzato

Figure 4, page 18: Brenntag (private loan), photo: Mayk Azzato

Figure 5, page 21: Brenntag (private loan), photo: Mayk Azzato

Figure 6, page 24/25: Straube, Julius. Amtlicher Wegemesser Für Den Landespolizeibezirk Berlin Und Die Zum Droschkenfahrbezirk Gehörigen Vororte Zu Den Droschken-Ordnungen Für Berlin Vom 16. Febr. 1905, [Für] Charlottenburg [Vom] 21. Febr. 1905, [Für] Schöneberg [Vom] 27. Febr. 1905, [Für] Lichtenberg [Vom] 27. März 1909 Und Deren Abänderungs-Verordnungen. Geographisches Institut und Landkarten-Verlag Jul. Straube, 1910

Figure 7, page 26: Brenntag

Figure 8, page 27: Brenntag, photo: Bengsch Werbeagentur

Figure 9, page 30: Vossische Zeitung, Berlin, Nr. 251 Morgenausgabe, 19.05.1914, p. 10

Figure 10, page 33: Brenntag, photo: Mayk Azzato

Figure 11, page 38/39: Brenntag, photo: Mayk Azzato

Figure 12, page 40: Brenntag, photo: Mayk Azzato

Figure 13, page 41: Brenntag (private loan), photo: Mayk Azzato

Figure 14, page 43: Brenntag (private loan)

Figure 15, page 44: Brenntag, photo: Mayk Azzato

Figure 16, page 50: Brenntag

Figure 17, page 52: © Getty Images/ Imagno/ brandstaetter images, BildNr. 167627415

Figure 18, page 56: Freude und Arbeit: offizielles Organ des Internationalen Zentralbüros Freude und Arbeit = Joy and work = Joie et travail / Zentralamt für Internationale Sozialgestaltung, Berlin, Heft Nr. 5, 1938, p. 688

Figure 19, page 58: Brenntag, photo: Mayk Azzato

Figure 20, page 60: Brenntag, in: Weekly Magazine, 18. August 1945

Figure 21, page 76: Brenntag advertisement from 1952, published in: Firmenhandbuch Chemische Industrie in der Bundesrepublik und in West-Berlin, 1952, p. 68

Figure 22, page 77: Brenntag, photo: Mayk Azzato

Figure 23, page 83: Brenntag, photo: Mayk Azzato

Figure 24, page 87: Brenntag, photo: Mayk Azzato

Figure 25, page 89: Brenntag

Figure 26, page 90: Fotoarchiv Ruhr Museum, Wilhelm Reimers

Figure 27, page 96: Brenntag

Figure 28, page 97: Brenntag

Figure 29, page 112: Helmut Uebbing: Die Brenntag wird verkauft, in: Frankfurter Allgemeine Zeitung, Montag, 16. November 1964, all rights reserved © Frankfurter Allgemeine Zeitung GmbH, Frankfurt/ Main. Provided by Frankfurter Allgemeine Archiv.

Figure 30, page 127: Brenntag

Figure 31, page 129: Brenntag

Figure 32, page 130: Brenntag: Ihr Partner im Markt. 1874–1974, Düsseldorf 1974, fig. 9

Figure 33, page 131: Brenntag

Figure 34, page 135: Brenntag: Ihr Partner im Markt. 1874–1974, Düsseldorf 1974, fig. 2

Figure 35, page 141: Brenntag: Ihr Partner im Markt. 1874–1974, Düsseldorf 1974, fig. 8

Figure 36, page 146: Hugo Stinnes AG, Geschäftsbericht 1973, p. 6

Figure 37, page 147: Brenntag: Ihr Partner im Markt. 1874–1974, Düsseldorf 1974, fig. 13

Figure 38, page 155: Stinnes AG, Geschäftsbericht 1986, p. 18

Figure 39, page 156: Brenntag

Figure 40, page 157: Brenntag

Figure 41, page 158: Brenntag

Figure 42, page 161: Brenntag

Figure 43, page 168: Stinnes AG, Geschäftsbericht 1988, p. 45

Figure 44, page 184: Brenntag

Figure 45, page 193: Brenntag, photo: Arnd Drifte

Figure 46, page 198: Brenntag, photo: André Langer

Figure 47, page 198: Brenntag, photo: André Langer

Figure 48, page 210: Brenntag

Figure 49, page 217: Brenntag

Figure 50, page 219: Brenntag, photo: Chris Hirschhäuser

Index

Individuals

Corporate and Public Bodies

Note: The company Name *Brenntag* is not listed separately